The Long Encounter

The Long Encounter

SELF

AND EXPERIENCE

IN THE WRITINGS

OF HERMAN MELVILLE

By Merlin Bowen

 THE UNIVERSITY OF CHICAGO PRESS

CHICAGO & LONDON

FOR AL AND DOROTHY

Library of Congress Catalog Card Number: 60-7232

THE UNIVERSITY OF CHICAGO PRESS, CHICAGO & LONDON
The University of Toronto Press, Toronto 5, Canada

© *1960 by the University of Chicago. All rights reserved. Published 1960
Second Impression 1963.
Composed and printed by* THE UNIVERSITY OF CHICAGO PRESS
Chicago, Illinois, U.S.A.

Introduction

                                  With his very first book, *Typee*, Herman Melville found himself on the best-seller list. As one to whom good fortune had been long in coming, he was of course gratified. But there was a price attached, he soon discovered: he was fixed henceforth in the public mind as a writer of South Sea romances. It was not, he came increasingly to feel, the sort of success he wanted. When, some ten years and nine books later, he closed his career as a professional writer, he did so in large part out of anger at this label and at the expectations that went with it. Today, after more than a century, his popular fame is still that of a writer of sea stories, though of whaling now rather than beachcombing. In either case, the label is misleading. It may be questioned whether his books are stories or novels at all, in the customary meaning of those words: certainly plot and character are not their strong points. Nor do all of them have to do with the sea. But there is one thing that all of them have in common, and that is a concern with the problem of self-discovery, self-realization. And here—however different he was in other respects—Melville was at one with his age, with such men as Emerson, Thoreau, Hawthorne, and his exact contemporary Whitman, whose more leisurely career was just opening as his own seemed prematurely closing. If we are to understand him, we must meet him on this, the ground of his principal concern, and survey his work from here.

This study calls attention, therefore, to the part played by the concept of selfhood in the writings of Herman Melville and attempts to show, in an examination of particular works, how this persistent concern helped to determine his subject matter, his imagery, his view of character, the shape of his narratives, and his at times equivocal attitude toward his material. No claim is made, of course, that this approach—or any other—will provide one with "the Talismanic Secret" by which all problems of Melville interpretation can be solved. But one may hope that some new insights may result from this approach and that the separate works will be found to throw light upon each other when seen as so many dramatic representations of the encounter of the self and the not-self, of the single human person and all that is set over against him—the total reality of nature, mankind, and God. For it was in terms of this conflict that the human experience, from first to last, presented itself to Melville.

To begin with a clear definition of the self would be good, if it were possible. But what the self actually is, neither Melville nor perhaps anyone else has ever satisfactorily defined, except in terms of what it is not. We may say, however, that it appears in Melville's work (and particularly in his imagery) as something that is both given and achieved: as an aboriginal, stable, though ever elusive center of identity on the one hand, and on the other as a realization in action of the full human and individual potential. A man is both his inmost sense of himself and the outward declaration of that sense in his interaction with the opposing world. The very character which that world assumes for him is in large part an expression of and a clue to his personality. For identity comes through one's realization of separateness from this outer world. The more highly developed one's sense of self (as distinguished from mere blatant and unreflective egotism), the keener the awareness of one's separateness from the not-self, of the basic hostility or indifference of the universe. And with this awareness will come the problem of the choice—or of the adoption, at any rate—of a life-attitude, a policy or course of action, in the following-out of which each man realizes himself and his destiny. In all of Melville's major works, accordingly (if we except the heroless *Confidence-Man*), and in most of his minor ones, we find ourselves looking on at the pitting, in some sense, of the single individual against the universe. It is this encounter, understood as a problem both of perception and of action, that lies at the center of all of Melville's work.

If this is so, we may hope to learn something by looking at the body of Melville's work in terms of this encounter, with regard both to what remains constant throughout and to what may vary from work to work. The assumption upon which this study proceeds is that there is a great deal that remains constant, that throughout most of a long life Melville maintained a relatively unchanging view of the nature of the experienced world and of the part it plays in the shaping and completion of the individual identity. To assume this is in no way to deny the reality of change, of development. Like every thoughtful man, Melville reshaped and qualified his beliefs in the light of continuing experience, and in part we may read the evidence of that reshaping in his work. But the change was never revolutionary; there is no sign of sudden conversion or recantation at any point, not even in *Billy Budd,* written in the closing years of his life. After *Pierre,* it is true, a definite current becomes more and more apparent—a movement away from open protest toward a quieter but always positive and life-affirming stoicism. But the seeds of this attitude were present from the first in the irony tempering the defiance of Babbalanja, of Ahab, of Pierre. And its clearest expression is to be found not in *Billy Budd* but in the much more fully elaborated statement of *Clarel,* for which reason I have chosen to end this study with a brief account of that poem rather than of Melville's final and in some ways most puzzling work.

The plan of the following chapters is simple and perhaps self-evident. In Part I an attempt is made to draw together from all of Melville's writings the materials for an account of the two actors, protagonist and antagonist, of this drama. The first chapter, "The Unknown Self," gathers up whatever is said or implied in these books about the meaning and value of the self insofar as it can be apprehended introspectively and apart from the encounter. Images and statements are here disengaged, it is true, from their particular dramatic contexts—though never, it is hoped, at the cost of ignoring ironic qualification or special circumstance—and so allowed to contribute to a single and as yet undifferentiated account of the self.

The second chapter, "The Opposing Other," attempts to trace the outlines of what is again, in the last analysis, a single large picture: Melville's vision of the external world. But since that vision is a complex one, it is presented in separate accounts of how that single universe presents itself to two types of people, the optimists and the pessimists, among Melville's characters. Melville himself (as he explicitly reminds us) belongs to neither group. Reality wears always for him, in the most light-hearted as in the bitterest of his books, the double aspect of bright and dark; wherever the picture is simplified to the one aspect or the other, we shall find evidence that it is not Melville speaking but one of his characters, and this within a context clearly implying a qualification upon the statement. But this is not to say that Melville sees the dark and bright in equal balance. If we are to judge by the quality of his imagery, his treatment of characters, the outcome of his plots, and the explicit comment of his narrators, it is clear that the dark far outweighs the bright. Still, the two compose, for the judicious viewer, a single picture; and it is by their awareness of this fact that we are meant to judge the perceptiveness and the wholeness (if not always the greatness) of particular characters.

With Part II, "The Meeting," we move from the problem of perception and judgment to the problem of action, and consider the characterizing responses to life made by those characters who are presented as having to some significant extent taken the dimensions of reality's dark side. These strategies which the self adopts toward its adversary are seen as basically three in number and are identified as defiance, submission, and an "armed neutrality" that is distinct from either. In the choice he makes of these strategies, and in the subsequent conduct of his life, each personality declares and completes himself. A degree of schematism is perhaps unavoidable under this method, but let it be noted that the three categories—broadly conceived as they are—are not offered as accounting for all of Melville's characters but only for the morally awakened, the dark-seers. Neither the imperceptive mass nor the depraved (Jackson or Claggart) nor the radically innocent (Billy Budd or Amasa Delano) has any place here.

Most of Part II of this study is given over to analyses of

particular works and characters, organized under the general
rubric of the three strategies. In one case, that of *Pierre*, the
discussion will be found to be both detailed and extended—
disproportionately so, some may feel. My justification (if it
be accepted as such) is that in *Pierre* Melville has given us a
much more elaborate and intricately worked out treatment of
this theme of self-discovery than in any other work. Looked at
in this light, too, the book may be seen (with all its faults) as
a more controlled and a more carefully designed work than it
is commonly taken to be.

To the preceding account of what the present study does attempt, it may be well to append a statement of some of the
things it deliberately makes no effort to do.

First of all, then, it does not purport to be a historical inquiry of any kind. It neither attempts to locate the sources of
Melville's ideas and attitudes in the events of his personal life
nor to reconstruct the pattern of that life from the evidence
of the works themselves. The first is a useful and, within limits, a defensible sort of inquiry, though aiming at other ends
than those here proposed. The second sort of historical inves-
tigation is one which, in its crude form, has happily gone out
of fashion. That critics should have undertaken such a task
once, when objective biographical materials were scarce and
little was known of Melville's habits of composition, is under-
standable. In the absence of authentic history, myth will always step in. Thus, in the twenties and thirties, a number of
biographer-critics, bent upon creating a writer "complex, massive, and original" enough to be capable of *Moby-Dick*, methodically dismantled the other books and used these materials as biographical data, often without either submitting them
to historical tests or observing the aesthetic function they had
performed in their proper place. The result was of course
more revelatory of the biographers than of their subject. The
patient labors, since that time, of a number of excellent historical scholars—among them, Charles R. Anderson, Wil-

liam H. Gilman, Jay Leyda, and Leon Howard—have done much to preserve a later generation of critics from falling into the same errors.

A more sophisticated approach than the one just examined is that which looks upon Melville's books as so many successive chapters in their author's intellectual or spiritual biography. Several able and sensitive critics (outstandingly William Ellery Sedgwick) have studied the books in this light and have discovered for us meanings and relationships that we might otherwise have missed and for which we must always remain grateful. But this approach too has its misleading assumptions and its intrinsic dangers from which I have attempted to steer clear, if only to fall into my own. That Melville's mind "unfolded within itself" and that his vision broadened and deepened with time, few perhaps will wish to deny. One may assume this of every serious artist, every thoughtful man. But we have less reason to assume that the record of this growth stands complete for us in the series of art works which the artist has left. The poet or novelist is not *ipso facto* a diarist, is not held by the terms of his art to set down a running account of his interior life. The critic, therefore, who looks to find a coherent story imbedded in these works will be forced himself to supply, however unconsciously, some of the links in his chain. For a good story is one with a pattern and a proper ending: it does not move disjointedly, leap gaps, reverse its direction, or break off abruptly in the way that life is so apt to do. Nor are the systematic spiritual biographers the only ones to assume the existence of such a completed pattern in the author's life and work. The common misinterpretation (as it seems to me) of *Billy Budd* offers a case in point. This last of Melville's works is frequently regarded as a kind of death-bed recantation of his earlier protests, a sort of relativist *nunc dimittis*. Had the book come a decade or so earlier in its author's career, it is probable that these same critics would have taken a quite different view of it and made more of its many likenesses to the earlier works than of its differences from them. But as it is, the book stands in a climactic position in the story of its author's growth and so is expected to provide a final turn to the whole action. Melville's life, these critics feel, must, like Shakespeare's in *The Tempest*, find its summing-up in a last definitive statement transcending all his earlier formulations. Possibly most of us have felt this to a degree. But the *must*, let us note, is a requirement not of life or of logic but only of our own misplaced aesthetic expectations: we have composed a story which needs such an ending to round itself out. And when all is done, *Billy Budd* and *The Tempest* remain as self-contained poetic wholes to be dealt with each in its own terms.

More recently it has been the fashion to search Melville for "significances for our own time"—for what has been called, through an editor's misreading of Melville's handwriting, the "usable truth." This has been no part of my concern, since it is my belief that art speaks to all times, if not in each work to all problems. I have been as little concerned to bring his writings into conformity with this or that school of thought, absolutist or relativist. "Metaphysical" as Melville's interests were, he was not drawn to the abstract or the systematic as such, nor did he feel himself bound to a philosophical consistency. But to say he was not a philosopher is not to condescend to him (an impertinence of which more than one aspiring critic has been guilty) nor in any way to deny the seriousness and importance of his ideas. The ideas are there as part of the very substance of his art. But any attempt to fix and systematize them ends only in a weakening of one's sense of the dynamic complexity of Melville's attitude toward life, of his refusal of all static positions, and his acceptance (as Charles Feidelson, Jr., has so well put it) of "the problematic, the inconclusive, and the contradictory" as the true and only face of experience.

It will be observed that I make no effort in these pages to

sum up, to judge, or even to make explicit use of, the wealth
of criticism and scholarship available in this field. This omis-
sion will be understood, I hope, as rather the unavoidable
consequence of my aim and my method than the expression
of any rash ambition to begin the entire labor over again sin-
glehanded. Given the scope of this study and the wish to illustrate and support my statements as fully as possible from
Melville's writings themselves, I could not with any adequacy
or thoroughness have represented the views of others without
impairing the coherence of my own work. I must not therefore let slip this occasion to express my very deep sense of
gratitude for the many facts and insights made available to
me (whether or not I have made the best use of them) in a
number of books which must always remain invaluable to the
student of Melville. From among these, let me name specif-
ically Lewis Mumford's *Herman Melville* (New York: Harcourt, Brace, 1929), Willard Thorp's *Herman Melville: Representative Selections* (New York: American Book Co., 1938),
F. O. Matthiessen's *American Renaissance* (New York: Oxford University Press, 1941), William Ellery Sedgwick's
Herman Melville: The Tragedy of Mind (Cambridge, Mass.:
Harvard University Press, 1944), Howard P. Vincent's *The
Trying-Out of Moby-Dick* (Boston: Houghton Mifflin, 1949),
Newton Arvin's *Herman Melville* (New York: Henry Holt,
1950), William H. Gilman's *Melville's Early Life and Redburn* (New York: New York University Press, 1951), Jay
Leyda's *The Melville Log* (New York: Harcourt, Brace,
1951), Leon Howard's *Herman Melville* (Berkeley: University of California Press, 1951), and Merrell R. Davis' *Melville's Mardi: A Chartless Voyage* (New Haven: Yale University Press, 1952). Those who are familiar with the field will
be aware (and at points perhaps where I am not) how deeply
I am indebted to these and to a variety of other critics and
scholars.

Less apparent but no less real is my debt to those who have

helped me in a more personal way by their confidence and encouragement, their criticism and advice, in the preparation of this volume. I take this occasion, then, to express my heart-felt thanks especially to Napier Wilt and Robert E. Streeter of the University of Chicago, to Harrison Hayford of North-western University, and to Merton Sealts of Lawrence College. Each of these has given to the consideration of my problems far more of his time than either duty or common courtesy could require; all have been generous in their approval, frank in their differences and reservations, specific in their sugges-tions for improvement. Many of these suggestions I have adopted and this book is, I know, the better for them. Where I have not been able thus to profit by instruction, let the blame, if any, fall upon my head alone.

For the same reason, I must be content to stand and take the fire of my critics with regard to those points (in my dis-cussions of *Pierre*, *The Confidence-Man*, and *Billy Budd* es-pecially) where I have clearly departed from the commonly accepted interpretation. Novelty of opinion is not something to be sought after in these matters. I can only say that my own departures have been made with some misgivings and only after long and thoughtful consideration of the alternatives. My own view being now set forth with some fulness, I can be corrected where correction is needed and thus allowed, even in my errors, to contribute to a better understanding of the works in question.

Finally, I owe it to my readers to state what I hope may be accomplished by still one more general study of Melville. One should not be expected at this date, and in a field so thor-oughly worked as this, to turn up much that is wholly new or astounding. Indeed, discoveries of this sort may reasonably be held suspect from the first as more likely originating in the critic's "intense and procreative enthusiasm" than in the art-ist's work itself. But even where one deals with materials al-ready attentively examined and from many quite different positions, it is still possible by a relatively slight alteration of standpoint to open up new perspectives and to see old things in new relations. This is my chief hope for the usefulness of the present study. To the extent that it is successful in what it attempts to do, it may help other readers to see Melville's works not only (though this is fundamental) in its own uniquely individual character but in the larger context of his work as a whole—the total expression of his characteristic vision of reality. A fuller sense of the complexity of that vision may also have the effect of discouraging the tendency— still far too common—to identify Melville unqualifiedly with one or another of his characters. There are times, moreover, when our response to certain of these characters (Ahab, Pierre, or Captain Vere) is troubled by a sense of something equivocal in Melville's handling of them; and here again an appeal to the larger context may prove—though never in itself decisive—illuminating and suggestive. Finally, by showing the relation of many of Melville's images and symbols to ideas of great and continuing concern to him, this study may do something to discourage the sort of arbitrary interpretation and uncontrolled system-building to which an interest in symbolism per se too often conducts. Should it appear that any one of these purposes has been realized in a significant degree, the labor that has gone into these pages will have been well spent.

What this book is about

PART I

The Antagonists

1. The Unknown Self

"There have been men in all ages," Coleridge once remarked, "who have been impelled as by an instinct to propose their own nature as a problem, and who devote their attempts to its solution." Herman Melville, by his own testimony and that of his friends, appears to have been such a man, and the greater number of his writings may be viewed as so many artistic attacks upon this problem. In *Mardi*, his first deliberately serious book, the philosopher Babbalanja admits that " 'though I have now been upon terms of close companionship with myself for nigh five hundred moons, I have not yet been able to decide who or what I am.' "[1] Much of *Mardi* is concerned—to its considerable detriment as a dramatic whole—with meditations and discourses upon various aspects of this question. Ahab and Pierre, in their turn, strive constantly to " 'probe the circle's center,' " to distinguish the personal from the impersonal. And more than twenty years later, near the end of Melville's writing career, the young hero of *Clarel* may be seen still searching for the key—no longer under the palms of a romanticized Polynesia but amid the sterile rubble of Palestine, the birthplace of the Christian faith.

Analytically regarded, Babbalanja's problem may be looked upon as twofold, involving the question of man's nature and the question of personal identity—man as distinguished from not-man, I as distinct from Other. Babbalanja may well have been puzzled: these are reefs upon which navigators more systematic than he have run hopelessly aground. For the *what*, though in theory subject to definition, is most apt in the actual attempt to end either in empty formalism or in a mere multiplication of the paradoxes of dualism; while the *who*, by reason of the very singularity it aims at, can find its answer only in an act of intuitive (and therefore incommunicable) apprehension. Nor can a mind grounded in the traditions of Western thought easily consider either question apart from such closely related and baffling problems as the meaning of good and evil, the nature of God and the created universe, and the ground and scope of man's reason, will, and aspirations.

Small wonder, then, that Babbalanja, in despair of a reasoned answer, was at last driven to give up the tormenting riddle in exchange for a simple faith that asks no questions.

[1] *The Works of Herman Melville* (16 vols.; Standard Edition; London: Constable & Co., 1922–24), *Mardi*, II, 155 (chap. cxliii). Unless otherwise noted, all references hereafter to the text of Melville's writings will be to this edition. For the convenience of readers to whom the Standard Edition may not be readily accessible, the chapter number (usually enough to locate a passage within two or three pages) has been added in parentheses after volume and page designation in each citation.

Melville himself, however (though he fared little better), did not give up. Central to nearly everything he wrote from 1849 on lies an awareness of this mystery, a sense of the simple yet undiscoverable self maintaining and realizing itself in the midst of a hostile universe—"the one warm spark in the heart of an arctic crystal."

AS LETTERS
SEALED UP

By degrees and by indirection only does man approach the self. It is, like Ahab's jagged-edged and galling Crown of the Lombards, something to be felt rather than seen or grasped: " 'I, the wearer, see not its far flashings; but darkly feel that I wear that, that dazzlingly confounds.' "[2] In the beginning, though, we have not even this sense of our identity. For the mind of man is not naturally or immediately reflexive, and our first awareness is always an awareness of others. It is from without, in the inexplicable faces and actions of others, that the mystery of personality first confronts us. Only in the gradual realization of our exclusion and pain and aloneness do we attain to that image of the self which thereafter seems to us so radical and so central to all our experience.

So it must have been for the young Melville of 1844–46, fresh from the active life of the whaleboat and the gun deck. His first two novels are, as one might expect, relatively unconcerned with the complexities of the world within. Of the two, the more superficial by far is the second—*Omoo*, a rambling picaresque travelogue. *Typee*, though much of its charm arises from its very faithfulness to the surface—practical, comic, or romantic—of Polynesian life, gives us occasional flashes of a deeper insight. The beautiful but voiceless birds of the valley, for instance, seem to the narrator emblematic

[2] *Moby-Dick*, I, 209 (chap. xxxvii).

of the islanders themselves, cut off from him by the wall of language and so made indistinguishable from the dumb mystery of nature.[3] It is the threat, it would seem, of the absorption of his personality into this universal blank of savagery that awakens in him so disproportionate a terror at the suggestion of a ritual tattooing.[4] And the final revelation of cannibalism at the heart of Fayaway's unfallen world comes to Tommo with the shock of a familiar door opening suddenly upon darkness.

There are these glimpses in *Typee*, but it would be a mistake to suggest that they characterize the book. Looking at it and at *Omoo* in the perspective of the later works, one realizes that their materials have not yet been subjected to that intense scrutiny and contemplation by which experience is compelled to disclose to the artist its underlying depths and ambiguities.

But beginning with *Mardi*, the next novel, one finds expressed again and again in Melville's writings a conviction of the deceptiveness (or incompleteness, at least) of man's presented surface, a sense of the "tiered galleries" branching out in mine-like darkness beneath. " 'We are only known by our names; as letters sealed up, we but read each other's superscriptions.' "[5] This is a truth not limited in its application to exceptional or to highly complex men. A disarming simplicity is found to be the common and instinctive guise of child and sage, of "the subtlest bad man, and the purest good man."[6] And when this is realized, one is confronted with an undecipherable "Egypt [in] every man's and every being's face."[7] Those with whom necessity forces us to deal—and in matters often of life and death—are and must remain utter

[3] *Typee*, p. 291 (chap. xxix).

[4] *Ibid.*, pp. 294–95 (chap. xxx); see also *Omoo*, pp. 32–33 (chap. vii).

[5] *Mardi*, II, 86 (chap. cxxvi).

[6] *Pierre*, p. 314 (Book XV, chap. ii).

[7] *Moby-Dick*, II, 83 (chap. lxxix).

strangers to us: " 'Nobody knows who anybody is. The data which life furnishes, toward forming a true estimate of any being, are as insufficient to that end as in geometry one side given would be to determine the triangle.' "[8]

An awareness of this withheld dimension becomes first evident in *Mardi* at the encounter with the raft, that point at which the bluff and carefree narrative of the opening chapters gives way to the darker history of Taji, the injured demigod:

> The old priest, like a scroll of old parchment, [was] covered all over with hieroglyphical devices, harder to interpret . . . than any old Sanscrit manuscript. And upon his broad brow, deep-graven in wrinkles, were characters still more mysterious, which no Champollion nor gipsy could have deciphered.[9]

Ishmael and Ahab, in their turn, find a like mystical significance in the cryptic tattooings of Queequeg, who

> in his own proper person was a riddle to unfold; a wondrous work in one volume; but whose mysteries not even himself could read, though his own live heart beat against them; and these mysteries were therefore destined in the end to moulder away with the living parchment whereon they were inscribed, and so be unsolved to the last. And this thought it must have been which suggested to Ahab that wild exclamation of his, when one morning turning away from surveying poor Queequeg—"Oh, devilish tantalization of the gods!"[10]

But the riddle must nevertheless be attempted. And when, with whatever caution, we have gathered from the outward signs a seeming image of the person within, that image is all too often contradicted in the more authoritative declaration of "the living act, the undoubted deed." It is worth noting that among Melville's radically evil characters—Jackson, Bland, Babo, the confidence man, and Claggart—only the

8 *The Confidence-Man,* p. 255 (chap. xxxvi).

9 *Mardi,* I, 151 (chap. xl).

10 *Moby-Dick,* II, 251 (chap. cx).

first (and earliest drawn) seems unequivocally to be what he is. Evil elsewhere wears the mask of good (as frequently pain-twisted good wears that of evil) and so imposes upon that simple innocence which sees only "the clean-swept deck, and oft-painted planks . . . above the water-line" and not the vessel's greater part, "with all its store-rooms of secrets, forever slid[ing] along far under the surface."[11]

But if the innocent lack insight, it must be added that experience, too, proves a far from infallible guide in these matters. The green boy Redburn is no more mistaken in the true character of his captain than is the veteran seaman Captain Delano in that of the sinister-seeming Spaniard, Benito Cereno. To enter and leave the labyrinth of another being requires a clue experience alone cannot give. "I am not certain," remarks an "honest scholar" in *Billy Budd*, "whether to know the world and to know human nature be not two distinct branches of knowledge."[12]

Books, the fruit of long study and of considered experience, may seem to provide us with a deeper insight. And so, in rare instances, they do—but only "covertly and by snatches": accidental glimpses of Truth, that "scared white doe in the woodlands."[13] In no book, not even in Shakespeare, may one hope to find a sufficient guide through the endless twistings of human nature. Novelists and dramatists exist, it is true, for whom the triumphant claim is made that they throw "open, sometimes to the understandings even of school misses, the

11 *White-Jacket*, p. 503 ("The End").

12 *Billy Budd*, in *The Portable Melville*, ed. Jay Leyda (New York: Viking Press, 1952), p. 674. All references to *Billy Budd* hereafter are to the text printed in this volume, the latest and most accurate transcription of Melville's manuscript available at the time of going to press. Harrison Hayford and Merton Sealts are working on a new edition, to be published in the near future.

13 "Hawthorne and His Mosses," in *Billy Budd and Other Prose Pieces*, p. 131.

last complications of that spirit which is affirmed by its Creator to be fearfully and wonderfully made"; but their achievement will impress only those who have forgotten that it is
not real people who are so dealt with, but "mere phantoms
which flit along a page, like shadows along a wall."[14]

But in the nineteenth century it is not art or philosophy
or religion but science which has staked out as its peculiar
domain the field of "reality." Moral reality, however, seems
to fall (if we ignore the utilitarians' "felicific calculus")
largely outside the limits of science. For this "King Commonplace" of the age concerns itself less with man's proper
study than with the trivialities of quantitative description:
counting the lenses in a dragonfly's eye or the muscles in a
flea's leg,[15] and identifying as " 'Jura limestone, every spur' "
the stone of the Mount of Temptation.[16] " 'Hast yet put a
usurer under your lens, to find his conscience?' " Babbalanja
asks the virtuoso Oh-Oh. " 'Or a libertine, to find his heart?' "[17]

There do exist, of course, those who boldly undertake such
researches. These are the practitioners of the pseudo sciences
—"those sallies of ingenuity, having for their end the revelation of human nature on fixed principles . . .—palmistry,
physiognomy, phrenology, psychology."[18] Midway through
Moby-Dick, Ishmael amuses himself by surveying the whale
physiognomically and phrenologically—neither of which deliberate studies reveals anything at all beyond what is already
known: the face is featureless and inscrutable, the skull presents for "reading" no bumps even remotely attributable to
the "mere handful" of brains buried twenty feet within. "Leav-

14 *The Confidence-Man*, pp. 89–91 (chap. xiv).

15 *Mardi*, II, 71 (chap. cxxii).

16 *Clarel*, I, 247 (Part II, canto xix).

17 *Mardi*, II, 71 (chap. cxxii).

18 *The Confidence-Man*, p. 91 (chap. xiv).

ing this hint to operate as it may with the phrenologists," Ishmael thereupon dismisses the attempt as hopeless.[19]

Not in the findings of science or of pseudo science, then, nor in the intuitions of the artist, nor by our own experience, have we any hope "of infallibly discovering the heart of man." For that heart "partakes of the unravelable inscrutableness of God," its maker,[20] and "whatever is truly wondrous and fearful in [it], never yet was put into words or books."[21] Glibness with regard to it is the surest mark of ignorance or fraud, uncertainty and fragmentary utterance the almost necessary garb of truth. Those

profounder emanations of the human mind, intended to illustrate all that can be humanly known of human life; these never unravel their own intricacies, and have no proper endings; but in imperfect, unanticipated, and disappointing sequels (as mutilated stumps) hurry to abrupt intermergings with the eternal tides of time and fate.[22]

From across the dead body of Pierre, the dark intruder Isabel calls to his one-time friends: " 'All's o'er, and ye know him not!' "[23] And Ahab too, his mortal wound unstanched (" 'For who can find it in the deep-loaded hull?' "), carries his unread secret with him down into that " 'awful waterland' " of his antagonist. But simplicity is no less a barrier to our sight, and innocence is in the end as baffling as guilt. Bartleby's mild gaze of dead-wall indifference and Billy Budd's glance of virginal self-assurance meet our eyes with the same impenetrability as the "unabashed" stare which Babo's severed head—"that hive of subtlety"—fixed upon his enemies and victims from across the Plaza in Lima.

[19] *Moby-Dick*, II, 81–86 (chaps. lxxix–lxxx).

[20] *Pierre*, p. 199 (Book VII, chap. viii).

[21] *Moby-Dick*, II, 246 (chap. cx).

[22] *Pierre*, p. 199 (Book VII, chap. viii); see also *Moby-Dick*, I, 179 (chap. xxxii).

[23] *Pierre*, p. 505 (Book XXVI, chap. vii).

CENTRIPETAL AND
CENTRIFUGAL

Excluded as we are, then, from the re-
cesses of another's being, what do we find as we turn our gaze
inward, each toward that walled reality of which he, if anyone,
must be sole witness? An unimagined vastness, in the first
place, but a vastness which carries only a hint of that which
is still to come. For

heaven [has] wisely ordained, that on first entering into the
Switzerland of his soul, man shall not at once perceive its tremendous immensity; lest illy prepared for such an encounter,
his spirit should sink and perish in the lowermost snows. Only
by judicious degrees, appointed of God, does man come at last
to gain his Mont Blanc and take an overtopping view of these
Alps; and even then, the tithe is not shown; and far over the
invisible Atlantic, the Rocky Mountains and the Andes are yet
unbeheld. Appalling is the soul of a man! Better might one be
pushed off into the material spaces beyond the uttermost orbit
of our sun, than once feel himself fairly afloat in himself.[24]

And in the second place, we find contradiction. Man feels
himself driven now this way, now that, by the most antithetical needs and compulsions. Dimly he senses himself to be one,
yet the evidence argues that he is also twain:

a more cunning compound, than an alchemist's—yet a hundred
weight of flesh, to a penny weight of spirit; soul and body glued
together, firm as atom to atom, seamless as the vestment without
joint, warp or woof—yet divided as by a river, spirit from flesh;
growing both ways, like a tree, and dropping thy topmost
branches to earth. . . . I give thee up, oh Man! thou art twain—
yet indivisible; all things—yet a poor unit at best.[25]

An awareness of this ill-sorted union, this uneasy and shifting balance, is everywhere evident in *Mardi*, as in the later

[24] *Ibid.*, p. 396 (Book XXI, chap. i).
[25] *Mardi*, II, 131 (chap. cxxxvi).

books. The islander Samoa is tattooed only on one "vertical half of his person . . . ; the other side being free from the slightest stain. Thus clapped together, as it were, he looked like a union of the unmatched moieties of two distinct beings."[26] The poet Yoomy is "so capricious a mortal; so swayed by contrary moods; . . . so made up of a thousand contradictions," as to defy description.[27] On the first isle visited by the companions, the boy king Peepi is said to be daily subject to the inner dictates of a different regent from among the twenty "heroes, sages, simpletons, and demi-gods" whose spirits he has inherited from his father.[28] The melancholy king Donjalolo of Juam spends his life "vacillating between virtue and vice; to neither constant, and upbraided by both; his mind, like his person in the glen, . . . continually passing and repassing between opposite extremes."[29] The meditative Babbalanja is similarly divided. He is able to smile at the weakness of those who " 'rant of etherealities: and long tarry over [their] banquets' "; yet his own follies and the haunting sense of a " 'something going on in me, that is independent of me' " drive him to hypothesize an " 'incomprehensible stranger' " prowling and dodging about within him.[30] How thoroughgoing this internal conflict at times seemed to Melville may be judged in the comic Manicheeism of that passage in which Babbalanja, parodying the steps of Socrates' refutation of Simmias in the *Phaedo*, "proves" that "our souls belong to our bodies, not our bodies to our souls."[31]

The familiar dualism of the Platonic-Christian tradition

---

[26] *Ibid.*, I, 112–13 (chap. xxx).

[27] *Ibid.*, p. 230 (chap. lxv).

[28] *Ibid.*, pp. 236–38 (chap. lxvii).

[29] *Ibid.*, p. 262 (chap. lxxiii).

[30] *Ibid.*, II, 155–57 (chap. cxliii).

[31] *Ibid.*, pp. 214–15 (chap. clv).

underlies, it is true, nearly everything that Melville wrote. It would be a mistake, however, to attempt to reduce that dualism to a simple good-evil dichotomy of soul and body. Man's fate admittedly hangs upon the outcome of that continuing civil war between reason and the passions; but one must note that Melville's sympathies were not invariably on the side of the higher faculty. For he was enough of a Romantic to realize that the mind too can play the villain and, by its tyrannizing over the affections, end in as fatal a disorder as the anarchy it would supplant. This being so, "the running battle of the star and clod" is not to be resolved by the old strategy of ascetic self-denial. Salvation—if salvation indeed is to be had —will lie not in purification by the exclusion of a large part of life but in wholeness approached through a generous inclusiveness; it will consist not in an unconditional surrender of body to soul, but in a development and balance of the powers of heart and head.

Melville himself is not of course to be credited with this revolutionary restatement of man's ancient dilemma. For at least a generation before he began to write, the concept of "heart and head" had existed as a commonplace of thought and as such had played its part, during the last quarter of the eighteenth century, in the gradual undermining of the arbitrary rule of mind. What was implicit in the phrase, however consciously realized in any single instance, was an admission that man's darker half—that unsystematizable complex of instinctual ties and compulsions—had a dignity of its own and a right to be named in the same breath with the "godlike exercise" of reason. What had heretofore been scorned as man's "lower nature" was now, dressed in the new semantic dignity of "heart," acknowledged as a permanent and constitutive part of his personality.

The exact stages of this transformation, so important in the intellectual and artistic history of Europe in the eighteenth century, one need not pause here to trace out in detail. It will be sufficient to the present purpose to note the central importance for Melville of this concept of heart and head and to indicate briefly some of the values associated with it throughout his work; later pages will consider more closely the part it plays in an understanding of certain characters and of their differing responses to life.

It needs to be clear at the outset that "heart and head" is for Melville neither a philosophical nor a psychological distinction, properly speaking, but an artistic one. For the primary concern of art is not with analysis and precise definition but with synthesis and the representation of experience. One must not expect, therefore, in Melville's employment of the terms, a settled denotation or a fixed value; rather, they will remain as fluid and as richly connotative as the primary symbols—light and dark or sea and land—of his imagination. Depth and complexity are what is aimed at, not a neat and obvious consistency.

What returned Melville again and again to this concept of head and heart was his sense of an inescapable division within the soul itself—a duality within a duality. Beyond the familiar strife of body and soul there lay, he felt, a yet deeper and more irreconcilable conflict: the opposition of the speculative reason and the natural affections, of the centrifugal and the centripetal, the godlike and the merely human. Man is pulled two ways, not merely between good and evil but between two antithetical goods, each a necessary part of his very nature.

The rule of the heart appears at its simplest in the life of the unreflecting savage, guided from moment to moment by impulse and floated along by "the mere buoyant sense of a healthful physical existence."[32] At the opposite pole, the rule of the head is to be seen in all the clearness of caricature in the picture of Emerson as one whose "brains descend down into his neck, & offer an obstacle to a draught of ale or a

[32] *Typee*, p. 170 (chap. xvii).

mouthful of cake."[33] For the mass of men, however, life lacks
the simplicity found at either extreme: they are born into
contention and must make each his separate settlement with
the warring powers. The negotiation may well prove the business of a lifetime.

Of the two powers, the active and masculine principle is
the head—that compulsion within man to doubt, to seek, to
question, to reject, to detach himself from all that seems to
be known and to return, a voluntary Ishmael, naked to the
wilderness. The compulsion is, of course, not always heeded.
Often enough, men are ignorant of its very existence until
aroused from their complacency by the shock of a strong
personal grief. Astonished then, they marvel at their long intellectual sleep. The old half-truths and irrelevancies, they
suddenly realize, will no longer do: a hunger has been awakened which only the ultimate answers can satisfy. " 'I will not
add [cries Babbalanja], I will diminish; I will train myself
down to the standard of what is unchangeably true.' "[34] It is
this hunger that leads the young Pierre forth from the gates
of his childhood's paradise, that forces Taji on through the
outer reef, that holds the unrelenting Ahab to the track of his
enemy, that conducts Clarel from desert to desert and even
beyond his last hope's burial in the Valley of Dry Bones. Few
are the men who wholly escape this longing: it draws us all
at times at least so far as "the extremest limit of the land"
and carries certain of us far beyond this mark—a wilful few
(Pierre among them) even into those farthest reaches of
desolation where the long search ends in a realization that
the question itself is not wholly comprehensible. But to whatever limit we may later follow it, it is the head which first
discloses to us the integral part of evil in our world and so

---

[33] Letter to Evert Duyckinck, March 3, 1849, reprinted in Eleanor Melville
Metcalf, *Herman Melville, Cycle and Epicycle* (Cambridge, Mass.: Harvard
University Press, 1953), p. 59.

[34] *Mardi*, II, 80–81 (chap. cxxiv).

ends forever that earlier childlike trust in the easy compatibility of reality and our dearest aspirations.

The uninstructed heart is, on the other hand, all but hopelessly innocent and unendowed with any instinct for the detection of life's ambushed malignancies. The feminine in man, it is its nature not to question but to accept and to trust. It lives by impulse and emotion rather than by thought. The physical evils of pain and loss it looks upon as accidental and temporary; moral evil seems to it an illusion, a mere theoretic thing. It imposes its own benevolence and warmth upon the inhuman world about it. Aggressiveness is as foreign to its nature as to its expectation. It seeks not action and risk but rest and security. Not for it are the rigors of the wilderness, "the horrors of the half-known life": it holds its place (so long as its sovereignty be not surrendered) amid the familiar, the domestic, the seemingly all-understood. Contentment and the quiet joy of possession are its marks.

But it is just here, in the heart's affections, in its docility, its ready consenting to "the infinite entanglements of all social things" that the head encounters the chief obstacle to that total commitment which alone will satisfy it. Struggling to free himself from the hold of his humanities, Ahab gives the carpenter a set of mock specifications for " 'a complete man after a desirable pattern: . . . no heart at all, brass forehead, and about a quarter of an acre of fine brains.' "[35] The ties that hold us to the breathing human beings whom we love are the same ties, the head realizes, that fetter us to the compromises and half-truths of our past: there can be no freeing ourselves of the one and clinging to the other. The fully awakened soul dares not, it feels, shirk the "inevitable keen cruelty [of] the loftier heroism. [For] it is not heroism only to stand unflinched ourselves in the hour of suffering; but it is heroism to stand unflinched both at our own and at some

[35] *Moby-Dick*, II, 238 (chap. cviii).

loved one's united suffering."[36] Nothing less will satisfy than
that the heart altogether foreswear its old allegiances and
permit its energies to be conscripted wholly into the service
of the head. Truth places the soul under the necessity to work
its way always into the landward wind, to sheer off from the
reefs of "safety, comfort, hearthstone, supper, warm blankets,
friends, all that's kind to our mortalities," and jealously "to
keep the open independence of her sea."[37] By the nature of
his calling, the seeker is an *Isolato*, "not acknowledging the
common continent of man, but . . . living on a separate continent of his own."[38] Like the fanatically vengeful Indian-hater
of frontier legend, he must settle his temporal affairs, take
leave of his kin, and to all purposes vanish from the haunts
of men. Here is the significance of Taji's final desertion of
his companions, of Father Mapple's drawn-up pulpit ladder,
of Ahab's refusal of the anguished plea of the "Rachel," of
Pierre's principled abandonment of Lucy. Nothing must be
permitted to stand between the mind and its object. "If a man
must wrestle, . . . it is well that it should be on the nakedest
possible plain."[39]

As the dedicated seeker will not be hindered in his pursuit
by the irrelevancies of any supposed duty to others, so neither
will he permit himself to be helped. He is determined to be
himself "not only his own Alpha and Omega, . . . but all the
intermediate gradations."[40] Need of any sort appears to him
as weakness, and the acknowledgment of the least obligation
becomes an affront to his individuality, a wound to his free
will. With Ahab, he is driven to curse " 'that mortal inter-
indebtedness' " by which he is " 'down in the whole world's

36 *Pierre*, pp. 248–49 (Book X, chap. ii).

37 *Moby-Dick*, I, 132–33 (chap. xxiii).

38 *Ibid.*, p. 149 (chap. xxvii).

39 *Pierre*, p. 413 (Book XXII, chap. i).

40 *Ibid.*, p. 363 (Book XVIII, chap. ii).

books' " and " 'owe[s] for the flesh in the tongue [he] brag[s] with.' "[41] It is not enough that the bread he eats should be made from the grain of his own field: he would escape, if possible, the humiliation of knowing that the seed had first to be borrowed from the harvest of some earlier planter.[42] Even the insufficiency of one's single sex appears as a kind of "Cosmic jest or Anarch blunder" by which "self-hood itself seems incomplete."[43]

To such a mind all books, all previously evolved ideas, are essentially foreign—mere incidental helps at best. The soul attains to its maturity only as it learns in "stillness and se-clusion . . . to think untraditionally and independently; re-ceiving all nature's sweet and savage impressions fresh from her own virgin, voluntary, and confiding breast."[44] And of all impertinences, the chief is that would-be intermediary, the priest—that "pretended envoy extraordinary [but] . . . mere man" who offers to divert the thunderbolt from your hearth by interposing his patented three-tined "pipestem between clay and sky."[45]

Nor is it only against his fellows that the head would have man assert and maintain his independence. There rules within him a "crowned and sceptred instinct," a "divine unidentifi-ableness," to which he may acknowledge no superior whatever. " 'Talk not to me of blasphemy, man; I'd strike the sun if it insulted me,' " cries Ahab.[46] He must, "like Russia or the British Empire, [declare] himself a sovereign nature (in him-self) amid the powers of heaven, hell, and earth" and insist "upon treating with all Powers upon an equal basis."[47] It is

[41] *Moby-Dick*, II, 240 (chap. cviii).

[42] *Pierre*, p. 363 (Book XVIII, chap. ii).

[43] "After the Pleasure Party," in *Poems*, p. 257.

[44] *Moby-Dick*, I, 91–92 (chap. xvi).

[45] "The Lightning-Rod Man," in *The Piazza Tales*, p. 179.

[46] *Moby-Dick*, I, 204 (chap. xxxvi).

[47] Letter to Nathaniel Hawthorne, 1851, in Metcalf, *op. cit.*, p. 105.

thus that we see Ahab at the summit of his daring: indifferent alike of good and evil, he stands erect in the midst of his terror-stricken crew, his foot upon the kneeling Parsee, his left hand grasping the lightning-links, his face turned fearlessly upward to where "God's burning finger" rests upon the masthead of his ship.[48] Man must first be faithful to the divinity within him, and of a God who chooses to come not as love but as "mere supernal power," clearly the "right worship is defiance."

For it is according to eternal fitness, that the precipitated Titan should still seek to regain his paternal birthright even by fierce escalade. Wherefore whoso storms the sky gives best proof he came from thither! But whatso crawls contented in the moat before that crystal fort, shows it was born within that slime, and there forever will abide.[49]

But though man's divinity be granted, it must be confessed to be at bottom no better than a demi-divinity—a sort of godhood on sufferance. Events are forever reminding us of the alloy in our nature. In the grip of some "reckless sky-assaulting mood," we may find ourselves at first, like the enthusiast Pierre,

all eagerness to cast off the most intense beloved bond, as a hindrance to the attainment of whatever transcendental object that usurper mood so tyrannically suggests. Then the beloved bond seems to hold us to no essential good; lifted to exalted mounts, we can dispense with all the vale; endearments we spurn; kisses are blisters to us; and forsaking the palpitating forms of mortal love, we emptily embrace the boundless and the unbodied air. We think we are not human; we become as immortal bachelors and gods; but again, like the Greek gods themselves, prone we descend to earth; glad to be uxorious once more; glad to hide these godlike heads within the bosoms made of too-seducing clay.[50]

48 *Moby-Dick*, II, 281–82 (chap. cxix).
49 *Pierre*, p. 483 (Book XXV, chap. v).
50 *Ibid.*, p. 252 (Book X, chap. iii).

Infinite though his aspirations may seem, each man finds at last that he "cannot overshoot the earth's orbit" and escape its field of gravitation. A force grounded in his own nature compels him sooner or later, if he is to live, to "lower, or at least shift, his conceit of attainable felicity; not placing it anywhere in the intellect or the fancy; but in the wife, the heart, the bed, the table, the saddle, the fireside."[51] He who attempts, in the white heat of his anger or enthusiasm, to ignore the reality of these "lower" claims does so at the risk of casting himself hopelessly adrift. It is not good for man to live alone, says Genesis. And it may be added that "our God is a jealous God; He wills not that any man should permanently possess the least shadow of His own self-sufficient attributes."[52] Therefore it is with Ahab as it was with Pip: "the intense concentration of self in the middle of . . . a heartless immensity" leads not to the transcendence only but to the loss of all human values. Pierre, too, having torn himself from all restraining hands in order to follow "the directing compass of his mind" to its ultimate pole, finds himself finally stranded at a moral nowhere incapable of sustaining life.[53]

Thus, "centripetal is ever too much for centrifugal." But the impetus of the outward thrust, though held down to earth, nevertheless continues and subjects the fabric of that "containing thing," our earthly nature, to the most dangerous stresses:—"Ah, muskets the gods have made to carry infinite combustions, and yet made them of clay!"[54]

When, in the soul of "a man of greatly superior natural force, with a globular brain and a ponderous heart,"[55] the two currents of the earthbound and the sky-aspiring meet in violent conflict, the result is heroism. The event comes but

51 *Moby-Dick*, II, 172 (chap. xciv).

52 *Pierre*, p. 364 (Book XVIII, chap. ii).

53 *Ibid.*, p. 231 (Book IX, chap. i).

54 *Ibid.*, p. 150 (Book V, chap. vii).

55 *Moby-Dick*, I, 91–92 (chap. xvi).

rarely, however, since always the great mass of mankind will be found deficient in the one respect or the other. The unintelligent, the spiritually timorous, the youthful, the thus-far fortunate whom grief has not yet awakened—these are they whose lives are ruled by the heart. Although they are in many instances admirable people (as witness Starbuck, Billy Budd, and Captain Amasa Delano), there remains something incomplete about them; they fall short of the full stature of man. Still, the possibility of growth is often there.

Of a lower sort altogether is the product of that opposite disorder of swollen head and feeble heart: mere monsters, " 'dwarfs, staggering under heads overgrown.' " Degeneration and not growth is the prospect here; for this is a deficiency in the very principle of life itself. " 'Pah! the brains grow maggoty without a heart; but the heart's the preserving salt itself, and can keep sweet without the head.' "[56] Driven by no generous or self-forgetful impulse, such minds lack a motive to the search for truth and devote their strength instead to problems of calculation and mere earthly prudence. For these moral cretins, Melville reserves his deepest scorn—a scorn unrelieved by any touch of the pity he keeps for the Jacksons and the Claggarts, whose far deeper evil, though chiefly intellectual in its nature, yet draws its strength from the fierceness of an embittered heart. For here, even at these inhuman depths, there is more of heroism to be found than in the reasoned "non-benevolence" and cold spiritual utilitarianism of a Mark Winsome or a Plotinus Plinlimmon. "What man, who is a man, does not feel livelier and more generous emotions toward the great god of Sin—Satan—than toward yonder haberdasher, who only is a sinner in the small and entirely honorable way of trade?"[57] And God Himself (in the person of the confidence man[58]) turns away in disgust from

---

[56] *Pierre*, p. 445 (Book XXIII, chap. iv).

[57] *Ibid.*, p. 248 (Book X, chap. ii).

[58] See below, pp. 117–18.

the sight of His handiwork in Egbert, the Yankee mystic's practical disciple, whose shrewd head is "kept cool by the under ice of the heart."[59]

The first and necessary mark of the heroic nature, then, is that it be on both sides richly endowed:

"Cerebrum must not overbalance cerebellum; our brains should be round as globes; and planted on capacious chests, inhaling mighty morning-inspirations. We have had vast developments of parts of men; but none of manly wholes. Before a full-developed man, [the world] would fall down and worship."[60]

Yet this completeness is almost necessarily self-destructive. Man is a creature, it seems, who can approach perfection only in the moment of his dissolution: when "the inmost leaf of the bulb" has been unfolded, "the flower must fall to the mould."[61] There is in mortal greatness something of the character of a divine infliction. The coming of Isabel's letter to Pierre is presented as the annunciation of that fatal " 'world-disdaining counsel' " of perfection which thereupon "foetally" takes shape within him:

Impregnations from high enthusiasms he had received; and the now incipient offspring which so stirred, with such painful, vague vibrations in the soul; this, in its mature development, when it should at last come forth in living deeds, would scorn all personal relationship with Pierre, and hold his heart's dearest interests for naught.

Thus, in the Enthusiast to Duty, the heaven-begotten Christ is born; and will not own a mortal parent, and spurns and rends all mortal bonds.[62]

To Ahab also comes this "unbidden and unfathered birth," making of Christmas Day itself "Hell-day and an eaten liver

---

[59] *The Confidence-Man,* p. 297 (chap. xli).

[60] *Mardi,* II, 322–23 (chap. clxxx).

[61] Letter to Nathaniel Hawthorne, June 29, 1851, reprinted in Metcalf, *op. cit.,* p. 110.

[62] *Pierre,* p. 149 (Book V, chap. v).

forever." Nor is it possible for us to ignore at whose command it is that the insatiable bird tears at the defier's vitals: "God help thee, old man, thy thoughts have created a creature in thee; and he whose intense thinking thus makes him a Prometheus; a vulture feeds upon that heart forever; that vulture the very creature he creates."[63] The doom of such men was sealed at the beginning, their ruin already accomplished in the choice of the irreconcilable elements of which they were composed.

IN THE CAVE
OF MAN

But there are other ways, too, in which man rends and punishes himself. The heart is not always victim: it knows how to torment as well as to suffer, to mislead and perplex as well as to guide aright. To the novice in truth or to the "ungovernably good-natured," such a thought falls little short of blasphemy. Evil—supposing it to exist at all—is clearly of the head, they feel, goodness of the heart. Pierre, poised at the brink of his fatal choice, is of this number. " 'The heart! 'tis God's anointed; let me pursue the heart!" he cries[64]—and knows nothing of the betrayal even then being prepared for him within that heart's recesses. A less candid seeker (Derwent, the unshakably optimistic clergyman of *Clarel*) later echoes the same faith in the prayer:

> "Behead me—rid me of pride's part
> And let me live but by the heart!"

only to draw from a companion the embittered query:

> "Hast proved thy heart? first prove it. Stay:
> The Bible, tell me, is it true,
> And thence deriv'st thy flattering view?"[65]

[63] *Moby-Dick*, I, 253 (chap. xliv).
[64] *Pierre*, p. 127 (Book V, chap. i).
[65] *Clarel*, II, 29 (Part III, canto vi).

The proving, if conscientiously carried out, is not likely to be reassuring. " 'I curiously look into my secrets; and grope under my ribs,' " reports Babbalanja. " 'I have found that the heart is not whole, but divided.' "[66] Savagery lives there as next neighbor to gentleness, and war to peace: Fayaway, we need to remember, is the sister of cannibals, and Quee-queg's soothing peace pipe serves him also as a tomahawk. Queequeg himself, the very type of the savior heart, can yet join the wild Daggoo and Tashtego in an eager sympathy with Ahab's murderous purpose.

To many (Pierre is an example), this revelation of the heart's duplicity comes with as profound a shock as that which accompanied their first glimpse into the inhuman voids of the physical universe. For with the disclosure that it is as capable of loving evil as good, the heart shows itself to be no more an integer than is fractioned man himself and to furnish no solider a basis for our hopes. The soaring mind, called back to earth, discovers in the heart not only the expected simplicities of "life's sunlit surface," but below that surface a dark and knotted intricacy of unguessed motives and desires. Man's holiest affections and his blindest appetites lie entangled here, and he who would attempt to sort them in that darkness will find no end to his labors.

In many, even the most trivial, affairs of life, we find it difficult precisely and certainly to locate the motive of our action in any rationally purposed end. What, then, of more complex and vital matters, impinging upon a multiplicity of unseen interests and passions? The conviction of moral accountability exists almost universally among men and would seem to presuppose the reality of an intelligent and deliberate choice.

Yet so strange and complicate is the human soul; so much is confusedly evolved from out itself, and such vast and varied accessions come to it from abroad, and so impossible is it always

[66] *Mardi*, II, 351 (chap. clxxxiii).

to distinguish between these two, that the wisest man were rash, positively to assign the precise and incipient origination of his final thoughts and acts. Far as we blind moles can see, man's life seems but an acting upon mysterious hints. . . . For surely no mere mortal who has at all gone down into himself will ever pretend that his slightest thought or act solely originated in his own defined identity.[67]

It is in the depths of the undefined that our actions are shaped, and all that we know of the shaping motives we catch in occasional faint gleams from below. How can one tell, for instance, whether a generous act of his doing arises from genuine altruism or from a disguised self-love? Who will undertake in all cases to distinguish the signatures of pride and self reverence, of hatred and a hopeless love, of ruthless egotism and a selfless dedication to truth? For what reason, Taji asked himself, was the old priest slain: that the maiden Yillah might be freed? or that the slayer might enjoy her?[68] The same question torments Pierre as he examines his motive in championing Isabel.

The heart, one finds, is capable of endless subterfuges and dissimulations. The searcher into motives must be alert against the stratagems of

> "Good done with ill intent—reversed:
> Best deeds designed to serve the worst."[69]

Spontaneity itself falls under suspicion. What of that "godlike longing" whose fervor moves us to sacrifice the happiness of those whom we love? Can we be certain of its purity? Pierre, though he nonetheless held to his determined course, felt he could not:

"Lo! by my conduct I seem threatened by the possibility of a sin anomalous and accursed, so anomalous, it may well be the

---

[67] *Pierre*, p. 246 (Book X, chap. i).

[68] *Mardi*, I, 156–57 (chap. xlii).

[69] *Clarel*, I, 319 (Part II, canto xxxvi).

one for which Scripture says, there is never forgiveness. Corpses behind me, and the last sin before, how then can my conduct be right?"[70]

But even the absence of self-interest—were it possible for us to be assured of that—would offer no guarantee of the purity of our motives. For evil is often disinterested and finds its sufficient satisfaction "in the very easy way of simply causing pain to [others]."[71] There is a "rabies of the heart" as well as a mania of the brain,[72] and what man will dare to think himself totally immune to it? The best of conscious intents offers but little protection against the possibility of an involuntary "chemical preparation in the soul for malice, as chemical preparation in the body for malady."[73] Granted that the great desideratum is the "free development of [our] inmost nature," one must acknowledge that the enterprise is not wholly free of risk: " 'if some men knew what was their inmost natures, instead of coming out with it, they would try their best to keep it in.' "[74]

Considering, then, the tortuousness of this lightless maze, one can sympathize with Ahab's wry wish for " 'a sky-light on top of [man's] head to illuminate inwards' " rather than the customary pair of " 'eyes to see outwards.' "[75] But the wish has even less point than one would have imagined. For what illumination will help us in dealing with a mystery of which "every revelation [partakes] more of significant darkness than of explanatory light?"[76]

Deep, deep, and still deep and deeper must we go, if we would find out the heart of a man; descending into which is as de-

[70] *Pierre*, p. 286 (Book XIV, chap. i).

[71] *The Confidence-Man*, p. 78 (chap. xii).

[72] *Billy Budd*, in *The Portable Melville*, p. 676.

[73] *The Confidence-Man*, p. 199 (chap. xxvi).

[74] *Ibid.*, p. 289 (chap. xl).

[75] *Moby-Dick*, II, 238 (chap. cviii).

[76] *Ibid.*, p. 231 (chap. cvi).

scending a spiral stair in a shaft, without any end, and where that endlessness is only concealed by the spiralness of the stair, and the blackness of the shaft.[77]

To the light-dazzled eye of reason, the greater part of this underworld must remain forever obscure. By feeling only and by intuition, the mind's peripheral vision, may we hope to be guided along "the endless, winding way,—the flowing river in the cave of man."[78]

During nearly half a century, as the imagery of his work everywhere testifies, Melville's imagination was haunted by an awareness of these depths. Nothing, says Babbalanja, " 'can so appall, as we ourselves. We are full of ghosts and spirits; . . . [whole] graveyards full of buried dead, that start to life before us.' "[79] Ishmael can only guess at what it is within him and his shipmates that so responds to the deadly lure of the white whale: "The subterranean miner that works in us all, how can one tell whither leads his shaft by the ever shifting, muffled sound of his pick?"[80] And though some attempt may be made to explain rationally the origin and nature of Ahab's monomania, yet when this has been done, it must be admitted that his

larger, darker, deeper part remains unhinted. But vain to popularize profundities, and all truth is profound. Winding far down from within the very heart of this spiked Hotel de Cluny where we here stand—however grand and wonderful, now quit it;—and take your way, ye nobler, sadder souls, to those vast Roman halls of Thermes; where far beneath the fantastic towers of man's upper earth, his root of grandeur, his whole awful essence sits in bearded state; an antique buried beneath antiquities, and throned on torsoes![81]

77 *Pierre*, p. 402 (Book XXI, chap. ii).

78 *Ibid.*, p. 151 (Book V, chap. vii).

79 *Mardi*, II, 323 (chap. clxxx).

80 *Moby-Dick*, I, 233 (chap. xli).

81 *Ibid.*, p. 231 (chap. xli).

Through "the hid chambers underlying the Claggarts" of this world prowl half-seen assassin figures.[82] And not beneath the Claggarts only:

> In Piranezi's rarer prints,
> Interiors measurelessly strange,
> Where the distrustful thought may range
> Misgiving still—what mean the hints?
> Stairs upon stairs which dim ascend
> In series from plunged bastilles drear—
> Pit under pit; long tier on tier
> Of shadowed galleries which impend
> Over cloisters, cloisters without end;
> The height, the depth—the far, the near;
> Ring-bolts to pillars in vaulted lanes,
> And dragging Rhadamanthine chains;
> These less of wizard influence lend
> Than some allusive chambers closed.
>   Those wards of hush are not disposed
> In gibe of goblin fantasy—
> Grimace—unclean diablerie:
> Thy wings, Imagination, span
> Ideal truth in fable's seat:
> The thing implied is one with man,
> His penetralia of retreat—
> The heart, with labyrinths replete.[83]

In the inner world as in the outer, illusion underlies illusion and the real is ever deeper than we had thought. Like Ahab, we watch our picture in the water sink and sink the more we strive "to pierce the profundity,"[84] until at last this image of our identity is lost in the abyss. It is at such times that we are visited by the "atheist thought" that "perhaps, after all, there is no secret," and that below that "little lower layer" to which we have penetrated, there exists—in man as in na-

[82] *Billy Budd,* in *The Portable Melville,* p. 680.

[83] *Clarel,* I, 316 (Part II, canto xxxv).

[84] *Moby-Dick,* II, 327 (chap. cxxxii).

ture—"nothing but surface stratified on surface," like the successive skins of an onion. The hollow vortices of Descartes have their counterparts, it seems, in the world of spirit, and virtue and vice may be in the end no more than " 'two shadows cast from one nothing.' "[85] The ultimate nightmare grips us: "By vast pains we mine into the pyramid; by horrible gropings we come to the central room; with joy we espy the sarcophagus; but we lift the lid—and no body is there!— appallingly vacant as vast is the soul of a man!"[86]

THE STILL CENTER

But the sense of our selfhood is too strong in us for such an anarchic vision to persist. The conviction returns of an "indefinite regent," a "captive king" ruling in the remotest depths of our nature, far below the level "of all hereditary beliefs and circumstantial persuasions."[87] Here, whatever the tumult of the upper world, our "own proper and inaccessible being" sits enthroned, beyond the reach of outrage or dishonor. Here, "buried among the holiest privacies of the soul," lives that "innate dignity" which can keep from degradation even the flogged sailor at the gangway,[88] "that immaculate manliness we feel . . . so far within us, that it remains intact though all the outer character seems gone."[89] In the face of the most shattering onslaught of circumstance, " 'always one dark chamber in [us] is retained by the old mystery,' "[90] and it is here that the unseen essential self reposes, as within that inmost room of Willamilla's concentric-corridored palace where, safe "in [his]

[85] *Pierre*, p. 382 (Book XIX, chap. ii).
[86] *Ibid.*, p. 397 (Book XXI, chap. i).
[87] *Ibid.*, p. 122 (Book V, chap. i).
[88] *White-Jacket*, p. 177 (chap. xxxiv).
[89] *Moby-Dick*, I, 143–44 (chap. xxvi).
[90] *Mardi*, II, 157 (chap. cxliii).

impenetrable retreat, centrally slumbered the universe-rounded, zodiac-belted, horizon-zoned, sea-girt, reef-sashed, mountain-locked, arbor-nested, royalty-girdled, arm-clasped, self-hugged, indivisible Donjalolo, absolute monarch of Juam."[91]

But to this still center, the soul's tideless and "landlocked Mediterranean,"[92] few of us have access entire and unobstructed. In ignorant childhood, it is true, we were permitted to live for a time in untroubled possession of our "insular Tahiti, full of peace and joy"; but long since made distrustful of its beauty, we have pushed off from that isle and come into the midst of "all the horrors of the half known life."[93] Supported though we may be thereafter by "a sense of uncapitulatable security" welling from that invisible source, we yet dwell less in the reality than in the memory of that repose. We will count ourselves fortunate when, by the chance turning of a key, our "own secret golden treasuries" are for a brief moment thrown open to us:

Oh, grassy glades! Oh, ever vernal endless landscapes in the soul; in ye—though long parched by the dead drought of the earthy life,—in ye, men yet may roll, like young horses in new morning clover; and for some few fleeting moments, feel the cool dew of the life immortal on them. Would to God these blessed calms would last.[94]

But they do not. Moments such as these are interludes only, the insights they offer the mere permitted and temporary accidents of fortune. The soul can place her trust in no such random charity but must continue to seek, as the true business of her life, the conquest and the settled occupation of her own buried citadel.

There will be hardship and danger in the attempt. Like Prospero's realm, like the "Enviable Isles" of fable, this core

---

91 *Ibid.*, I, 279 (chap. lxxix).

92 *Ibid.*, II, 53 (chap. cxix).

93 *Moby-Dick*, I, 349 (chap. lviii).

94 *Ibid.*, II, 264 (chap. cxiv).

of quiet is guarded by tempests: "Through storms you reach
[it] and from storms are free."[95] The thought is of frequent
recurrence in Melville. Ishmael's boat, whirled by a harpooned
and pain-maddened whale through ring after frantic ring of
"the grand armada" of leviathans, slows at last and comes
quietly to rest in "that enchanted calm which they say lurks
at the heart of every commotion." There, in the entranced
clear deeps beneath, he sees—while the business of death goes
forward everywhere at the circumference—the unintermitted
work of birth and generation:

And thus, though surrounded by circle upon circle of consterna-
tions and affrights, did these inscrutable creatures at the centre
freely and fearlessly indulge in all peaceful concernments; yea,
serenely revelled in dalliance and delight. But even so, amid the
tornadoed Atlantic of my being, do I myself still for ever centrally disport in mute calm; and while ponderous planets of un-
waning woe revolve round me, deep down and deep inland there
I still bathe me in eternal mildness of joy.[96]

Art lays its unplumbed foundations in these waters, and
the great work of art becomes itself an emblem of the soul
that has shaped it:

. . . [M]ost grand productions of the best human intellects ever
are built round a circle, as atolls (i.e., the primitive coral islets
which, raising themselves in the depths of profoundest seas, rise
funnel-like to the surface, and present there a hoop of white rock,
which though on the outside everywhere lashed by the ocean, yet
excludes all tempests from the quiet lagoon within), digestively
including the whole range of all that can be known or dreamed.[97]

The labor of the artist seems often hopeless, for the reality
he seeks lies deep: it must be dived for in the sea and dug
for in the earth. An incredible amount of "earthy rubbish has
first to be troublesomely handled and thrown out" of the

---

95 "The Enviable Isles," in *Poems*, p. 241.
96 *Moby-Dick*, II, 135–36 (chap. lxxxvii).
97 *Pierre*, p. 394 (Book XXI, chap. i).

shaft before the rich vein can be tapped.[98] Yet the labor must be endured, for creation both begins and ends in the experience of self-possession:

"When Lombardo set about his work, he knew not what it would become. He did not build himself in with plans; he wrote right on; and so doing, got deeper and deeper into himself; and like a resolute traveler, plunging through baffling woods, at last was rewarded for his toils . . . , [coming] out into a serene, sunny, ravishing region; full of sweet scents, singing birds, . . . prophetic voices."[99]

And once established there, the artist knows (for the time, at least) a self-sufficiency like that of "the circus-running sun" who "needs no sustenance but what's in himself."[100] All external compulsion fallen away, as when the wind's pressure is suddenly withdrawn, he moves now with an effortless ease. Melville himself, in the afterglow of *Moby-Dick*'s creation, knew this feeling of completeness and spoke of it to Hawthorne:

A sense of unspeakable security is in me this moment, on account of your having understood the book. I have written a wicked book, and feel spotless as the lamb. Ineffable socialities are in me. I would sit down and dine with you and with all the gods in old Rome's Pantheon. It is a strange feeling—no hopefulness is in it, no despair. Content—that is it; and irresponsibility; but without licentious inclination. I speak now of my profoundest sense of being, not of an incidental feeling.[101]

But the victories of the artist are not so lasting as they seem, and he is permitted to share but briefly in the self-sufficiency of his product. (The triumph here celebrated will in a few short months be all but forgotten among the an-

[98] *Ibid.*, p. 359 (Book XVIII, chap. i).

[99] *Mardi*, II, 326 (chap. clxxx).

[100] *Moby-Dick*, II, 125–26 (chap. lxxxvii).

[101] Letter to Nathaniel Hawthorne, November, 1851, reprinted in Metcalf, *op. cit.*, pp. 128–29.

guished uncertainties of *Pierre*.) In the finished work of art the artist sees, it is true, the image of his own fulfilment; but that fulfilment exists in symbolic prefiguration only and not in living actuality. For though the work of art has moved, in the course of its creation, out of time and into a world of unvarying perfection, yet it has done so, paradoxically, at the cost of incurring a kind of finitude in the exhaustion of its possibilities for growth and change. Man, on the other hand, is by the mere fact of his continued living denied the privilege of this fixed repose. He is condemned to change, but the same sentence makes him capable also of an endless growth: "his whole mortal life brings not his immortal soul to maturity; nor will all eternity perfect him."[102] His life proceeds by imbalances constantly redressed, and the soul's still center is at first no more than the incredibly fine point of the fulcrum upon which all rests. By experience, by the teaching of pain, by reflection, by the deepening of his sympathies, and by the long practice of a stoic discipline, the realm of quiet may be gradually enlarged. It is not to be attained, however, through the denial of any part of man's nature. A Nirvana of ignorance or of insensibility presents a less than human goal: man's task is to weigh and to bring to a poise the realities both of head and heart. Small wonder, then, if the long-desired stillness, once achieved, is found to be no true stasis but a trembling, ever precarious balance.

Difficult as is the discovery and full possession of our profoundest being, we are yet sustained in that labor by a never quite failing consciousness of the thing we seek. There is that within us, we instinctively know, which the world cannot defile: like the doubloon's virgin gold, it remains "untouchable and immaculate to any foulness" though "nailed amidst all the rustiness of iron bolts and the verdigris of copper spikes."[103] Nor can the mind's red flames and leaping shadows

102 *Mardi*, I, 268 (chap. lxxv).
103 *Moby-Dick*, II, 189 (chap. xcix).

reach in so far: "in the pitchiest night the ship's black hull still houses an illumination," and in that flood of white and purest light we may, like the sleeping sailors of the "Pequod," find refreshment.[104] Taught by this quiet, we may even perceive beyond the known paths of submission and defiance a third course—the path of indifference. Embittered Enceladus is not, after all, the sole type and figure of the outcast god. There is also

> That Rama whom the Indian sung—
> A god he was, but knew it not;
> Hence vainly puzzled at the wrong
> Misplacing him in human lot.
> Curtailment of his right he bare
> Rather than wrangle; but no less
> Was taunted for his tameness there.
> A fugitive without redress,
> He never the Holy Spirit grieved,
> Nor the divine in him bereaved,
> Though what that was he might not guess.

Nor can we guess, in our own lives. But what is possible for us is, like Rama, at all times to acknowledge and respect that obscured divinity, to desire and seek his revelation, and quietly to maintain in the face of all hardships and indignities the simple

> . . . consciousness of self.
> Though black frost nip, though white frost chill,
> Nor white frost nor the black may kill
> The patient root, the vernal sense
> Surviving hard experience
> As grass the winter. Even that curse
> Which is the wormwood mixed with gall—
> Better dependent on the worse—
> Divine upon the animal—
> That cannot make such natures fall.[105]

[104] *Ibid.*, p. 183 (chap. xcvii).
[105] *Clarel*, I, 130–31 (Part I, canto xxxii).

2. *The Opposing Other*

But though the thing we seek lies within us, our path to it is anything but direct. Mere introspection, unlighted by experience, proves beyond a certain point worse than useless to us. Stared at, the images vanishes, like Ahab's reflection in the water. Melville develops this point most elaborately in his account of Donjalolo, the captive king of Juam.[1] Locked by traditional law within his cliff-walled pleasure-valley, this enervated Rasselas makes no effort to escape but passes his life in a perpetual transit from shadow to shadow, dodging the direct rays of the sun. It is the principal business of his court to guard him at

[1] *Mardi,* I, 252–90 (chaps. lxxi–lxxxii).

all times from the rough touch of reality. Everything is done for him, even to smoking, girl attendants breathing the aromatic fumes into his face. Fleetingly, in the intervals of his self-indulgence, Donjalolo is troubled by curiosity concerning the outer world, though never to the point of seeking experience in his own person. At the most, he will cross-examine returned travelers in an effort (invariably futile) to come at truth by proxy. And on the failure of each such attempt, he returns to the melancholy round of his pleasures. Appropriately enough, this "self-hugged . . . absolute monarch" is sterile: "for all his multitude of wives, he had never an heir."

A comparable sterility awaits those of us who would rest in a simple contemplation of self. For our identity is something that takes shape for us only through interaction with all which opposes it. Neither in life nor in art are we sufficient to ourselves:

Had Milton's been the lot of Casper Hauser [the wild boy of Germany], Milton would have been as vacant as he. For though the naked soul of man doth assuredly contain one latent element of intellectual productiveness; yet never was there a child born solely from one parent; the visible world of experience being that procreative thing which impregnates the muses; self-reciprocally efficient hermaphrodites being but a fable.[2]

The road to a fuller discovery of self leads outward, therefore, into this same "visible world of experience." What we are is necessarily to be defined upon the background of what we are not: the *I* has meaning only by reference to an *Other*. With the realization of this truth, the immediate problem is no longer "What am I?" but "What is this universe in which I find myself?" The second question is not markedly easier than the first, for implicit within it lie a thousand other questions having to do with the nature, attitude, and effect upon us of particular men, of society and its institutions, of the natural world, and of the God with Whom all began. The answers we individ-

[2] *Pierre*, p. 361 (Book XVIII, chap. i).

ually propose to these questions are at once consequences of what we are and determinants of what we shall become.

Nearly the first thing we learn from our contact with this universe is that its nature is mixed: it shows itself as both good and bad, tender and merciless, life-giving and death-dealing. The many polarities of the natural world—day and night, summer and winter, land and sea—make this everywhere evident to us:

> At variance . . . move
> The spleen of nature and her love:
> At variance, yet entangled too—
> Like wrestlers. Here in apt review
> They call to mind Abel and Cain—
> Ormuzd involved with Ahriman
> In deadly lock.[3]

But it is by our inability to hold this simple truth in mind that we most frequently go astray. For our individual experience of life does not show us these opposing aspects in anything like a just or symmetrical balance. Circumstance differs from man to man and from day to day, as do also the facts of temperament. Each of us, therefore, forms his own partial and imperfect picture of reality and all too often insists upon that picture—optimistic or pessimistic—as the true and complete account. What follows from this error will shape itself as tragedy, pathos, or bitter comedy, in accordance with each man's mental and emotional endowment.

Experience and reflection may in time redress the balance and help us to a truer estimate. "Evil and good they braided play/Into one cord."[4] And the wise man is not he who can discern and cleverly disentangle the one strand from the other but he who can see it always as one cord, who can keep the two aspects fused in a single integral vision of life:

[3] *Clarel*, II, 21 (Part III, canto v).

[4] *Ibid.*, p. 174 (Part IV, canto iv).

> Curled in the comb of yon billow Andean,
> Is it the Dragon's heaven-challenging crest?
> Elemental mad ramping of ravening waters—
> Yet Christ on the Mount, and the dove in her nest![5]

Such a view neither denies the existence of evil nor attempts to force it into a subordinate role as part of a benevolent general design. It frankly acknowledges that evil is more than the mere absence of good: it is a positive and active force working against the good. The two strands must be kept at all times distinct, yet neither is to be seen in isolation from the other.

From *Typee* on, all of Melville's books are marked by an aspiration, at least, toward this single vision. The wild anger with which certain of his heroes hurl themselves against the injurious gods ought not to blind us to the fact that Melville himself remains always to some degree reserved, not finally committed. Our attention is repeatedly directed, in both *Moby-Dick* and *Pierre*, to elements of extravagance and blindness as well as heroism in the characters of the protagonists. And during his later years especially, Melville held steadily before him —as is evident in *Clarel*—the ideal of a balanced view of life. In a letter of 1885, written to thank an admirer for the gift of a volume of James Thomson's poems, he makes clear that despite a large measure of sympathy, he and the gloomy Londoner look upon the world from quite different standpoints:

Your friend was a sterling poet, if ever one sang. As to pessimism, altho neither pessimist nor optimist myself, nevertheless I relish it in the verse if for nothing else than as a counterpoise to the exorbitant hopefulness, juvenile and shallow, that makes such a bluster in these days—at least in some quarters.[6]

Poise and not passion, it would appear, is the desired state. From the time of *Israel Potter*, Melville gives an increasingly

[5] "Pebbles VI," in *Poems*, p. 244.

[6] Letter to James Billson, January 22, 1885, in Eleanor Melville Metcalf, *Herman Melville, Cycle and Epicycle* (Cambridge, Mass.: Harvard University Press, 1953), p. 268.

prominent place in his writing to the figures of the patient sufferer and the stoic realist whom neither elation nor despair can
drive from a conviction of the unitary nature of experience.

But only in rare instances and with difficulty does human
nature rise to this level of insight and firmness. Of far more
frequent occurrence are the enthusiasts and the rebels, those
partisans of bright or dark for whom life must be always the
one thing or the other. And it is of these that we must first
speak.

GREEN AND GOLDEN
WORLD

Before the whole can be grasped, the
parts must be seen. And though it be granted that reality's two
aspects lie entwined in the least part of our experience, yet the
two are not equally apparent. To perceive the dark and to assign to it its just part in the whole is by far the more difficult
task. For "happiness courts the light, so we deem the world is
gay; but misery hides aloof, so we deem that misery there is
none."[7]

The darker truths rarely come to us in our youth. To be
young is to be in some measure deluded: one is dazzled by
life's glitter and variety and carried along by one's own exu-
berant vitality. Each of us begins as an optimist, and no one
more obviously so than the carefree young adventurer who
saunters through most of *Typee*, *Omoo*, and *White-Jacket*.
(That marked discrepancies have been found between this figure and that of the historical Melville is less important than
the fact that this is the picture that Melville wished his audi-
ence to have of him.) Looking at these books in the perspective of his later works, we today are likely to fasten our attention upon certain dark and portentous shadows in the background to the extent that we may fail to appreciate fully the

[7] "Bartleby," in *The Piazza Tales*, p. 40.

overflowing heartiness and good humor that made these books so acceptable to the general public of their day. But looked at simply in themselves, they are clearly the work of a young man delighted with living, confident of the future, sensuously alive and reaching out for every kind of experience.

A glance at his letters of the period gives further evidence of the high value Melville placed upon fine food, drink, cigars, and good fellowship. The appetites, he firmly believed, should keep step with the intellect. His "poetical creed" notwithstanding, he tells Hawthorne, he cannot feel it as inevitable that "the brain eats out the heart"; it is his "*prose* opinion that in most cases, in those men who have fine brains and work them well, the heart extends down to hams."[8] Asceticism never, either then or later, held the slightest charm for Melville. In the exhortation he addresses, in *Pierre*, to the devotees of cold water and the Graham cracker, we seem to hear Rabelais speaking with the voice of St. Paul:

Feed all things with food convenient for them,—that is, if the food be procurable. The food of thy soul is light and space; feed it then on light and space. But the food of thy body is champagne and oysters; feed it then on champagne and oysters; and so shall it merit a joyful resurrection, if there is any to be. Say, wouldst thou rise with a lantern jaw and a spavined knee? Rise with brawn on thee, and a most royal corporation before thee; so shalt thou in that day claim respectful attention.[9]

Even the admirable Hawthorne strikes Melville as insufficiently earthy: "He doesn't patronize the butcher—he needs roast-beef, done rare."[10] Nevertheless, it is Hawthorne (in unexpectedly convivial mood) and a basket of champagne (for "I won't believe in a Temperance Heaven") that occupy the center of Melville's imagined paradise: "We shall [he informs his no doubt startled friend] . . . cross our celestial legs in the

---

8 Letter to Nathaniel Hawthorne, June, 1851, in Metcalf, *op. cit.*, p. 109.

9 *Pierre*, p. 417 (Book XXII, chap. i).

10 Letter to Evert Duyckinck, February 12, 1851, in Metcalf, *op. cit.*, p. 99.

celestial grass that is forever tropical, and strike our glasses and our heads together, till both musically ring in concert. . . . ."[11]

The picture has, despite its oddity, a certain teasing familiarity. One might almost take it—but for the champagne—as a reminiscence of life among the Typees during Melville's first weeks on Nukuheva. One recalls, too, that to the imagination of Rolfe, the most Melvillean of the desert pilgrims of *Clarel*, the thought of Paradise comes as a memory of the untroubled Polynesian world he had known in youth and so unaccountably fled.[12]

What one remembers most vividly of *Typee* is its sympathetic presentation of a life of simple instinct and spontaneity. It puts before us a world we all seem somehow to remember, in which the bond between man and nature is still unbroken, the archangel's flaming sword not yet interposed. When Tommo, descending the cliff into tree-hidden Typee valley, puts aside a branch and catches, as it seems to him, "a glimpse of the gardens of Paradise," his eye takes in the huts of the islanders, scattered "here and there amidst the foliage," simply as part of the one natural scene.[13] One is reminded, perhaps not too incongruously, of a similar interpenetration of nature and art in the opening of Wordsworth's "Tintern Abbey":

> These plots of cottage-ground . . .
> . . . .
> [which] lose themselves
> 'Mid groves and corpses. . . .
> These hedgerows, hardly hedgerows, little lines
> Of sportive wood run wild: these pastoral farms,
> Green to the very door; and wreaths of smoke
> Sent up, in silence, from among the trees!

[11] Letter to Nathaniel Hawthorne, June 29, 1851, *ibid.*, p. 108.

[12] *Clarel*, II, 140–41 (Part III, canto xxix).

[13] *Typee*, p. 64 (chap. vii) ; see also p. 262 (chap. xxvi).

Arrived at the valley floor, Tommo find his first impressions everywhere confirmed. The naked boy and girl he encounters in the forest are as much at ease in their surroundings as any animals. The birds and the small golden lizards of the valley, he later observes, display no fear whatever of man: he moves among them as little noted as any other creature.[14]

Nor has the islander much more need to labor than these birds and lizards:

> The penalty of the Fall presses very lightly upon the valley of Typee; for, with the one solitary exception of striking a light, I scarcely saw any piece of work performed there which caused the sweat to stand upon a single brow. As for digging and delving for a livelihood, the thing is altogether unknown. Nature had planted the breadfruit and the banana, and in her own good time she brings them to maturity, when the idle savage stretches forth his hand, and satisfies his appetite.[15]

In this favored climate, the "wide-slaughtering typhoon" of other regions is unknown: the weather "can hardly be said to have any vicissitudes." The worst that nature seems to be capable of is a small non-stinging species of fly:

> There are no animals of any kind on the island, unless it be decided that the natives themselves are such. The mountains and the interior present to the eye nothing but silent solitudes, unbroken by the roar of beasts of prey, and enlivened by few tokens even of minute animated existence. There are no venomous reptiles, and no snakes of any description.[16]

Man himself, at least within the limits of his own tribe, presents no greater danger to his kind. Crime is unknown in this world where nature supplies every want:

> In the darkest nights they slept securely, with all their wordly wealth around them, in houses the doors of which were never fastened. The disquieting ideas of theft or assassination never dis-

[14] *Ibid.*, pp. 284–85 (chap. xxix).
[15] *Ibid.*, p. 262 (chap. xxvi).
[16] *Ibid.*, p. 286 (chap. xxix).

turbed them. Each islander reposed beneath his own palmetto thatching, or sat under his own breadfruit tree, with none to molest or alarm him. There was not a padlock in the valley, nor anything that answered the purpose of one.[17]

As little cause for violence is provided by sexual jealousy. No sign of such a passion is to be seen in Typee. By an easy but regular system of plural marriage, "A baneful promiscuous intercourse of the sexes is . . . avoided, and virtue, without being clamorously invoked, is, as it were, unconsciously practiced." A fraternal feeling marks every observable relation of the islanders:

> During my whole stay on the island I never witnessed a single quarrel. . . . The natives appeared to form one household, whose members were bound together by the ties of strong affection. The love of kindred I did not so much perceive, for it seemed blended in the general love; and where all were treated as brothers and sisters, it was hard to tell who were actually related to each other by blood.[18]

Running through all, he finds, is a universal and inexhaustible delight in the mere act of living. Untroubled by any of "those thousand sources of irritation that the ingenuity of civilized man has created to mar his own felicity," a spirit of "perpetual hilarity [reigned] through the whole extent of the vale. There seemed to be no cares, griefs, troubles, or vexations in all Typee. The hours tripped along as gaily as the couples down a country dance."[19]

Not even religion occasions any great discomfort. So long as a decent regard is had for the niceties of the taboo, the individual is free to do pretty much as he pleases. As for theology, the natives

are either too lazy or too sensible to worry themselves about abstract points of religious belief. While I was among them they

---

[17] *Ibid.*, p. 270 (chap. xxvii).

[18] *Ibid.*, pp. 256–58 (chap. xxvi) ; p. 275 (chap. xxvii).

[19] *Ibid.*, p. 168 (chap. xvii).

never held any synods or councils to settle the principles of their faith by agitating them. An unbounded liberty of conscience seemed to prevail.[20]

Worship (of a sort) is accorded a variety of gods, but it has been made clear to them from the start that this is a man-centered world to which they have been granted a wholly probational admission. If anyone here may be said to be priest-ridden, it is rather the gods than the people. The latter, made slack by a "long prosperity of breadfruit and coconuts," may with impunity scant their religious duties. But let some "poor devil of a deity" withhold his co-operation only a little, and he is beaten, scolded, and shut up in a box until he learns better. In general, Typee's

luckless idols . . . received more hard knocks than supplications. I do not wonder that some of them looked so grim, and stood so bolt upright, as if fearful of looking to the right or to the left lest they should give any one offence. The fact is, they had to carry themselves *"pretty straight,"* or suffer the consequences.[21]

As regards the people themselves, however, perhaps the most remarkable thing of all is the complete absence from their society of coercion or (the absurdities of the taboo aside) of external law. How different from the state of civilized man, among whom "truth and justice, and the better principles of our nature, cannot exist unless enforced by the statute-book!"[22]

It may reasonably be inquired, how were these people governed? How were their passions controlled in their everyday transactions? It must have been by an inherent principle of honesty and charity toward each other. They seemed to be governed by that sort of tacit common-sense law which, say what they will of the inborn lawlessness of the human race, has its precepts graven on every breast. The grand principles of virtue and honor, however they may be distorted by arbitrary codes, are the same all the world over:

20 *Ibid.*, pp. 229–30 (chap. xxiv).

21 *Ibid.*, p. 239 (chap. xxiv).

22 *Ibid.*, pp. 269, 272 (chap. xxvii).

and where these principles are concerned, the right or wrong of any action appears the same to the uncultivated as to the enlightened mind. It is to this indwelling, this universally diffused perception of what is *just* and *noble,* that the integrity of the Marquesans in their intercourse with each other is to be attributed.[23]

We have here the central tenet of the young Melville's optimistic faith: man is not Adam in ruins but a being divinely guided (when uncorrupted by creeds or institutions) by the instinctive promptings of his own nature. The idea is of course not new with Melville. Rousseau and Godwin, among others, had long since given it a wide currency, and in the hands of the anti-Calvinist religious thinkers of the past half-century it had become almost a commonplace. In adopting it to the extent that he does in his early works, Melville is simply moving with the current of his age. He presents this view most fully and explicitly in certain of the philosophical discussions of *Mardi.* There the writings of the sage Bardianna are cited to remind us that "we need not be told what righteousness is; we were born with the whole Law in our hearts."[24] For the primitive Christians of Serenia, the love of God is spontaneous and untaught: " 'We love him [Christ] from an instinct in us;—a fond, filial, reverential feeling.' " So too the Serenians' charity for their fellow men: " 'By the abounding, the needy are supplied. Yet not by statute, but from dictates, born half dormant in us, and warmed into life by [Christ]. These dictates we but follow in all we do; we are not dragged to righteousness; but go running.' "[25] The inward voice speaks through our reason as well as our conscience. Seeking abroad after wisdom, we forget that

"much of the knowledge we seek, already we have in our cores. Yet so simple it is, we despise it; so bold, we fear it.

"In solitude, let us exhume our ingots. Let us hear our own

[23] *Ibid.,* pp. 269–70 (chap. xxvii).

[24] *Mardi,* II, 303 (chap. clxxv).

[25] *Ibid.,* pp. 367–68 (chap. clxxxvii).

thoughts. The soul needs no mentor but [God]; and [God], without proxy. Wanting Him, it is both the teacher and the taught. Undeniably, reason was the first revelation; and so far as it tests all others, it has precedence over them. It comes direct to us, without suppression or interpolation; and with [God's] indisputable imprimatur."[26]

Granted that reason is no infallible guide to the fulness of truth, we must impute this failure less to the imperfection of the instrument than to the immensity of the object to which it is perhaps improperly applied: " 'Fellow-men; the ocean we would sound is unfathomable; and however much we add to our line, when it is out, we feel not the bottom.' "[27] And though all the seekers after the ultimate except Taji end by accepting the reality of that fact and acknowledging the mind's true work to be the attainment of the good life, they do not thereby repudiate the birthright of reason, for " 'Right-reason, and Alma [Christ], are the same; else Alma, not reason, would we reject.' "[28]

Time will darken this picture of man for Melville. But never by any display of human meanness or malignity will he be driven into a settled despair of his kind. Hero, sot, saint, or murderer—over all is spread the "one royal mantle of humanity."[29] For " 'we all wear crowns, from our cradles to our graves, and though in *double-darbies* in the *brig*, the commodore himself can't unking us.' "[30] Within each of us there speaks, however intermittently, a noble instinct (call it conscience or reason) which has no counterpart in nature; and all our best endeavors are undertaken at its prompting. It is this which teaches us to reverence "the essential dignity of man" and to denounce the assaults of tyranny upon it as "religious-

26 *Ibid.*, p. 301 (chap. clxxv).

27 *Ibid*

28 *Ibid.*, pp. 370–71 (chap. clxxxvii).

29 *Moby-Dick*, I, 144 (chap. xxvi).

30 *White-Jacket*, p. 296 (chap. lvi).

ly, morally, and immutably *wrong*," even though backed by the full authority of custom and law;[31] to bleed "with keenest anguish at the undraped spectacle of a valor-ruined man" and with "our costliest robes" run to cover from our sight and his own whatever "ignominious blemish" fate may have disclosed in him.[32]

To emphasize as we have the predominantly optimistic view of man offered in *Typee* and *Omoo* is not to deny that these books present a darker side. The civilization which Europe and America had brought to Polynesia is pictured as a rapacious and destructive force, unnatural in its vices, rigid and sterile in its virtues.[33] Yet it is to civilized men in Europe and America that Melville appeals for justice to the islanders: "Let the savages be civilized, but civilize them with benefits, and not with evils; and let heathenism be destroyed, but not by destroying the heathen."[34] Evil exists, but so does the possibility of reform and amelioration. The question of the source of social evil (so fatal a question to primitivism) remains unasked, nor is there any evidence that Melville as yet suspects that source to be "the all-engendering heart of man" himself.[35]

Life's brighter aspect thus presented itself to the young Melville, not only in his intuition of what man essentially is, but in the prospect of what he may yet be. The words *democracy, progress,* and the *future* were above all others the shibboleths of nineteenth-century America, and it would be remarkable if the unsophisticated sailor-author of those years were wholly to have escaped their force. It ought not to surprise us, then, if in the earlier books we find these topics treated with an at times quite surprising naïveté.

31 *Ibid.*, p. 182 (chap. xxxv).

32 *Moby-Dick*, I, 144 (chap. xxvi).

33 *Typee*, pp. 262–68 (chap. xxvi); *Omoo*, pp. 218–29 (chap. xlviii).

34 *Typee*, p. 263 (chap. xxvi).

35 "Hawthorne and His Mosses," in *Billy Budd and Other Prose Pieces,* p. 128.

In *White-Jacket,* for instance, the case for the abolition of
naval flogging is made to rest not on the dignity of man alone
but on an almost mystical faith in the inevitability of progress:

The world has arrived at a period which renders it the part of
Wisdom to pay homage to the prospective precedents of the Future
in preference to those of the Past. The Past is dead, and has no
resurrection; but the Future is endowed with such a life, that it
lives to us even in anticipation. The Past is, in many things, the
foe of mankind; the Future is, in all things, our friend. In the
Past is no hope; the Future is both hope and fruition. The Past
is the textbook of tyrants; the Future the Bible of the Free. Those
who are solely governed by the Past stand like Lot's wife, crystal-
lized in the act of looking backward, and forever incapable of
looking before.
    Let us leave the Past, then, to dictate laws to immovable China.
. . . But for us, we will have another captain to rule over us—that
captain who ever marches at the head of his troop and beckons
them forward, not lingering in the rear, and impeding their march
with lumbering baggage-wagons of old precedents.[36]

(A mocking echo of this procession will come back to us in
Clarel's account, a quarter of a century later, of that other
cheerful marcher, Derwent, the liberal cleric:

> Thought's last adopted style he showed;
> Abreast kept with the age, the year,
> And each bright optimistic mind,
> Nor lagged with Solomon in rear,
> And Job, the furthermost behind—
> Brisk marching in time's drum-corps van
> Abreast with whistling Jonathan.)[37]

But at the moment there is not the slightest hint of derision. It
is our nation's happy destiny, we are told, to lead the family
of man into this new Promised Land:

[36] *White-Jacket,* p. 188 (chap. xxxvi).
[37] *Clarel,* I, 172 (Part II, canto i).

[We] Americans are the peculiar, chosen people—the Israel of our time; we bear the ark of the liberties of the world. . . . God has predestinated, mankind expects, great things from our race; and great things we feel in our souls. The rest of the nations must soon be in our rear. We are the pioneers of the world; the advance-guard, sent on through the wilderness of untried things, to break a new path in the New World that is ours. In our youth is our strength; in our inexperience, our wisdom. At a period when other nations have but lisped, our deep voice is heard afar. Long enough have we been sceptics with regard to ourselves, and doubted whether, indeed, the political Messiah had come. But he has come in *us*, if we would but give utterance to his promptings. And let us always remember that with ourselves, almost for the first time in the history of earth, national selfishness is unbounded philanthropy; for we cannot do a good to America but we give alms to the world.[38]

With only a slight alteration of tone, the voice here could be mistaken for Emerson's. The same confusion is perhaps less likely with regard to a similar passage in *Redburn* where the imagery mounts to an even more fevered pitch: "The deep-sea lead, that first struck these soundings, brought up the soil of Earth's Paradise. Not a Paradise then, or now; but to be made so . . ."; and we may with confidence look forward to "the world's jubilee morning" when, "at God's good pleasure," we shall see "a new Pentecost" descend in flames upon the other races of men with the unifying gift of a single tongue, which shall be (conveniently) "the language of Britain."[39]

It is not of course suggested that this sort of thing is typical of Melville at any time. Rather, it is Melville pleading a case, Melville carried away for the moment by his own natural exuberance. These same books, viewed either as wholes or in their separate parts, furnish evidence enough that already he knew better than to "insist upon the universal application of a tem-

---

[38] *White-Jacket*, p. 189 (chap. xxxvi).
[39] *Redburn*, p. 217 (chap. xxxiii).

porary feeling or opinion."[40] Philosophical consistency, it is true, is no very sound criterion for art. Yet one cannot but wonder that the man who had already written the satiric Vivenza chapters of *Mardi*[41] could set down paragraphs like these and not be driven to exclaim, as he later did in the margin of one of Emerson's cheerful pages, "What stuff all this is!"[42]

And indeed, in the books following *White-Jacket*, the note is never sounded without its unmistakable overtone of irony. So it is, for instance, in that passage of mock celebration of the green and golden, seemingly never-ending summer world of Pierre's youth:

> Oh, praised be the beauty of this earth; the beauty, and the bloom, and the mirthfulness thereof! We lived before, and shall live again; and as we hope for a fairer world than this to come; so we came from one less fine. From each successive world, the demon Principle is more and more dislodged; he is the accursed clog from chaos, and thither, by every new translation, we drive him further and further back again. Hosannahs to this world! so beautiful itself, and the vestibule to more. Out of some past Egypt, we have come to this new Canaan; and from this new Canaan, we press on to some new Circassia. Though still the villains, Want and Woe, followed us out of Egypt, and now beg in Canaan's streets; yet Circassia's gates shall not admit them; they, with their sire, the demon Principle, must back to chaos, whence they came.[43]

By the time this was written, Melville's youth was wholly behind him and he had too little patience with the naïveté of his hero. "The questionable apple of knowledge" had been bitten to the core and he was no longer able to forget that " 'evil is the chronic malady of the universe [which] checked in one place, breaks forth in another.' "[44] This is not to say that for

[40] Letter to Nathaniel Hawthorne, June, 1851, in Metcalf, *op. cit.*, p. 110.

[41] *Mardi*, II, 225–52 (chaps. clviii–clxii).

[42] Jay Leyda, *The Melville Log* (New York: Harcourt, Brace & Co., 1951), II, 648.

[43] *Pierre*, pp. 43–44 (Book II, chap. iv).

[44] *Mardi*, II, 244 (chap. clxi).

> Whate'er the light musician tenders;
> So warblest thou lay after lay
> Scarce self-derived; and (shroud before)
> Down goest singing toward Death's Sea.[50]

A less poignant instance of the naïveté of boyhood is to be seen in the young hero of *Redburn*. The prevailingly comic tone of the first half of this book arises from a carefully maintained disproportion between the illusions of the protagonist and the hard realities of life in a merchantman forecastle. Early adversity had taught Redburn "to think much and bitterly before [his] time," but unfortunately these reflections have done little to sharpen his sight for the smooth dishonesty of his captain or the vice and cruelty of his fellows. The latter strike him as "men of naturally gentle and kind dispositions" only a little soured for the time by "hardships, and neglect, and ill-usage."[51] The more sophisticatedly evil Captain Riga seems to him "a fine, funny gentleman, full of mirth and good humor," who would no doubt be delighted to have him drop in at the cabin for a social call.[52] These and other errors of the young sailor are in a familiar comic tradition of the period and seem often amusing enough; but the world which continues to reveal to the boy depth after depth of infamy and heartlessness is anything but comic. And at the book's end we are reminded that although he, "Wellingborough Redburn, chance[d] to survive," his friend and English counterpart, young Harry Bolton, did not.

But of all Melville's youthful heroes, the most tragically deluded is that "dewy boy" whose ambiguous portrait is given us in the early chapters of *Pierre*. In *Redburn,* the narrator's handling of the protagonist has been indulgent, even tender; but here the note of satire is so pronounced that the reader is often uncertain what attitude he is meant to adopt toward

[50] *Clarel*, II, 19 (Part III, canto iv).

[51] *Redburn*, p. 10 (chap. ii) ; p. 59 (chap. ix).

[52] *Ibid.*, pp. 85–91 (chap. xiv).

Pierre. Are we to see in him an authentic American Adam, or simply a caricature of the genteel romantic hero of magazine fiction? Unfortunately, we are never able wholly to exclude either element, but in Books I and II the balance inclines toward caricature.

Born to position and affluence, his mind shaped by the combined forces of culture and a simple country life, endowed with perfect health and considerable beauty of person, secure in the memory of a godlike father and the love of a "pedestaled mother," happy in the prospect of his approaching marriage, and utterly confident of the future, Master Pierre Glendinning of Saddle Meadows presents a picture too idyllic for belief. And that Melville himself was unable to believe in its reality is all too evident in the artificiality of both language and character. What he has been unable truly to imagine, he is driven to borrow; and what he borrows from the sentimental literature of the day, he is constantly tempted to burlesque. The result is an unfortunate mixture of tones which remains unresolved until after the hero's expulsion from the earthly paradise of Saddle Meadows. As we read these chapters now, it is easy to see why for thirty years thereafter Melville did not attempt another picture of youthful innocence, and when he did, gave us in Billy Budd a figure with the large simple outlines and the deep suggestiveness of myth. What in Pierre had been presented as ignorance, a mere negation, becomes in Billy the positive phenomenon of an innocence as radical and as mysterious as the evil it confronts. Reverence replaces the note of amused condescension that troubled us in the earlier book. The difference, however, ought not to blind us to the fact that innocence is in both cases shown to be deadly to its possessor.

But it is impossible to make of these instances a universal rule. For it must be admitted that certain men do exist whom fortune chooses (for a time, at least) to spare; and for these men, far beyond the period of their youth, nature's bright aspect remains her only one. Granted that "sailor or landsman, there is some sort of a Cape Horn for all," yet there are men for whom the passage of that dangerous strait is long postponed and there are still other "lucky livers, to whom, by some rare fatality, [their] Cape Horns are placid as Lake Lemans."[53] Of this number, clearly, is that prosperous and vainglorious vessel, the "Bachelor," upon whose revelry Ahab turned his back with the same scorn that his fellow-sufferer, Paul Jones, reserved for all "cuddled natures made humdrum by long exemption from pain."[54] And such a one par excellence among men was that spotless passenger of the "Fidèle," the gentleman with the gold sleeve buttons:

Such goodness seemed his, allied with such fortune, that, so far as his own personal experience could have gone, scarcely could he have known ill, physical or moral; and as for knowing or suspecting the latter in any serious degree . . . by observation or philosophy; for that, probably, his nature, by its opposition, was imperfectly qualified, or from it wholly exempted.[55]

More numerous than the "lucky livers," however, are those best described as the "ungovernably good-natured." Happy-go-lucky Stubb comes to mind at once. "Good-humored, easy, and careless," the second mate of the "Pequod" is one who will undertake to run with the sun through the zodiac's full circle of calamities " 'and yet [come] out of it all alive and hearty. . . . Oh, jolly's the word for aye!' "[56] And when his last moment comes, he goes to his death jesting both at Starbuck's prayer and at the grinning monster about to stave in his ship.[57] Even in the midst of the greater catastrophe, one finds a moment to regret that Stubb ever chose to ship aboard Ahab's grim vessel. He would have served so happily under

---

[53] *White-Jacket*, p. 137 (chap. xxvi).

[54] *Moby-Dick*, II, 266–68 (chap. cxv) ; *Israel Potter*, p. 120 (chap. xiv).

[55] *The Confidence-Man*, pp. 45–46 (chap. vii).

[56] *Moby-Dick*, I, 145 (chap. xxvii) ; II, 191–92 (chap. xcix).

[57] *Ibid.*, p. 365 (chap. cxxxv).

the jovial captain of the "Samuel Enderby," who had lowered once for the white whale, lost an arm to him, and cheerfully putting it down to profit and loss, turned to the pursuit of more manageable game.[58] Charlie Millthorpe, one of Pierre's foils, offers another instance of good nature: a boyhood of grinding poverty and the daily sight of misery and sickness seems to have had no other effect upon this resilient youth than to heighten his native bumptiousness and cheery good humor.[59]

Membership in this group is not, however, incompatible with a degree of what is commonly considered a sound intellectual maturity. Captain Amasa Delano is perhaps the best example. Described as "a person of a singularly undistrustful good nature, not liable, except on extraordinary and repeated incentives, and hardly then, to indulge in personal alarms, any way involving the imputation of malign evil in man,"[60] he is nevertheless the sober and responsible master of a successful trading vessel. Aboard the half-derelict Spanish ship he encounters in the harbor of Santa Maria, he proves almost fatally blind to the true state of affairs; but that blindness is a consequence not of any deficiency of mind but of certain sentimental prejudices arising from a too "benevolent heart." The mere presence of evil in the universe he will not venture to deny, but its power to harm he sees as held in check by an "ever-watchful Providence." The Lucifer-like figure of the rebel slave Atufal is, after all, in chains (or seems to be), and Delano's "charmed eye" placidly includes him as a mere subordinate detail of "the benign aspect of nature, taking her innocent repose in the evening."[61] Portents of the truth—of the subtly dissembled reign of evil aboard the "San Dominick" —drift in upon him only to be dismissed as incredible:

58 *Ibid.*, pp. 198–202 (chap. c).

59 *Pierre*, pp. 383–89 (Book XX, chap. i).

60 "Benito Cereno," in *The Piazza Tales*, p. 67.

61 *Ibid.*, p. 139.

From no train of thought did these fancies come; not from within, but from without; suddenly, too, and in one throng, like hoar frost; yet as soon to vanish as the mild sun of Captain Delano's good-nature regained its meridian.[62]

And even after events have forced the malignant Babo to drop his mask of benevolence and openly strike at the life of the Spanish captain—even then Delano cannot learn from experience but persists in regarding such manifestations of evil as rare and isolated incidents:

"You generalize, Don Benito [he later tells the still horror-stricken Spaniard]; and mournfully enough. But the past is passed; why moralize upon it? Forget it. See, yon bright sun has forgotten it all, and the blue sea, and the blue sky; these have turned over new leaves."[63]

So also, Don Benito might have reminded him, had Don Alexandro Aranda, owner of the cargo of slaves carried by the "San Dominick," who had assured him at embarkation that "no fetters would be needed with his blacks"[64] and who had ended the voyage as a skeleton figurehead lashed to the vessel's prow.

To describe these several varieties of "provincial[s] and sentimentalist[s] in Truth,"[65] Melville had a half-jocular term of his own. He refers to them upon occasion as "bachelors," by which epithet he seems to imply not only that they are free of family responsibilities but that they have ascended no higher than the first degree of knowledge and perceive as yet only the surface of truth. We may include here (although his ignorance, it is true, is in large part wilful) "the care-free bachelor Abrazza" of *Mardi* who keeps always to the sunlit side of his island, ignores the ills of his subjects, and will hear at his banquet table no mention of pain or death.[66] "Bachelor,"

[62] *Ibid.*, p. 93.   [63] *Ibid.*, p. 168.   [64] *Ibid.*, p. 81.

[65] *Moby-Dick*, II, 71 (chap. lxxvi).

[66] *Mardi*, II, 316–45 (chaps. clxxix–clxxxvi).

again, is the name of the seventh ship spoken by Ahab: that fortunate, oil-rich, flag-bedecked vessel bound home for Nantucket without ever having encountered the white whale— " 'Only heard of him; but don't believe in him at all.' "[67] And the well-ordered ship commanded by the Captain Amasa Delano of whom we have spoken bears the name of "Bachelor's Delight."[68] To any one of these we might without unfairness attribute the words assigned by Melville to the hospitable young gentlemen of London's Temple, that "very Paradise of Bachelors":

> The thing called pain, the bugbear styled trouble—those two legends seemed preposterous to their bachelor imaginations. . . . How could they suffer themselves to be imposed upon by such monkish fables? Pain! Trouble! No such thing. Pass the sherry, sir.[69]

Of a somewhat more distrustful but still imperfectly hardened temper is Pitch, the "Missouri Bachelor" of *The Confidence-Man,* who for all his painful experience with dishonesty in the young, cannot wait to be shown before investing his confidence in his thirty-sixth hired boy.[70]

It is the chief danger of an optimistic view of life that it leads one into a too-unguarded trust in the benignities of a world that is, after all, "not without some man-traps." More safety, if less piety, may be found in an attitude marked by a certain suspicion of both man and God. Providence no doubt exists, but with interregnums; and experience teaches that that "grand and glowing creature" man is often in his particular manifestations "no better than he should be." He who wholly commits himself into the hands of either God or man courts the sad fate of China Aster, who accepted too unques-

---

[67] *Moby-Dick*, II, 268 (chap. cxv).

[68] "Benito Cereno," in *The Piazza Tales*, p. 136.

[69] "The Paradise of Bachelors," in *Billy Budd and Other Prose Pieces,* p. 237.

[70] *The Confidence-Man*, p. 140 (chap. xxi), pp. 154–71 (chap. xxii).

And in the midst of his meditation one night, the yard dropped
from beneath him and only a swift clutch at the rigging saved
him from being, in an all too literal sense, "[fused] . . . into
the universe of things."[77]

Ishmael, though similarly tempted, was more watchful.
Manning the masthead of the "Pequod" in the serene spring
weather of the tropics, he kept in mind what sort of wakening
is reserved for the dreamer at that post:

Lulled into such an opium-like listlessness of vacant, unconscious
reverie is this absent-minded youth by the blending cadence of
waves with thoughts, that at last he loses his identity; takes the
mystic ocean at his feet for the visible image of that deep, blue,
bottomless soul, pervading mankind and nature; and every strange,
half-seen, gliding, beautiful thing that eludes him; every dimly
discovered, uprising fin of some undiscernible form, seems to him
the embodiment of those elusive thoughts that only people the
soul by continually flitting through it. In this enchanted mood,
thy spirit ebbs away to whence it came; becomes diffused through
time and space; like Cranmer's sprinkled Pantheistic ashes, forming at last a part of every shore the round globe over.

There is no life in thee, now, except that rocking life imparted
by a gently rolling ship; by her, borrowed from the sea; by the
sea, from the inscrutable tides of God. But while this sleep, this
dream is on ye, move your foot or hand an inch; slip your hand
at all; and your identity comes back in horror. Over Descartian
vortices you hover. And perhaps, at mid-day, in the fairest weather,
with one half-throttled shriek you drop through that transparent
air into the summer sea, no more to rise for ever. Heed it well, ye
Pantheists![78]

77 *White-Jacket*, pp. 96–98 (chap. xix). That Melville himself knew the attraction of the pantheistic mood is apparent in the postscript to one of his
1851 letters to Hawthorne (in Metcalf, *op. cit.*, p. 110). After scoffing at the
"nonsense" of Goethe in effect telling a sufferer from toothache to "live in the
all," he adds: "That 'all' feeling, though, there is some truth in. You must
have often felt it, lying on the grass on a warm summer's day. Your legs seem
to send out shoots into the earth. Your hair feels like leaves upon your head.
This is the *all* feeling. But what plays the mischief with the truth is that men
will insist upon the universal application of a temporary feeling or opinion."

78 *Moby-Dick*, I, 198 (chap. xxxv).

DARK HINDOO HALF
OF NATURE

To some other dreamers the stroke of
misfortune comes less catastrophically, but with an equal finality cutting them off from the pleasant world they have hitherto
known. Such a transforming stroke for Taji was the disappearance of Yillah, for Pierre the reception of Isabel's letter,
for the Southerner Ungar of *Clarel* the shot at Sumter opening
"the fissure in the [nation's] hearth." For each of these the
familiar world took on from that hour a different and a darker
aspect, and in "the light of that gloom" truths before unsuspected became suddenly visible. " 'Woe it is, that reveals these
things. He knows himself, and all that's in him, who knows
adversity.' "[79]

In the experience of the deeper griefs, the soul undergoes
a kind of catalysis that defies rational explanation:

That holy office [of purgation and enlightenment] is not so much
accomplished by any covertly inductive reasoning process, whose
original motive is received from the particular affliction; as it is
the magical effect of the admission into man's inmost spirit of a
before unexperienced and wholly inexplicable element, which like
electricity suddenly received into any sultry atmosphere of the
dark, in all directions splits itself into nimble lances of purifying
light; which at one and the same instant discharge all the air of
sluggishness and inform it with an illuminating property.

In the very swiftness and immediacy with which these insights
present themselves to us there lies an immense power of conviction. Seized by it, we will admit no thought of qualification
or of a need to look beyond for a final and more inclusive
term. We know with the certainty of mystical apprehension:

[Those] objects which before, in the uncertainty of the dark,
assumed shadowy and romantic outlines, now are lighted up in all

[79] *Mardi*, II, 324 (chap. clxxx).

their substantial realities; so that in these flashing revelations of grief's wonderful fire, we see all things as they are.[80]

And the conviction lingers. Our particular anger may expand, as it did in the mutilated Ahab, to a general rage which seems selfless but is in truth the pitch of egotism. Like dis-illusioned Pierre, we view life through a "rarefied atmosphere" which causes "the most immemorially admitted maxims of men [to] begin to slide and fluctuate, and finally become wholly inverted."[81] Like Ungar, we may enter upon what seems to us a totally new existence:

> Reading and revery imped his pain,
> Confirmed, and made it take a flight
> Beyond experience and the reign
> Of self; till, in a sort, the man
> Grew much like that Pamphylian
> Who, dying (as the fable goes)
> In walks of Hades met with those
> Which, though he was a sage of worth,
> Did such new pregnancies implant,
> Hadean lore, he did recant
> All science he had brought from earth.[82]

And yet, for all our new-found certainty, we are mistaken. The soul's long journey is at this point hardly more than begun and life's "substantial realities" are still figured to us as in a glass darkly. Among the truths still undisclosed to us is that contraries can (and indeed do) exist side by side. Darkness, we have learned, is both real and permanent; but this does not mean that the sun is to be dismissed as an illusion: it continues to shine even when our gaze is fixed upon the earth's eternal cone of shadow. If we are fortunate, time and a quieter mind may bring this truth home to us.[83]

---

[80] *Pierre*, p. 123 (Book V, chap. i).

[81] *Ibid.*, p. 231 (Book IX, chap. i).

[82] *Clarel*, II, 177–78 (Part IV, canto v).

[83] *Pierre*, p. 237 (Book IX, chap. iii).

But whether or not this further insight is later granted, a step has nevertheless been taken. And from this new vantage ground more of truth can be seen than was evident before. The pessimist may, like the optimist, see something less than the whole picture, but he can with some reason argue that his " 'too-sober view is [at least] nearer true than the too-drunken.' "[84] For though the tortoise of reality has two sides, yet that side which is usually and naturally uppermost is, after all, the black and not the bright.[85]

Let us, then, look more closely at this black side, and first as it most visibly confronts us—in the features of external nature.

What do we find here? What character is to be read in the face of nature? The answer (if we accept Melville's considered and reiterated judgment) is clear: we find ferocity, universal pain, and death. The world of nature is a haunted world, stalked everywhere by the specter of physical evil. More, it is a world that seems often diabolically possessed, its simplest objects informed by demonism, its beauties masks for nameless evils. Melville's imagination, ever "quick to sense a horror," touched upon object after object of the natural world, expanding each until it became as it were coextensive with the whole. Each in its turn—the sea, the shark, the whale, the iceberg, the desert—is made to body forth "that intangible malignity that has been from the beginning"[86] and that forever sets itself against the fact of life.

In its formlessness, its immensity and unsearchable depths, its vast power, its union of fecundity and ferocity, the sea is the very image of nature. Nothing can conquer or comprehend it. It has been a terror from the beginning:

[84] *The Confidence-Man*, p. 180 (chap. xxiv).

[85] "The Encantadas," in *The Piazza Tales*, pp. 188–89.

[86] *Moby-Dick*, I, 228 (chap. xli).

The first boat we read of, floated on an ocean, that with Portuguese vengeance had whelmed a whole world without leaving so much as a widow. That same ocean rolls now; that same ocean destroyed the wrecked ships of last year. Yea, foolish mortals, Noah's flood is not yet subsided; two thirds of the fair world it yet covers.[87]

And in eternal darkness, "a thousand fathoms beneath the sunlight," it keeps its trophies of "unrecorded names and navies." There "in her murderous hold this frigate earth is ballasted with bones of millions of the drowned."[88] No reason exists to hope that the future will be different. For "however baby man may brag of his science and skill . . . , yet for ever and for ever, to the crack of doom, the sea will insult and murder him."[89]

Man has perhaps no right to expect a different treatment, for in the sea's domain he is by nature an alien and an intruder. But the sea "is also a fiend to its own offspring, . . . sparing not the creatures which itself hath spawned. Like a savage tigress that tossing in the jungle overlays her own cubs, so the sea dashes even the mightiest whales against the rocks, and leaves them there side by side with the split wrecks of ships." Divine Providence would seem at such times to have withdrawn Its hand and left the sea to its own senseless rage: "No mercy, no power but its own controls it. Panting and snorting like a mad battle steed that has lost its rider, the masterless ocean overruns the globe."[90]

But again it will seem to give every evidence of deliberate cunning and malign purpose: "Consider the subtleness of the sea; how its most dreaded creatures glide under water, unapparent for the most part, and treacherously hidden beneath the loveliest tints of azure."[91] From beneath such "soft Turk-

---

[87] *Ibid.*, p. 348 (chap. lviii).

[88] *Ibid.*, II, 38 (chap. lxx).

[89] *Ibid.*, I, 347 (lviii).

[90] *Ibid.*

[91] *Ibid.*

ish-rugged waters" as these, his snow-white hump dabbled with greenish foam and bright dancing bubbles, Moby Dick rose to meet Ahab.[92] And in the phosphorescent stillness of the night sea, the "ghastly White Shark" at times vaguely shows, "stealing along like a spirit in the water, with horrific serenity of aspect," revealing no more than "glimpses now and then of his bottomless white pit of teeth."[93]

It is not to be thought that these terrors are exceptional. Destruction here is the very rule of life: "Consider, once more, the universal cannibalism of the sea; all of whose creatures prey upon each other, carrying on eternal war since the world began."[94] Not even Leviathan can escape, being marked down as the prey of the smaller but more ferocious thrashers and killers. ("Exception might be taken to the name bestowed upon this [last] whale, on the ground of its indistinctness. For we are all killers, on land and on sea. . . .")[95] Man, as predatory as his fellow creatures, enters into alliance with the whale's natural enemies. And when he has done his work and turned the monster's "peeled white body" adrift,

Slowly it floats more and more away, the water round it torn and splashed by the insatiate sharks, and the air above vexed with rapacious flights of screaming fowls, whose beaks are like so many insulting poniards in the whale. The vast, white headless phantom floats further and further from the ship, and every rod that it so floats, what seem square roods of sharks and cubic roods of fowls, augment the murderous din. For hours and hours from the almost stationary ship that hideous sight is seen. Beneath the unclouded and mild azure sky, upon the fair face of the pleasant sea, wafted by the joyous breezes, that great mass of death floats on and on, till lost in infinite perspectives.[96]

[92] *Ibid.*, II, 333–34 (chap. cxxxiii).

[93] *Mardi*, I, 48 (chap. xiii).

[94] *Moby-Dick*, I, 348 (chap. lviii).

[95] *Ibid.*, p. 176 (chap. xxxii).

[96] *Ibid.*, II, 34 (chap. lxix).

If no creature in the sea is too large to have enemies, so none is so small as to lack victims. Everything lives on something else. But there is such a thing as degree even here. And for sheer naked voracity and frightfulness, nothing on land or sea can match the phenomenon of the shark. These "vultures of the deep" are born ravenous and, though gorging their whole lives through, are never filled. They will feed, if the opportunity offers, upon each other; wounded, they will turn and wolf down their own entrails; killed and drawn up on deck, they will seem for a time to continue to eat by reflex.[97] Their very numbers make them appear more horrible. The sea is alive with these ministers of death: "Trust me, there are more sharks in the sea than mortals on land."[98] Swarming in their thousands about a whale carcass at night, they present a vision of universal corruption, as though "the whole round sea was one huge cheese, and those sharks the maggots in it."[99]

The ferocity of nature appears most unmistakably in the shark, but it is in the whale that she most clearly exhibits her overwhelming power, her "pyramidical silence," her self-sufficient indifference. Largest of all creatures, present or past, the whale is "a mass of tremendous life, only to be adequately estimated as piled wood is—by the cord; and all obedient to one volition, as the smallest insect." His gigantic tail combines the delicate sensitivity of a girl's fingertips and "the strength of a thousand thighs." In that one organ "the confluent measureless force of the whole whale seems concentrated to a point. Could annihilation occur to matter, this were the thing to do it." Less consistently vicious than the shark—wholly inoffensive at times—he is yet capable of a malice even more frightening by its pointlessness and its seemingly "wilful, deliberate" character.[100]

[97] *Ibid.*, p. 26 (chap. lxvi)

[98] *Mardi*, I, 46 (chap. xiii).

[99] *Moby-Dick*, II, 25 (chap. lxvi).

[100] *Ibid.*, II, 71 (chap. lxxvi) ; p. 94 (chap. lxxxi) ; p. 119 (chap. lxxxvi) ; I, 262 (chap. xlv).

Mystery surrounds him. He seems ubiquitous in time and space. The presence of his huge bones among the earliest fossils makes it hard to imagine a time when he did not exist: he has come "floundering down upon us from the head-waters of the Eternities."[101] And his "island bulk" today rises and sinks in all the world's oceans. The sperm whale, viewed from the front, has nothing that can be called a face—only a featureless, "dead, impregnable, uninjurable wall," behind which the directing brain is hidden away "like the innermost citadel within the amplified fortifications of Quebec."[102] The harpooner, poised in the whaleboat's prow, looks up into a "broad firmament of a forehead, pleated with riddles; dumbly lowering with the doom of boats, and ships, and men."[103] To Ahab it seems the imprisoning wall of appearances, " 'shoved near to me' " and shutting off the truth, " 'the dead, blind wall [that] butts all inquiring heads at last.' "[104] It is the meaningless face of nature, the inert mass of what is, against which the questioner hurls himself in vain, like "the impetuous ship" in the dream driving head on into the iceberg's "dead indifference of walls."[105]

Significantly, the whale is voiceless.[106] He has "moved amid this world's foundations" and knows the darkest secrets of "that awful water-land" below; yet to all questions he returns the same sphinxlike silence. Palpably real as he is, his very outlines are imperfectly known: "afloat, the vast bulk of him is out of sight"; killed and moored to the ship, his body loses its natural shape. Accordingly, "you must needs conclude that the great Leviathan is the one creature in the world which must remain unpainted to the last."[107] Like Nature, he eludes all

101 *Ibid.*, II, 219–24 (chaps. civ–cv).

102 *Ibid.*, p. 71 (chap. lxxvi) ; p. 84 (chap. lxxx).

103 *Ibid.*, p. 83 (chap. lxxix).

104 *Ibid.*, I, 204 (chap. xxxvi) ; II, 300 (chap. cxxv).

105 "The Berg," in *Poems*, pp. 240–41.

106 *Moby-Dick*, II, 114 (chap. lxxxv).

107 *Ibid.*, I, 336 (chap. lv).

formulas and must be encountered by each man for himself: "Only in the heart of quickest perils; only . . . within the eddyings of his angry flukes; only on the profound unbounded sea, can the fully invested whale be truly and livingly found out."[108] His claim to the world is far older than man's: "I am horrorstruck at [the] antemosaic, unsourced existence of the unspeakable terrors of the whale, which, having been before all time, must needs exist after all humane ages are over."[109]

But the whale is life, of a sort, at least. And there is something still older and more lasting than this: the domain of death and non-being, within which the whole history of life must be included as a barely noticed episode. Of this, the desert is the best emblem: the stony, waterless, heat-blasted, leafless and all but lifeless land—"the unleavened nakedness of desolation."[110] Its threat is a permanent reality. Today as before the building of the pyramids, "A long billow of desert [forever] hovers as in act of breaking, upon the verdure of Egypt."[111] Art may intrude her order but briefly upon that chaos:

> "Petra's there,
> Down in her cleft. Mid such a scene
> Of Nature's terror, how serene
> That ordered form. Nor less 'tis cut
> Out of that terror—does abut
> Thereon: there's Art."[112]

But knock now at Petra's door and there comes no answer. Man finds no refuge here. The desert is older even than religion: "the diabolical landscapes [of the] great[er] part of Judea must have suggested to the Jewish prophets, their ghastly theology."[113] The gentle Christ, for all His victory on the

108 *Ibid.*, II, 218 (chap. ciii).

109 *Ibid.*, p. 222 (chap. civ).

110 Herman Melville, *Journal of a Visit to Europe and the Levant,* ed. Howard C. Horsford (Princeton: Princeton University Press, 1955), p. 137.

111 *Ibid.*, p. 119.

112 *Clarel*, I, 299 (Part II, canto xxx).

113 *Journal of a Visit to Europe and the Levant*, p. 151.

Mount of Temptation, has left no lasting mark upon the king-
doms He looked upon; but His adversary has: far beyond the
limits of Palestine's "unchristened earth," Satan's "dead Me-
dusa stare / Petrific o'er the valley thrown, / Congeals Arabia
into stone."[114] And where the bare rock slopes down to the
scalded edges of "Lot's mortal sea"—"foam on [the] beach &
pebbles like slaver of mad dog"[115]—ocean and desert seem to
meet and mix, the world's first state and its last. Mortmain, the
parched wanderer, coming upon these once life-giving but now
poisonous waters, sees in them the features of Nature the murderous mother:

> "Be these the beads on the wives'-wine,
> Tofana-brew?—O fair Medea—
> O soft man-eater, furry fine:
> Oh, be thou Jael, be thou Leah—
> Unfathomably shallow!—No!
> Nearer the core than man can go
> Or Science get—nearer the slime
> Of Nature's rudiments and lime
> In chyle before the bone. Thee, thee,
> In thee the filmy cell is spun—
> The mould thou art of what men be:
> Events are all in thee begun—
> By thee, through thee!—Undo, undo."[116]

Scarcely less cursed are those "Enchanted Isles," the Galapagos, hopelessly fixed between flaming sky and burning sea:

Take five-and-twenty heaps of cinders dumped here and there in
an outside city lot; imagine some of them magnified into mountains
and the vacant lot the sea. . . . A group rather of extinct volcanoes
than of isles; looking much as the world at large might, after a
penal conflagration.

[114] *Clarel*, II, 25 (Part III, canto v) ; p. 7 (Part III, canto i).

[115] *Journal of a Visit to Europe and the Levant*, p. 136.

[116] *Clarel*, I, 320–21 (Part II, canto xxxvi).

The jackal and other scavengers are known to haunt the ruins of ancient cities, but

The Encantadas refuse to harbor even the outcasts of the beasts. Man and wolf alike disown them. Little but reptile life is here found: tortoises, lizards, immense spiders, snakes, and that strangest anomaly of outlandish nature, the *iguana*. No voice, no low, no howl is heard; the chief sound of life here is a hiss.

With neither spring nor autumn comes any shadow of change; century after century these "clinkered islands" remain "invariably the same: fixed, cast, glued into the very body of cadaverous death." Surely, "in no world but a fallen one could such lands exist."[117]

And when we turn from nature to look at man himself, here too we find all "shrouded in a blackness, ten times black." The discovery ought not, perhaps, to surprise us. If the tradition be true that this world is a fallen one, it is so as a consequence of man's fall. And whatever his more formal beliefs may be, there are "certain moods [in which] no man can weigh this world without throwing in something, somehow like Original Sin, to strike the uneven balance."[118]

Among the most grievous consequences of that primal fall, theologians have long held, is the maiming and darkening of the human intellect. Experience offers much to support such a view. And Melville, though often employing reason as a weapon against the rigidities of inherited doctrine (as, for instance, in the use made of syllogistic logic in *Mardi*[119] to confound orthodoxy with heresy), never loses sight of its limitations. The entire central action of *Mardi*, from the beginning of the voyage to the departure from Serenia, is a record of the philosopher Babbalanja's gradual discovery of the insufficiency of

[117] "The Encantadas," in *The Piazza Tales*, pp. 181–85.

[118] "Hawthorne and His Mosses," in *Billy Budd and Other Prose Pieces*, p. 129.

[119] *Mardi*, II, 123–25 (chap. cxxxv).

the speculative intellect as a guide to essential truth.[120] Reason, though it aspires to be a sun, is in actuality little more than a candle:

> Ay, in caves the miner see:
> His forehead bears a taper dim;
> Darkness so he feebly braves
> Which foldeth him![121]

We are the blind men of the fable, groping about among the banyan's tangle of roots and trunks: " 'The tree is too much for us all.' " Reason may at its best serve us to discover the errors of others, but it will not lead us to truth. For " 'truth is in things, and not in words.' " Like Pilate, we end in asking "What is truth?" and in acknowledging " 'that question [to be] more final than any answer.' "[122]

And even supposing that we were, miraculously, to win through to truth, by what means could we hope to make it practically effective in our lives? We are hampered by the irrational both within us and without. Obscure appetites (as Pierre learned) move beneath the surface of consciousness and silently determine our actions. Circumstances often block the realization of our best purposes: "Faith and philosophy are air, but events are brass."[123] One may have extensive knowledge of the realities of his situation and still be powerless to change it. "For in tremendous extremities human souls are like drowning men; well enough they know they are in peril; well enough they know the causes of that peril;—nevertheless, the sea is the sea, and these drowning men do drown."[124]

Shortly before the opening of the last act of Ahab's tragedy,

---

120 See especially *ibid.*, pp. 359–60 (chap. clxxxv) and pp. 369–72 (chap. clxxxvii).

121 "The Conflict of Convictions," in *Poems*, p. 19.

122 *Mardi*, II, 40–42 (chap. cxv) ; p. 128 (chap. cxxxv) ; I, 329 (chap. xciii).

123 *Pierre*, p. 403 (Book XXI, chap. ii).

124 *Ibid.*, p. 423 (Book XXII, chap. iii).

a sea hawk (the same "bird of heaven," it may be, that Tashtego's hammer would pull down with the sinking "Pequod")
snatches Ahab's hat from his head and carrying it to a great
height, drops it into the sea.[125] The incident is repeated in
Clarel, when the skullcap of that other insistent questioner,
Mortmain, is seized by an eagle, carried aloft and cast into the
dry gorge of Kedron where its owner is shortly to die.[126] In
both events, it is clear, we are meant to read the gods' disdain
of human reason.

Whatever the pretensions of his mind, man cannot be adequately understood in isolation from nature. He is, after all,
"but one member of a fighting world"; prudence dictates,
therefore, that like the experienced backwoodsman we maintain the same watchful attitude toward nature and all of " ' "her
creatures, . . . including panthers and Indians." ' "[127] Savage
man, even in paradisial Typee, is a phenomenon to be feared.
At his worst, acting not from need but "out of mere delight in
tyranny and cruelty, by virtue of a quality in him inherited
from Sycorax his mother,"[128] he can be more frightful than
any animal. The same Negro mothers whom Captain Delano
sentimentally admired at play with their sprawling infants
("There's naked nature, now; pure tenderness and love.")
have tortured their victims, he later learns, with a ferocity even
beyond that of their men.[129]

Civilization may cover over this ferocity but not remove it.
It is an ineradicable part of human nature and may reappear
at any moment. "Long exile from Christendom and civilization inevitably restores a man to that condition in which God
placed him, i.e., what is called savagery."[130] And with some,

125 *Moby-Dick,* II, 322–23 (chap. cxxx).

126 *Clarel,* II, 124–25 (Part III, canto xxv).

127 *Mardi,* II, 141 (chap. cxxxviii); *The Confidence-Man,* p. 194 (chap.
xxvi).

128 "The Encantadas," in *The Piazza Tales,* p. 239.

129 "Benito Cereno," *ibid.,* pp. 105, 163.

130 *Moby-Dick,* I, 343 (chap. lvii).

not even this stimulus is needed to reveal it. Paul Jones, prowling the floor of Franklin's Paris apartment, wears at all times the mark of the "thorough-bred savage":

So at midnight, the heart of the metropolis of modern civilization was secretly trod by this jaunty barbarian in broadcloth; a sort of prophetical ghost, glimmering in anticipation . . . of those tragic scenes of the French Revolution which levelled the exquisite refinement of Paris with the bloodthirsty ferocity of Borneo; showing that broaches and finger-rings, not less than nose-rings and tattooing, are tokens of the primeval savageness which ever slumbers in human kind, civilized or uncivilized.[131]

But beneath even the most circumspect exterior there will stir at times a longing for the old anarchy. The Yankee mystic, for example, is clearly moved by a deep natural empathy when he inquires of the Cosmopolitan:

"When charmed by the beauty of [the] viper, did it never occur to you to change personalities with him? to feel what it was to be a snake? to glide unsuspected in grass? to sting, to kill at a touch; your whole beautiful body one iridescent scabbard of death? In short, did the wish never occur to you to feel yourself exempt from knowledge, and conscience, and revel for awhile in the care-free, joyous life of a perfectly instinctive, unscrupulous, and irresponsible creature?"[132]

And one remembers that Melville himself, writing to Duyckinck of the insanity of a friend, confessed to a similar envy of the amoral state: "What sort of sensation permanent madness is may be very well imagined—just as we imagine how we felt when we were infants, tho' we can not recall it. In both conditions we are irresponsible & riot like gods without fear of fate."[133]

From the burden of conscience, all men probably at one

131 *Israel Potter*, pp. 81–82 (chap. xi).
132 *The Confidence-Man*, pp. 251–52 (chap. xxxvi).
133 Letter to Evert Duyckinck, April 5, 1849, in Metcalf, *op. cit.*, p. 60.

time or another long to be delivered. But few are they with the daring or the desperation to throw it off and boldly undertake a course of active and principled evil. The safer and far more common way is simply to pursue one's own self-interest and to allow evil to happen of itself. How nearly universal this stratagem is became frighteningly evident to the boy Redburn as stony indifference met all his attempts to solicit help for the starving mother and children he came upon in the Liverpool alley.[134] Reasons for the avoidance of charitable actions are not hard to come by. The wretched themselves are often too insulated by their own sufferings to feel for each other.[135] A truly platonic love, on the other hand, will not easily descend to the grubby doing of terrestrial good. The piety of the fortunate is most apt to express itself in a humble acceptance of the general frame of things: " 'Don't you think,' " the Yankee mystic soberly inquires, " 'that for a man to pity where nature is pitiless, is a little presuming?' " To meddle in the affairs of Providence is a dangerous business, for as " 'enmity lies couched in . . . friendship,' " so may not also " 'ruin in the relief' "?[136]

But if we avoid the indiscretions either of committing or of opposing evil, surely there can be no real harm in our profiting by it? It is, after all, one of the few compensations of this life that "There seems to be no calamity overtaking man that cannot be rendered merchantable." Starvation in Ireland can, with a little effort, be turned to the profit of the English shipowner. Suicides on the Liverpool docks, fished from the water by scavengers, bring in death a bounty they could rarely command when alive. And it is not impossible for an enterprising crimp to dispose of such merchandise at an even better price

[134] *Redburn*, pp. 231–37 (chap. xxxvii).

[135] *Ibid.*, p. 341 (chap. lii).

[136] *The Confidence-Man*, pp. 271–73 (chap. xxxix) ; p. 253 (chap. xxxvi) ; p. 270 (chap. xxxix).

by dragging it aboard an outbound ship as one of a last-minute lot of drunken sailors.[137]

But these are the mere "haberdashers" of evil—"sinners only . . . in the small and entirely honorable way of trade," cautious traders "on the coast of crime" who take what gains may be had without the risks of an outright landing.[138] A deeper evil exists which is at the same time more venturesome and more disinterested. Its ends may even be described as spiritual. For " 'Money . . . is [not] the sole motive to pains and hazard, deception and deviltry, in this world. How much money did the devil make by gulling Eve?' "[139]

In the actions of certain men we catch glimpses of a kind of malice so refined, so entirely gratuitous and unprovoked, as to defy explanation on grounds either of animal savagery or of the ordinary human love of self. The one phrase which seems adequate to it is the biblical one: "the mystery of iniquity."

For what can more partake of the mysterious than an antipathy spontaneous and profound such as is evoked in certain exceptional mortals by the mere aspect of some other mortal, however harmless he may be? if not called forth by this very harmlessness itself.[140]

Such is the antipathy of Jackson for Redburn and of Claggart for Billy Budd, though in the one case it expresses itself in open hatred and in the other in an envious love bordering at times on tears.[141]

Evil of this sort is invariably marked by intellectuality. Jackson, though "the foul lees and dregs of a man," is "marvellously clever [and] cunning" and knows the weaknesses of

[137] *Redburn*, p. 230 (chap. xxxvi) ; p. 379 (chap. lviii) ; pp. 315–18 (chap. xlviii).

[138] *Pierre*, p. 248 (Book X, chap. ii) ; *Clarel*, I, 320 (Part II, canto xxxvi).

[139] *The Confidence-Man*, p. 42 (chap. vi).

[140] *Billy Budd*, in *The Portable Melville*, pp. 672–73.

[141] *Redburn*, pp. 73–74 (chap. xii) ; *Billy Budd*, in *The Portable Melville*, pp. 677–78, 688–89.

human nature "to a kink"; Bland is equally intelligent, but a
gentleman with "a fine polish" and "a pliant, insinuating style
in his conversation"; the Negro Babo's head is "a hive of subtlety"; and the pale lofty brow of Claggart is a sign of his
"more than average intellect."[142] It is no coincidence that both
Claggart and Bannadonna, the heartless egotist of "The Bell-
Tower," die of a blow to the forehead.[143]

Natures like these "have no vulgar alloy of the brute in
them"; they make a reasonable show of virtues and are "without vices or small sins": their pride never stoops to so mean a
fault as avarice, nor does any gross touch of "the sordid or
sensual" hint of their deeper infamy. "An uncommon prudence
is habitual with the subtler depravity, for it has everything to
hide."[144] No obvious felonies betray them; they are guilty,
rather, of

> . . . sins scarce scored as crimes
> in any statute known, or code—
> Nor now, nor in the former times:
> Things hard to prove: decorum's wile,
> Malice discreet, judicious guile;
> Good done with ill intent—reversed:
> Best deeds designed to serve the worst;
> And hate which under life's fair hue
> Prowls like the shark in sunned Pacific blue.[145]

Evil of a voluntary and occasional nature it is possible to
bear with—perhaps even in some degree to understand. But
evil that is radical and organic is worse because irremediable:
integral to the agent's nature, it can end only with his final dissolution. So it was with Bland, "an organic and irreclaimable

---

[142] *Redburn*, p. 72 (chap. xii) ; *White-Jacket*, p. 232 (chap. xliv) ; "Benito
Cereno," in *The Piazza Tales*, p. 170; *Billy Budd*, in *The Portable Melville*,
p. 662.

[143] *Ibid.*, pp. 701–2; "The Bell-Tower," in *The Piazza Tales*, p. 270.

[144] *Billy Budd*, in *The Portable Melville*, pp. 674–75, 680.

[145] *Clarel*, I, 319 (Part II, canto xxxvi).

scoundrel, who did wicked deeds as the cattle browse the herb-age, because wicked deeds seemed the legitimate operation of his whole infernal organization."[146] So, too, with Claggart, "in whom was the mania of an evil nature, not engendered by vicious training or corrupting books or licentious living, but born with him and innate; in short 'a depravity according to nature.' "[147]

The phenomenon is more common, Melville intimates, than one might suppose. In chapter xxvi of *The Confidence-Man*, it takes on the dimensions of a general type—the Indian—and inspires the formulation of a new philosophy, "The Metaphysics of Indian-Hating." The Indian, as he appears in this fable of Colonel John Moredock, the Illinois Indian-hater, is wholly incorrigible: " ' "his race's portion by nature is total depravity." ' " He may not as yet be proved to be as murderous as Mocmohoc, but you will nevertheless be wise to step warily, for " ' "in the least harmful may lie his [Mocmohoc's] germ." ' " As he speaks with you in seeming and possibly sincere friendship, who knows " ' "what involuntary preparations may be going on in him for things as unbeknown in present time to him as [to you]—a sort of chemical preparation in the soul for malice, as chemical preparation in the body for malady." ' "[148] But in the wider world, unfortunately, this wariness does not always help, since the enemy's features rarely betray his Indian blood.

It is the great advantage of evil that it draws its strength not only from its own perfection but from that of its opposite. Innocence is made, as it were, a party to its own deception and overthrow. It was "owing to the generosity and piety of Amasa Delano, incapable of sounding such wickedness," as much as to Babo's "devices which offered contradictions to the true state of affairs," that the rebel slaves came as near to final vic-

146 *White-Jacket*, p. 234 (chap. xliv).

147 *Billy Budd*, in *The Portable Melville*, p. 675.

148 *The Confidence-Man*, pp. 192–202 (chap. xxvi).

tory as they did.[149] Claggart, too, found a helper in Billy's serene consciousness of right action and in the absence from his makeup of the least trace of "that intuitive knowledge of the bad which in natures not good or incompletely so foreruns experience."[150]

The wicked, moreover, show a singleness of purpose far surpassing that of ordinary men. They have their own perverted integrity. Unlike their victims, they rarely hesitate between right and wrong, the struggle of conscience being in their case already largely resolved. If guilt is felt at all, it never shows on the surface. Captain Delano's transitory suspicions light not upon the fiendish Babo but upon the innocent Don Benito; for the Spanish captain, compelled to share in the black's deception, gives "every token of craven discomposure" at the same moment that Babo's face looks up all openness and "humble curiosity." There is a strength in shamelessness. Jackson, the smallest and weakest man in the forecastle of the "Highlander," rules them all by his unparalleled "brass and impudence," his "unflinching face," and the sheer intensity of his hatred. And Bland, having served out his own jail sentence, returns to his policeman's tasks with an "erect and cordial assurance" that confounds his enemies.[151]

Assurance of this sort is of course rooted in an unshakable pride. Such men are self-sufficient, self-justifying. Like the shark, they hunt alone. No hunger for affection or for human companionship drives them, as at times it will the " 'diluted Indian-hater,' "[152] to throw themselves upon the mercy of their enemies. They keep their own counsels and accept their own misfortunes with something even of a stoic heroism. "The infernal nature," Melville once remarked, struck by the resolu-

---

[149] "Benito Cereno," in *The Piazza Tales*, pp. 163–64.

[150] *Billy Budd*, in *The Portable Melville*, pp. 687, 689.

[151] "Benito Cereno," in *The Piazza Tales*, pp. 94, 103; *Redburn*, p. 72 (chap. xii) ; *White-Jacket*, p. 233 (chap. xliv).

[152] *The Confidence-Man*, p. 201 (chap. xxvi).

tion shown by Edmund in *Lear*, "has a valor often denied to innocence."[153] He might have added that it has also, as befits its predatory role, an inexhaustible energy and an intellectual force against which "mere unaided virtue or right-mindedness" is wholly inadequate.

Immense as their power may appear, the number of the Blands, the Babos, and the Claggarts is admittedly small. One must not, however, suppose that theirs is the monopoly of evil. Total virtue is an even rarer thing than total depravity. What we have in the great majority of mankind is not the absence of evil but simply its presence in a less concentrated form. Diluted, the poison still has power to kill. Christ fell the victim of no single man but of that " '*human,* that unanimous cry, / "We're fixed to hate Him—Crucify!" ' "[154] By its universality alone, this less intense evil can be fully as appalling. Mortmain, the embittered philanthrope, knows this as he lies down to sleep unguarded in the wilderness, feeling "Safer than in the cut-throat town / Though on the church steps."[155] And Ungar, who represents the waning of the New World's humanitarian dreams as Mortmain of the Old World's hopes, greets the sound of a shot in the desert with the words:

"A gun:
A gun's man's voice—sincerest one.
Blench we to have assurance here,
Here in the waste, that kind is near?"[156]

The heart of man is, in Ungar's view, incorrigibly evil:

"What incantation shall make less
The ever-upbubbling wickedness!
Is this fount nature's?"[157]

[153] Leyda, *The Melville Log*, I, 290.

[154] *Clarel*, I, 185 (Part II, canto iii).

[155] *Ibid.*, p. 232 (Part II, canto xv).

[156] *Ibid.*, II, 166 (Part II, canto ii).

[157] *Ibid.*, p. 251 (Part IV, canto xxii).

Such a view of humanity looks through also between the lines of the sermon that Fleece, the Negro cook on the "Pequod," preaches to the sharks swarming about the whale carcass:

"Your woraciousness, fellow-critters, I don't blame ye so much for; dat is natur, and can't be helped; but to gobern dat wicked natur, dat is de pint. You is sharks, sartin; but if you gobern de shark in you, why den you be angel; for all angel is not'ing more dan de shark well goberned. Now, look here, bred'ren, just try wonst to be cibil, a helping yourselbs from dat whale. Don' be tearin' de blubber out your neighbor's mout', I say."

But the sharks are too busy rending the whale and each other to hear him, and the exasperated preacher dismisses his flock at last with the malediction: " 'Cussed fellow-critters! Kick up de damndest row as ever you can; fill your dam bellies 'till dey bust—and den die.' "[158]

With much the same bitterness, Melville looked into the abyss of anarchy opened by New York's draft riots of 1863 and hailed the arrival of martial law:

> Wise Draco comes, deep in the midnight roll
> Of black artillery; he comes, though late;
> In code corroborating Calvin's creed
> And cynic tyrannies of honest kings;
> He comes, nor parlies; and the Town, redeemed,
> Gives thanks devout; nor, being thankful, heeds
> The grimy slur on the Republic's faith implied,
> Which holds that Man is naturally good,
> And—more—is Nature's Roman, never to be scourged.[159]

Little more than a decade earlier, the author of *White-Jacket* had himself borne eloquent witness to this tenet of "the Republic's faith":

Join hands with me, then; and in the name of that Being in whose image the flogged sailor is made, let us demand of legislators, by what right they dare profane what God himself holds sacred.

158 *Moby-Dick*, II, 16–17 (chap. lxiv).
159 "The House-Top," in *Poems*, p. 64.

Is it lawful for you to scourge a man that is a Roman? asks the intrepid Apostle, well knowing . . . that it was not. And now, . . . is it lawful for you, my countrymen, to scourge a man that is an American?[160]

Neither statement, of course, is meant to offer us Melville's final and comprehensive view of human nature; each is qualified by its context. But in the years that followed *White-Jacket,* the shades in the picture became steadily more pronounced.

The optimist, in his rare moods of discouragement with his fellows, finds consolation in the thought that " 'the past is passed' " and the rich and untouched future still before him.[161] But one may hold such a belief only by a willing suspension of the principle of causality, by an insistence that events do not necessarily resemble their causes and that the child is simply the forerunner and not the father of the man—much as " 'The second teeth follow, but do not come from, the first . . . [which are] thrust from their place by the independent growth of the succeeding set.' "[162] In such a world, who can guess the infinite possibilities still before us?

"Supposing, respected sir [asks the man from the Philosophical Intelligence Office], that worthy gentleman, Adam, to have been dropped overnight in Eden, as a calf in the pasture; . . . how could even the learned serpent himself have foreknown that such a downy-chinned little innocent would eventually rival the goat in a beard? Sir, wise as the serpent was, that eventuality would have been entirely hidden from his wisdom."

"I don't know about that [the skeptical Pitch responds]. The Devil is very sagacious. To judge by the event, he appears to have understood man better even than the Being who made him."[163]

And he who today sees clearly what man is may venture also a shrewd guess at what he will be. Whatever Melville's later res-

---

160 *White-Jacket,* p. 177 (chap. xxxiv).

161 *Ibid.,* pp. 188–89 (chap. xxxvi) ; "Benito Cereno," in *The Piazza Tales,* p. 168.

162 *The Confidence-Man,* pp. 163–64 (chap. xxii).

163 *Ibid.,* p. 162 (chap. xxii).

ervations concerning science, he was first and last a strong believer in cause and effect. The doctrine of necessity seems early to have impressed him, and in *Mardi* his philosopher Babbalanja is at some pains to distinguish it in his hearers' minds from another closely related doctrine:

"Fatalism presumes express and irrevocable edicts of heaven concerning particular events. Whereas, Necessity holds that all events are naturally linked, and inevitably follow each other, without providential interposition, though by the eternal letting of Providence."[164]

The connections between events remain for the most part hidden and unsuspected:

Strike at one end the longest conceivable row of billiard balls in close contact, and the furthermost ball will start forth, while all the rest stand still; and yet the last ball was not struck at all. So, through long previous generations, whether of births or thoughts, Fate strikes the present man.[165]

That the law is thus casual and impersonal in its operation serves only to mark its unexceptional and inevitable character. Like Lee and his fellow patriots ("less fortunate, not less righteous, than we"), we are all "the fated inheritors" of the past.[166]

But one may guess that the full force of this insight came home to Melville only with the outbreak of the Civil War, that

> tempest bursting from the waste of Time
> On the world's fairest hope linked with man's foulest crime.[167]

In the poems called *Battle-Pieces*, at any rate, we note, to a far greater extent than in the stories and sketches of the mid-fifties, a growing awareness of the weight of necessity; and *Clarel*, written in the long recoil of that great event, is marked by an

164 *Mardi*, II, 121 (chap. cxxxv); see also pp. 238–45 (chap. clxi).

165 *Pierre*, p. 254 (Book XI, chap. i).

166 "Supplement" to *Battle-Pieces*, in *Poems*, p. 185.

167 "Misgivings," in *Poems*, p. 7.

almost oppressive sense of history. The whole poem is essentially a search through the detritus of the past for clues by which to decipher a meaningless present. In a period of seemingly endless material expansion, these doom-haunted pilgrims have renounced the promised land and turned back to the wilderness:

> "Nay, nay; your future's too sublime:
> The Past, the Past is half of time,
> The proven half."[168]

Generations have lived out their lives in the dark lee of Sinai and yet more in that still longer shadow falling with every sunrise across Lybia:

> Thou shadow vast
> Of Cheops' indissoluble pile,
> Typ'st thou the imperishable Past
> In empire posthumous and reaching sway
> Projected far across to time's remotest day?[169]

In such a perspective how foolish and presumptuous seem our boasts of progress. In what essential respect have we advanced beyond our ancestors? In knowledge? in political wisdom? in virtue? The answer stands in the pages of Ecclesiastes, "the fine hammered steel of woe":

> The thing that hath been, it is that which shall be;
> and that which is done is that which shall be done;
> and there is no new thing under the sun.

Twenty centuries ago Jesus walked here and announced a new kingdom to His disciples. But they too lived in the shadow of the past:

> "What dream they knew, that primal band
> Of gipsy Christians! But it died;
> Back rolled the world's effacing tide:
>
> . . . .

[168] *Clarel*, I, 49 (Part I, canto xii).
[169] *Ibid.*, pp. 216–17 (Part II, canto xi).

> .   .   . worse came—creeds, wars, stakes. Oh, men
> Made earth inhuman; yes, a den
> Worse for Christ's coming, since His love
> (Perverted) did but venom prove."

So it has been with Buddha, Confucius, and all other " 'Ethe-real visitants of earth, / Foiled benefactors' '' whose teachings, " 'light scratched, not graved on man's hard heart,' '' grow ever dimmer in the world's weather. Fossilized in institutions, the meaningless form alone remains: Saba's green palm of faith steeped in the bitter waters of Lot's sea—"free from decay / But dead." [170]

So entangled with alien interests has religion become that it is all but impossible to distinguish the kingdom of heaven from the kingdom of this world. A warship's chaplain—"the minister of the Prince of Peace serving in the host of the God of War"—is as truly a shareholder in the enterprise as the gunner, receiving his two-twentieth lay of the twenty-dollar bounty paid for each person aboard every enemy ship sunk by his vessel.[171] In such a world, the thought of Christ becomes a source not of comfort but of still deeper pain:

> "For this Thou bleedest, Anguished Face;
> Yea, Thou through ages to accrue,
> Shalt the Medusa shield replace:
> In beauty and in terror too
> Shalt paralyze the nobler race—"[172]

But to the great mass of men that face grows daily more unreal. We live today under the new dispensation of science and commonsense. Not Christ, but this world, has become the measure of all things; and any philosophy, it is felt, which " 'tends to produce a character at odds with it . . . must neces-

---

[170] *Ibid.*, p. 254 (Part II, canto xxi) ; II, 235 (Part IV, canto xviii) ; I, 309 (Part II, canto xxxiii).

[171] *Billy Budd*, in *The Portable Melville*, p. 727; *White-Jacket*, p. 196 (chap. xxxviii).

[172] *Clarel*, I, 53 (Part I, canto xiii).

sarily be but a cheat and a dream.' " No problem is meaningful to which a practical solution lies not at hand: " 'Sir [says
the Yankee mystic], man came into this world, not to sit down
and muse, not to befog himself with vain subtleties, but to gird
up his loins and to work.' "[173]

The task of science, in such a view, is not to understand
nature but to break and harness her. Such was the intent of
that "cynic solitaire," Bannadonna, in building his Babel-like
bell-tower with its manacled iron helot:

A practical materialist, what Bannadonna had aimed at was to
have been reached, not by logic, not by crucible, not by conju-
ration, not by altars; but by plain vice-bench and hammer. In short,
to solve nature, to steal into her, to intrigue beyond her, to pro-
cure someone else to bind her to his hand;—these, one and all,
had not been his objects; but, asking no favors from any element
or any being, of himself, to rival her, outstrip her, and rule her.
He stooped to conquer. With him, common sense was theurgy;
machinery, miracle; Prometheus, the heroic name for machinist;
man, the true God.[174]

The past, all prejudice and superstition, must be cleared away
in preparation for the new order. Hammer in hand, accordingly, the mocking geologist retraces the footsteps of Jesus
through the Holy Land, gathers disciples about him and

> With master-key unlocks the spells
> And mysteries of the world unmade,

announces new and more hygienic miracles, and issues his own
utilitarian fiat:

> "Let there be
> Rails, wires, from Olivet to the sea,
> With station in Gethsemane."[175]

[173] *The Confidence-Man,* pp. 263, 264 (chap. xxxvii).

[174] "The Bell-Tower," in *The Piazza Tales,* p. 268.

[175] *Clarel,* I, 250 (Part II, canto xx).

True, the new gospel (like the old) does not convince every-one; but most men at least acquiesce in it. The caravan fol-lows obediently on behind the riderless, self-important ass trot-ting at the head of the column: "O, world's advance! We wise limp after!"[176]

Is it objected that the picture is something less than fair, that in addition to her asses, " 'science has her eagles too' "?

> "Eagles? ay; but few.
> And search we in their aeries lone
> What find we, pray? perchance, a bone."[177]

Man looks here in vain for the satisfaction of his deeper needs. The microscope shows him nothing of the soul; Galileo's tele-scope brings heaven no nearer to him. The irrelevance of sci-ence springs (as the Dominican reminds his modernist col-league, Derwent) from the nature of its subject matter:

> "Science but deals
> With Nature; Nature is not God;
> Never she answers our appeals,
> Or, if she do, but mocks the clod.
> Call to the echo—it returns
> The word you send; how thrive the ferns
> About the ruined house of prayer
> In woods; one shadow falleth yet
> From Christian spire—Turk minaret:
> Consider the indifference there.
> 'Tis so throughout. Shall Science then,
> Which solely dealeth with this thing
> Named Nature, shall she ever bring
> One solitary hope to men?"[178]

" 'Science! Curse thee, thou vain toy,' " cries the frustrated Ahab, and tramples underfoot the quadrant that can tell him

[176] *Ibid.*, II, 36–37 (Part III, canto viii).

[177] *Ibid.*, I, 252 (Part II, canto xxi).

[178] *Ibid.*, p. 275 (Part II, canto xxv).

nothing of the ultimate, of the sun's " 'unknown, thither side.' "[179] The toil of learning is both difficult and pointless. Seen in the perspective of history, our advance into knowledge is like a movement through the Erie canal, constantly broken and interrupted by obstacles; and " 'after all these weary lockings-up and lockings-down, upon how much of a higher plain do you finally stand? Enough to make it an object?' "[180] The little we do learn serves only to deepen the mystery we cannot penetrate: "The light is greater, hence the shadow more."[181] But the mystery may be ignored, and most of us ignore it. Not for us is Bulkington's open sea, "shoreless, indefinite as God"; now

> "luminous on every hand,
> The breadths of shallow knowledge more expand.
> Much as a lightship keeper pines
> Mid shoals immense, where dreary shines
> His lamp, we toss beneath the ray
> Of Science' beacon. This to trim
> Is now man's barren office."[182]

Nor are we the better off that this knowledge, such as it is, is more widely diffused than before. The printing press is an improvement upon the pen, it is true, but much like that of the Colt revolver upon the single-shot pistol—" 'involving, along with the multiplication of the barrel, no consecration of the aim.' "[183] Man's own mind may be made an instrument for his enslavement. Simple literacy by itself is no more than

> "the ring in the bull's nose
> Whereby a pert boy turns and winds
> This monster of a million minds."[184]

---

179 *Moby-Dick*, II, 274–75 (chap. cxviii).

180 *The Confidence-Man*, pp. 255–56 (chap. xxxvi).

181 *Clarel*, II, 297 (Part IV, canto xxxv).

182 *Ibid.*, I, 255 (Part II, canto xxi).

183 *The Confidence-Man*, p. 221 (chap. xxix).

184 *Clarel*, II, 197 (Part IV, canto x).

In the growth of material arts, we may read a surer promise of man's debasement than of his improvement, for

> "Arts are tools;
> But tools, they say, are to the strong:
> Is Satan weak? weak is the Wrong?
> No blessed augury overrules:
> Your arts advance in faith's decay:
> You are but drilling the new Hun
> Whose growl even now can some dismay;
> Vindictive in his heart of hearts,
> He schools him in your mines and marts—
> A skilled destroyer."[185]

Ours is an age, however, not only of mechanical science but of humanitarian effort. And when we view the world in a social and political perspective, what do we see? We see again a mass of evils so vast as to out-reach our imagination. This "man-of-war world" of ours, "though boasting some fine fellows here and there, [is], upon the whole, charged to the combings of her hatchways with the spirit of Belial and all unrighteousness."[186] Suffering is both universal and eternal: "the most poisonous reptile of the marsh perpetuates his kind as inevitably as the sweetest songster of the grove; so, equally with every felicity, all miserable events do naturally beget their like. Yea, more than equally . . ."[187] A lifetime spent in such a world may dull the moral sense to the point where " 'wrongs seem almost natural as rights.' "[188] Many of these ills, moreover, are clearly ineradicable, being organic either to society itself or to the makeup of the particular sufferer—in either case "incurable, except when they dissolve with the body they live in."[189] In self-defense, the mind builds up its own scar tissue:

185 *Ibid.*, p. 246 (Part IV, canto xxi).
186 *White-Jacket*, p. 493 (chap. xci).
187 *Moby-Dick*, II, 229–30 (chap. cvi).
188 *Mardi*, II, 251 (chap. clxii).
189 *Redburn*, pp. 177–78 (chap. xxix) ; *White-Jacket*, p. 473 (chap. lxxxix),

So true it is, and so terrible, too, that up to a certain point the thought or sight of misery enlists our best affections; but, in certain special cases, beyond that point it does not. They err who would assert that invariably this is owing to the inherent selfishness of the human heart. It rather proceeds from a certain hopelessness of remedying excessive and organic ill. To a sensitive being, pity is not seldom pain. And when at last it is perceived that such pity cannot lead to effectual succor, common sense bids the soul be rid of it.[190]

Whatever our sympathy, the truth remains that " 'Tears are not swords.' "[191] "Like good, [evil] is an irremovable element. Bale out your individual boat, if you can, but the sea abides."[192] So it is that "Surrounded . . . by the wants and woes of our fellow-men, and yet given to follow our own pleasures, regardless of their pains [we are] like people sitting up with a corpse, and making merry in the house of the dead."[193]

But say we do attempt by a concerted action to remedy the ills of society—what then? Our first mistake, no doubt, will be that of underestimating our enemy:

> Events, they make the dreamers quail;
> Satan's old age is strong and hale,
> A disciplined captain, gray in skill,
> And Raphael a white enthusiast still.[194]

Infiltration of the reformers' ranks is not the least of Satan's stratagems:

> Along with each superior mind,
> The vain, foolhardy, worthless, blind,
> With Judases, are nothing loath

[190] "Bartleby," in *The Piazza Tales*, p. 42.

[191] *Mardi*, II, 251 (chap. clxii).

[192] "Rammon," in *Collected Poems of Herman Melville*, ed. Howard P. Vincent (Chicago: Packard & Co., 1947), p. 411. This prose fragment is not included in the Standard Edition's *Poems*.

[193] *Redburn*, p. 237 (chap. xxxvii).

[194] "The Conflict of Convictions," in *Poems*, p. 8.

> To clasp pledged hands and take the oath
> Of aim, the which, if just, demands
> Strong hearts, brows deep, and priestly hands.[195]

Our choice of means, too, may be such as to benefit our opponent's cause more than our own. Hating the ill as we do, and angry perhaps at the discovery of our folly in thinking "that Reason can / Govern the reasoning creature, man,"[196] we are occasionally tempted to the use of force. Violence alone, at certain times, seems to offer a prospect of success. But can we really hope to cure man's "many questionable wrongs" by recourse to "yet more questionable war"?

> "Come, thou who makest such hot haste
> To forge the future—weigh the past."[197]

Though the thought seem treasonable, it is yet true that "With certain evils men must be more or less patient."[198]

And quite aside from our choice of means, what is the end that we envision? An enlarged freedom? To what purpose? For " 'It is not the prime end, and chief blessing, to be politically free. And freedom is only good as a means; is no end in itself.' "[199] The past has seen the overthrow of many ancient tyrannies, and

> "what's the sequel? Verily,
> Laws scribbled by law-breakers, creeds
> Scrawled by the freethinkers, and deeds
> Shameful and shameless."[200]

Is equality our goal? The consequences of that, too, are not hard to imagine:

[195] *Clarel*, I, 188 (Part II, canto iv).

[196] "A Reasonable Constitution," in *Collected Poems*, p. 411. Not included in the Standard Edition's *Poems.*

[197] *Clarel*, I, 189 (Part II, canto iv).

[198] "Supplement" to *Battle-Pieces*, in *Poems*, p. 187.

[199] *Mardi*, II, 242 (chap. clxi).

[200] *Clarel*, I, 281–82 (Part II, canto xxvi).

> "Myriads playing pygmy parts—
> Debased into equality:
> In glut of all material arts
> A civic barbarism may be:
> Man disennobled—brutalised
> By popular science—atheised
> Into a smatterer. . . .
>   Yet knowing all self need to know
> In self's base little fallacy;
> Dead level of rank commonplace:
> An Anglo-Saxon China, see,
> May on your vast plains shame the race
> In the Dark Ages of Democracy."[201]

What is it, then, that we really wish for man? Can we even name it to ourselves? The frightening possibility recurs that, like Ishmael in his dream, we are "not so much bound to any haven ahead as rushing from all havens astern," that our ideals themselves may simply be part of the blind momentum of events.[202]

How transient, too, are our few and hard-won victories. Behind all, the power of necessity works on:

> "*That* steers the world, not man. States drive;
> The crazy rafts with billows strive."

Our moment of triumph comes and passes:

> "Prose overtakes the victor's songs:
> Victorious right may need redress:
> No failure like a harsh success.
> Yea, ponder well the historic page:
> Of all who, fired with noble rage,
> Have warred for right without reprieve,
> How many spanned the wings immense
> Of Satan's muster, or could cheat
> His cunning tactics of retreat

---

[201] *Ibid.*, II, 249–50 (Part IV, canto xxi).

[202] *Ibid.*, p. 242 (Part IV, canto xx).

And ambuscade? . . .

. . . .

. . . The flood ebbs out—the ebb
Floods back; the incessant shuttle shifts
And flies, and wears and tears the web."[203]

Measured by the years of man, these tides are slow. For five
hundred long years, Rome, " 'by courtesy of history, was re-
publican; yet, at last, her terrible king-tigers came, and spot-
ted themselves with gore.' "[204] Who can say what is in store for
our own land, whose free star now "leads up the constella-
tions"? Already once the "goblin-mountain" of civil war has
been upheaved through her green fields; and though the crater
be sunk once more, one does not easily forget the sight of that
"core of fire below."[205] The crust of solidity is thin indeed. The
mutineers of the Nore had only to wipe out the superimposed
union and cross of the British colors to disclose civilization's
permanent red ground of "unbridled and unbounded revolt."[206]

Freed (if he ever is) from the last visible external bond,
man has but placed himself more completely in the power of
that most subtle of tyrants—himself. Long held back, the final
irony of his life is here: "Seeking to conquer a larger liberty,
man but extends the empire of necessity."[207] The weight of the
past is heavy indeed, yet the past too was in some sense of
man's making:

> "Hypothesise [Ungar suggests]:
> If be a people which began
> Without impediment, or let
> From any ruling which foreran;
> Even striving all things to forget

[203] *Ibid.*, I, 190 (Part II, canto iv).

[204] *Mardi*, II, 241 (chap. clxi).

[205] "The Apparition," in *Poems*, p. 115.

[206] *Billy Budd*, in *The Portable Melville*, pp. 651–52.

[207] "The Bell-Tower," in *Selected Writings of Herman Melville* (New
York: Modern Library, 1952), p. 355. This and the other two epigraphs to
"The Bell-Tower" are omitted from the Standard Edition.

> But this—the excellence of man
> Left to himself, his natural bent,
> His own devices and intent;
> And if, in satire of the heaven,
> A world, a new world have been given
> For stage whereon to deploy the event;
> If such a people be—well, well,
> One hears the kettledrums of hell!"[208]

The small leaven of good is never enough to raise the huge inert mass, though it may at times serve the opposite purpose of salting and so preserving the ill. All too often it seems to us that

> Indolence is heaven's ally here,
> And energy the child of hell:
> The Good Man pouring from his pitcher clear,
> But brims the poisoned well.[209]

In such a view, inaction and a dumb resignation would seem the final wisdom:

> "The world is portioned out, believe:
> The good have but a patch at best,
> The wise their corner; for the rest—
> Malice divides with ignorance."[210]

Seeing the visible world of experience to be of this nature, we may well ask with young White-Jacket: "What then, . . . who is to blame in this matter?"[211] The question admits of more than one answer. Humanly speaking and in the short view, men must of course bear the responsibility for their particular misdeeds. Yet in another and a longer perspective it is also true that "to treat of human actions is to deal wholly with

---

[208] *Clarel*, II, 247 (Part IV, canto xxi).

[209] "Fragments of a Lost Gnostic Poem of the 12th Century," in *Poems*, p. 272.

[210] *Clarel*, I, 189 (Part II, canto iv).

[211] *White-Jacket*, p. 234 (chap. xliv).

second causes."[212] To an unknown degree, men act as they must, out of the compulsion of necessity or the pressures of their individual natures. That "there is an Indian nature" congenital in certain men is not to be doubted. "Branded on his yellow brow with some inscrutable curse," Jackson was as pitiable as he was hideous; Bland's wickedness "seemed the legitimate operation of his whole infernal organization"; and Claggart's hopelessly damned soul, "apprehending the good, but powerless to be it," had no recourse "but to recoil upon itself and like the scorpion for which the Creator alone is responsible, act out to the end the part allotted it."[213]

In the natural world, the significant cause is similarly remote. The shark is rapacious. But is he to be blamed either for this rapacity or for his imperfect success in governing it? "As well hate a seraph, as a shark. Both were made by the same hand."[214] And sustained, one might add, by the same watchful Providence, as witness "the multitudes of sharks . . . [rushing] to the fresh blood [of the dying whale], . . . thirstily drinking at every new gash, as the eager Israelites did at the new bursting fountains that poured from the smitten rock."[215] Nor is the shark the only offender. " 'Look! see yon Albicore! who put it into him to chase and fang that flying-fish?' "[216] Shall we condemn the rattlesnake for his " 'capacity for mischief' "? But if his " 'accountability is not by nature manifest,' " much the same must be admitted of man.[217] By what authority do we deny man the solace of irresponsibility? When a knife fight threatens in the forecastle of the "Pequod," the old Manxman answers the welcoming shout " 'A ring, a ring!' " with the

212 "Supplement" to *Battle-Pieces*, in *Poems*, p. 184.

213 *Redburn*, p. 134 (chap. xxii) ; *White-Jacket*, p. 234 (chap. xliv) ; *Billy Budd*, in *The Portable Melville*, p. 678.

214 *Mardi*, I, 47 (chap. xiii).

215 *Moby-Dick*, II, 54–55 (chap. lxxiii).

216 *Ibid.*, p. 330 (chap. cxxxii).

217 *The Confidence-Man*, p. 253 (chap. xxxvi).

cry: " 'Ready formed. There! the ringed horizon. In that ring Cain struck Abel. Sweet work, right work! No? Why then, God, mad'st thou the ring?' "[218]

It is the ancient and seemingly unanswerable question of how to reconcile with the indisputable existence of evil the notion of an all-good, all-powerful Creator still interested in His creation. True, we have been authoritatively admonished that God " 'is *in* all things, and himself *is* all things . . . But since evil abounds, and [God] is all things, then he cannot be perfectly good; wherefore, [God's] omnipresence and moral perfection seem incompatible.' "[219] An obvious way out of the dilemma would be to admit that God is not everywhere, that He rules "in a divided empire,"[220] in certain parts of which His power is not acknowledged. The rainbow set in the heavens for Noah and still incongruously gleaming over the Dead Sea wastes was perhaps never meant as a pledge of His effective power but simply of His benignity.[221] Accepting this, one may still look upon Him, as Queequeg did upon his pocket-god Yojo, as "a rather good sort of god, who perhaps [means] well enough upon the whole, but in all cases [does] not succeed in his benevolent designs."[222]

Yet it is something of a Pyrrhic victory if we are able to salvage a conviction of God's goodness only at the expense of His power. How much respect is it possible to have for a God of limited powers or, still worse, for an intimidated one, like Stubb's " 'old governor who daresn't catch [the devil] and put him in double-darbies, as he deserves, but lets him go about kidnapping people; aye, and signed a bond with him, that all the people the devil kidnapped, he'd roast for him?' "[223] May

[218] *Moby-Dick*, I, 221 (chap. xl).

[219] *Mardi*, II, 124–25 (chap. cxxxv).

[220] "Cock-A-Doodle-Doo!" in *Billy Budd and Other Prose Pieces*, p. 144.

[221] *Journal of a Visit to Europe and the Levant*, p. 136 n.; "The Lightning-Rod Man," in *The Piazza Tales*, p. 179.

[222] *Moby-Dick*, I, 84 (chap. xvi).

[223] *Ibid.*, II, 58 (chap. lxxiii).

it not even be thought preferable to choose the other horn of
the dilemma and take our stand upon

> "That ground where Durham's prelate stood
> Who saw no proof that God was good
> But only righteous"?[224]

Bishop Butler's resolution (here referred to) of this difficulty
has, after all, the Calvinistic virtue of a consistent God-cen-
teredness. What reason, Butler asks, has man to set up his own
welfare as the measure of the Divine perfection? A higher estimate of the Creator is that which considers Him as not merely
good but as "Just; that is, not simply benevolent, but righteous." For it is the mistake of a sentimental age

to think the only character of the Author of nature to be that of
simple absolute benevolence. This, considered as a principle of
action and infinite in degree, is a disposition to produce the greatest possible happiness, without regard to persons' behaviour, otherwise than as such regard would produce higher degrees of it. . . .
[But this] is not the thing here to be inquired into; but whether
in the constitution and conduct of the world, a righteous government be not discernibly planned out: which necessarily implies a
righteous governor. There may possibly be in the creation beings,
to whom the Author of nature manifests himself under the most
amiable of all characters, this of absolute benevolence; for it is the
most amiable, supposing it not, as perhaps it is not, incompatible
with justice: but he manifests himself to us under the character of
a righteous governor."[225]

Righteousness, then, may be all that it is fair to ask of the
Divinity. But this trait, though it may command admiration, is
not in itself particularly amiable. Melville turns an ironic eye
upon Bishop Butler's distinction both in *The Confidence-Man*
and in the account of Plotinus Plinlimmon in *Pierre*. However
eloquently the superiority of righteousness is argued, Melville

---

[224] *Clarel*, II, 29 (Part III, canto vi).

[225] Joseph Butler, *The Analogy of Religion: The Works of Joseph Butler*,
ed. W. E. Gladstone (Oxford: Clarendon Press, 1896), I, 64–65.

observes, weak humanity continues to prefer goodness and to hope that on this lower level, at least, the two conditions are "not . . . so incompatible as that a righteous man can not [also] be a good man"; and even the severe St. Paul has remarked in his Epistle to the Romans that although " 'Scarcely for a righteous man will one die, yet peradventure for a good man some would even dare to die.' "[226]

It is hard enough at times to persuade oneself that God is even a righteous governor. Experience offers us no very clear support of such a view, "since the common occurrences of life . . . never, in the nature of things, steadily look one way and tell one story, as flags in the trade-wind." A belief in Providence, if it is not to fluctuate like "the stock-exchange during a long and uncertain war," must rest upon faith rather than reason and observation. "It [is] of the essence of a right conviction of the divine nature, as with a right conviction of the human, that, based less on experience than intuition, it [rises] above the zones of weather."[227] An over-reliance upon experience may, on the contrary, come close to persuading us of the existence of an inverted Providence, permissive of good in the interest of evil:

> "Ill to fulfill
> Needful is good: good salts the ill."[228]

The Cosmopolitan cheerfully testifies to his belief in Providence as a great " 'Committee of Safety' " presiding over all the affairs of man and nature;[229] but he does not remind his hearer that it was under the Committee of Safety that France experienced the Reign of Terror. The workings of divine justice show very obscurely indeed through the distortions of our atmosphere, and faith is compelled to seek support in the thought of the compensations of a future life. But this too pre-

---

226 *The Confidence-Man*, p. 47 (chap. vii).

227 *Ibid.*, p. 84 (chap. xiii).

228 *Clarel*, I, 243 (Part II, canto xviii).

229 *The Confidence-Man*, p. 334 (chap. xlv).

sents us with certain difficulties, since it may prompt "the mischievous conceit" that "Providence [is] not now, but [is] going to be."[230]

Observation and reflection may lead to still other, most disturbing conclusions in this regard. The Psalmist has said, "The heavens declare the glory of God, and the firmament sheweth His handiwork." Are we not therefore justified in looking to the more accessible parts of His creation for further evidence of the divine nature? The deists of the eighteenth century looked and found that which they had hoped to find—abundant evidence of the ingenuity of the Great Mechanic. Bishop Butler, concerned with the defense of Scripture against rationalist charges of its inconsistency, took a more searching look at the deists' "natural revelation" and discovered here also, as in the Bible, unsuspected difficulties and contradictions, the sum of which—far from discouraging him—proved to him beyond a reasonable doubt the common authorship of Scripture and the natural order.[231] Melville, who seems to have read Butler with mingled respect and amusement, carries the bishop's reasoning a step further and argues from the imperfections of the creature to the imperfections of the Creator. The very indirectness of the evidence may itself, he suggests, be significant. God reveals in the whale, as once in the burning bush, not His face but only His "back parts," a practice imitated by the soured hermit Oberlus for the sufficient reason that "that was his better side, since it revealed the least."[232] The inconsistencies of human nature, Melville suggests, are reflections of what must by courtesy be called "the contrasts" of the divine nature.[233] At the moment when Pierre discovers the impurity of his motives in championing Isabel, the narrator exclaims:

230 *Ibid.*, p. 85 (chap. xiii).

231 Butler, *op. cit.*, pp. 9–10.

232 *Moby-Dick*, II, 123 (chap. lxxxvi); "The Encantadas," in *The Piazza Tales*, p. 237.

233 *The Confidence-Man*, p. 91 (chap. xiv).

—Ah, if man were wholly made in heaven, why catch we hell-glimpses? Why in the noblest marble pillar that stands beneath the all-comprising vault, ever should we descry the sinister vein? We lie in nature very close to God; and though, further on, the stream may be corrupted by the banks it flows through; yet at the fountain's rim, where mankind stand, there the stream infallibly bespeaks the fountain.[234]

The implication is clear: life is poisoned in its very wellspring, and the closer to the source the more contaminated the waters.

But what the stream's further reaches show us can also be frightening. We see in nature an " 'outrageous strength, with an inscrutable malice sinewing it,' "[235] and that malice seems to us chargeable less to the blind agent than to its principal. Evil is no accident: it proceeds from causes, and these in turn from a first cause. Queequeg, having nearly lost a hand to the "Pantheistic vitality" still lurking in the jaws of a supposedly dead shark, put the matter bluntly: " 'Queequeg no care what god made him shark, . . . wedder Fejee god or Nantucket god; but de god wat made shark must be one dam Ingin.' "[236] In Maramma, the center of Mardi's institutionalized religion, sharks deified and have altars, the stone shark mouth in the sacred spring is known as "the mouth of [God]," and to kill a shark is "deemed worse than homicide." " 'And what if they destroy human life?' say the Islanders, 'are they not sacred?' "[237] Babbalanja sees nothing novel in the attribution of a malicious intent to "the august gods"; he finds difficulty only in believing that they would stoop to inflict upon man the myriad petty ills that beset him.[238] To Ishmael, freely acknowledging his own savagery, the ruler of the universe appears as "the King of the Cannibals." [239] Pitch, the Missouri Bachelor,

234 *Pierre*, p. 151 (Book V, chap. vii).
235 *Moby-Dick*, I, 204 (chap. xxxvi).
236 *Ibid.*, II, 26 (chap. lxvi).
237 *Mardi*, II, 15 (chap. cviii).
238 *Ibid.*, I, 307–8 (chap. lxxxvi).
239 *Moby-Dick*, I, 343 (chap. lvii).

sees Him as a murderous swindler and rails at the optimists who deny that fact as " 'the green ones [who] . . . pace the rotten planks [of this world's ship], singing like . . . fool[s], words put into [their] green mouth[s] by the cunning owner, . . . who, heavily insuring it, sends his ship to be wrecked.' "[240] " 'Who's to doom,' " cries Ahab, " 'when the judge himself is dragged to the bar?' "[241] And as Peleg hints,[242] the name "Ahab" has connotations outrunning merely human wickedness; for this was the great king of Israel whom God deceitfully led to his death through the agency of a "lying spirit," as is set down in the eighteenth chapter of Second Chronicles —the same "mysterious passage," one cannot doubt, which Redburn assured the puzzled Negro cook "no one could explain; not even a parson."[243]

But in attributing deliberate malice to God, it may be that man simply betrays his own egocentrism. It is not established that man is the firmament's keystone, or even that he is significant enough to figure in the divine plan. Can we really be sure that God *has* a plan at all? " 'If He fears not, nor hopes,—He has no other passion; no ends, no purposes. He lives content; all ends are compassed in Him; He has no past, no future; He is the everlasting now; which is an everlasting calm. . . .' "[244]

A God thus perfect and complete is of course infinitely remote from His creation. Worship does not touch Him. The dying whale turns to the sun " 'how slowly, but how steadfastly, his homage-rendering and invoking brow.' " " '[H]ere, too, life dies sunward full of faith; but see! no sooner dead, than death whirls round the corpse, and it heads some other way.' "[245] Man cannot hope to approach or to understand such

240 *The Confidence-Man*, p. 159 (chap. xxii).

241 *Moby-Dick*, II, 330 (chap. cxxxii).

242 *Ibid.*, I, 99–100 (chap. xvi).

243 *Redburn*, p. 105 (chap. xvii).

244 *Mardi*, II, 359 (chap. clxxxv).

245 *Moby-Dick*, II, 270 (chap. cxvi).

a God; and the best and wisest men, by their greater awareness of this fact, will be the saddest.[246] Entreaties mean nothing to Him. The wooden idols of Maramma, with holes drilled straight through their heads from ear to ear, are to this extent true representations of Him.[247] He answers no one—not even the crucified Christ, Who

> "Crying out in death's eclipse,
> When rainbow none His eyes might see,
> Enlarged the margin for despair—
> *My God, My God, forsakest Me?*"[248]

The pretensions of the philosophers and the theologians notwithstanding, the truth is that a "profound Silence . . . [is the] only Voice of our God."[249]

Of this withdrawn and self-absorbed deity, we are given a dramatic prefiguration in the person of the philosopher Plotinus Plinlimmon, whose distant face looked down into Pierre's cubicle from a high window in the Apostles' tower. Studying it thus through two panes of glass, Pierre found it a face marked by a certain "cheerful content" that was not to be confused with either "Happiness or Delight," a face exhibiting a vaguely repellent quality of "non-Benevolence" that "was neither Malice nor Ill-will; but something passive," and wearing at all times an expression of "Inscrutableness." Inquiry revealed that Plinlimmon was without "family or blood ties of any sort." His self-sufficiency expressed itself not only in his air of "cheerful content," but in a repose never disturbed by labor and a silence broken only on rare occasions. Although reputed wise, "he never was known to open a book"; and "the sleazy works that went under his name . . . were nothing more than his verbal things, taken down at random, and bunglingly methodized by his young disciples." Gazing placidly down

---

[246] *Mardi*, II, 374–76 (chap. clxxxviii).

[247] *Ibid.*, pp. 37–38 (chap. cxiv).

[248] *Clarel*, I, 52 (Part I, canto xiii).

[249] *Pierre*, p. 290 (Book XIV, chap. ii).

into Pierre's study, Plotinus' face showed a detached amusement at the young author's despairing struggles:

Vain! vain! vain! said the face to him. Fool! fool! fool! said
the face to him. Quit! quit! quit! said the face to him. But when
he mentally interrogated the face as to why it thrice said Vain!
Fool! Quit! to him; here there was no response. For that face did
not respond to anything. . . . [That] face was something separate,
and apart; a face by itself.

And "mystic-mild" as it was, "to Pierre the face at last wore
a sort of malicious leer" which, whether subjective or objective, grew to be insufferable to him.[250]

If inaction and permissiveness most characterize God's gov-
ernance of His world, quite the opposite qualities stand forth
when we consider Him as Creator. The endless procession of
beings momently coming into existence and passing unnoted
into nothingness suggests a Creator mechanically and point-
lessly active, like Israel Potter in the London brickyard com-
pulsively slapping clay into forms:

[W]hat is a mortal but a few luckless shovelfuls of clay, moulded
in a mould, laid out on a sheet to dry, and ere long quickened into
his queer caprices by the sun? Are not men built into communities
just like bricks into a wall? Consider the great wall of China;
ponder the great population of Pekin. As man serves bricks, so
God him, building him up by billions into edifices of his purposes.
Man attains not to the nobility of a brick, unless taken in the
aggregate.[251]

The divine prodigality and irresponsibility is most vividly
realized for us in the image of the vine-grown whale skeleton
in the jungle:

It was a wondrous sight. The wood was green as mosses of the
Icy Glen; the trees stood high and haughty, feeling their living
sap; the industrious earth beneath was as a weaver's loom, with a
gorgeous carpet on it, whereof the ground-vine tendrils formed the

---

250 *Ibid.*, pp. 404–10 (Book XXI, chap. iii).
251 *Israel Potter*, pp. 206–7 (chap. xxiii).

warp and woof, and the living flowers the figures. All the trees, with all their laden branches; all the shrubs, and ferns, and grasses; the message-carrying air; all these unceasingly were active. Through the lacings of the leaves, the great sun seemed a flying shuttle weaving the unwearied verdure. Oh, busy weaver! unseen weaver!—pause!—one word!—whither flows the fabric? what palace may it deck? wherefore all these ceaseless toilings? Speak, weaver!—stay thy hand!—but one single word with thee! Nay— the shuttle flies—the figures float from forth the loom; the freshet-rushing carpet for ever slides away. The weaver-god, he weaves; and by that weaving he is deafened, that he hears no mortal voice.[252]

A like vision of the fortuitous, meaningless character of life is the source of Pip's desperate but liberating knowledge. Deserted on the open sea, Pip was

carried down alive to wondrous depths, where strange shapes of the unwarped primal world glided to and fro before his passive eyes; and the miser-merman, Wisdom, revealed his hoarded heaps; and among the joyous, heartless, ever-juvenile eternities, Pip saw the multitudinous, God-omnipresent, coral insects, that out of the firmament of waters heaved the colossal orbs. He saw God's foot upon the treadle of the loom, and spoke it; and therefore his shipmates called him mad.[253]

The carpenter of the "Pequod" is a type of this jack-of-all-trades God, "prepared at all points" to turn out bird cages, masts, legs, boats, oars, and coffins—"and alike indifferent and without respect in all." His versatility, however, argued no uncommon vivacity of intelligence. . . . For nothing was this man more remarkable, than for a certain impersonal stolidity as it were; impersonal, I say; for it so shaded off into the surrounding infinite of things, that it seemed one with the general stolidity discernible in the whole visible world; which while pauselessly active in uncounted modes, still eternally holds its peace, and ignores you, though you dig foundations for cathedrals. Yet was this half-hor-

---

[252] *Moby-Dick*, II, 213 (chap. cii).
[253] *Ibid.*, pp. 169–70 (chap. xciii).

rible stolidity in him, involving, too, as it appeared, an all-ramify-
ing heartlessness;—yet was it oddly dashed at times, with an old,
crutch-like, antediluvian, wheezing humorousness . . . .

. . . He was a stript abstract; an unfractioned integral; uncom-
promised as a new-born babe; living without premeditated reference to this world or the next. You might almost say, that this
strange uncompromisedness in him involved a sort of unintelli-
gence; for in his numerous trades, he did not seem to work . . .
by reason or by instinct . . . ; but merely by a kind of deaf and
dumb, spontaneous literal process. He was a pure manipulator; his
brain, if he had ever had one, must have early oozed along into
the muscles of his fingers.[254]

Ahab, later finding the carpenter at work calking Queequeg's
discarded coffin as a life-preserver, challenges him:

"Then tell me; art thou not an arrant, all-grasping, intermed-
dling, monopolizing, heathenish old scamp, to be one day making
legs, and the next day coffins to clap them in, and yet again life-
buoys out of those same coffins? Thou art as unprincipled as the
gods, and as much of a jack-of-all-trades."
"But I do not mean anything, sir. I do as I do."
"The gods again. . . ."[255]

It is this very lack of purpose that allows Israel Potter's life
to molder away like a cord of wood forgotten in a mountain
pasture, that creates souls like Bartleby and dispatches them
into life with no other goal than the Dead Letter Office of
oblivion.[256] The sight of fatherless Pip moves Ahab to angry
protest:

"There can be no hearts above the snow-line. Oh, ye frozen
heavens! look down here. Ye did beget this luckless child, and
have abandoned him, ye creative libertines. Here, boy; Ahab's
cabin shall be Pip's home henceforth, while Ahab lives."[257]

[254] *Ibid.*, pp. 233–34 (chap. cvii).
[255] *Ibid.*, pp. 308–9 (chap. cxxvii).
[256] *Israel Potter*, p. 224 (chap. xxvii); "Bartleby," in *The Piazza Tales*,
p. 65.
[257] *Moby-Dick*, II, 301–2 (chap. cxxv).

Yet Ahab too, aspiring to a more than human pitch of isolation and self-sufficiency, is fated to desert him and is in this
perhaps most like the God he accuses and emulates.

But the worst possibility is not that God may be unconcerned
for the welfare of His creatures, or permissive of evil either
for the sake of a larger good or because of His limited power,
or even that He may be upon occasion wilfully malicious. The
most appalling thought is that all our distinctions between
good and evil may be unreal in His eyes, that virtue and vice
may be no more than " 'two shadows cast from one nothing,' "258 and God Himself, like His universe, amoral and all-
inclusive. It is just this suggestion of final meaninglessness
and absence of all value that makes the phenomenon of whiteness at times so unbearable to Ishmael:

As in essence whiteness is not so much a color as the visible
absence of color, and at the same time the concrete of all colors;
is it for these reasons that there is such a dumb blankness, full of
meaning, in a wide landscape of snows—a colorless, all-color of
atheism from which we shrink? And when we consider that other
theory of the natural philosophers, that all other earthly hues . . .
are but subtle deceits, not actually inherent in substances, but only
laid on from without; so that all deified Nature absolutely paints
like the harlot, whose allurements cover nothing but the charnel-
house within; and when we proceed further, and consider that the
mystical cosmetic which produces every one of her hues, the great
principle of light, for ever remains white or colorless in itself, and
if operating without medium upon matter, would touch all objects,
even tulips and roses, with its own blank tinge—pondering all this,
the palsied universe lies before us a leper.259

It is this unprincipled and chameleon-like God, too unfixed
even to merit the epithet "malicious," who throughout the
bitter masquerade of *The Confidence-Man* diverts Himself by
toying, from behind one pasteboard mask or another, with the
hopes and fears and weaknesses of mankind. Presenting Him-

258 *Pierre*, p. 382 (Book XIX, chap. ii).
259 *Moby-Dick*, I, 243–44 (chap. xlii).

self to the passengers of the "Fidèle" first in the inoffensive and Christlike figure of the mute in white garments who, mocked by the crowd, falls asleep and is seen no more, the Arch Swindler moves in the course of the narrative through a spectrum of seven successive disguises (all of them "diddlers" of one sort or another and all of them tied to each other through the running motif of white and black) and ends in the role of the genial Cosmopolitan with his all-color harlequin's dress and a broadmindedness that refuses to entertain "any uncharitable prejudice [even] against the rattlesnake." The comedy draws to its appropriate close with a scene in which God and the devil—in the persons of the Cosmopolitan and a too-knowing boy peddler with flame-colored garments, sooty face, and a hard horny foot like a steer's hoof—co-operate with practiced ease to defraud a saintly old man of both his money and his faith and lead him off confused and foolish into the darkness of death.[260] But the supposed opponents are even closer to each other than is here implied: the Cosmopolitan himself has certain serpent-like traits[261] and speaks allusively of himself as continually going up and down the world, " 'from Teheran to Natchitoches,' " sipping, tasting, and smacking his lips over " 'that good dish, man,' " whether " 'served up à la Pole, or à la Moor, à la Ladrone, or à la Yankee.' "[262] Good and evil are indeed strands of the same

---

[260] *The Confidence-Man*, pp. 320–26 (chap. xlv).

[261] *Ibid.*, p. 251 (chap. xxxvi).

[262] *Ibid.*, p. 177 (chap. xxiv). The Satanic traits of the confidence man are fairly obvious and have been often remarked; the hints of his divinity, though many, are somewhat more subtle. One must not forget that it is the Christlike mute in white garments who introduces the masquerade and that it is his function to disarm (by the biblical exhortation "Charity thinketh no evil") the suspicion aroused by a placard warning the travelers against "a mysterious imposter, supposed to have recently arrived from the East; quite an original genius in his vocation, as would appear, though wherein his originality consisted was not clearly given; but what purported to be a careful description of his person followed" (pp. 1–2, chap. i). This same plea for confidence, to be echoed by each of the swindlers in turn, prepares the way first for the crippled Negro beggar (pp. 10–20, chap. iii) who first appears near

cord, and the contradictions of man but mirror the contrasts
of the Divine Nature.

the scene of the mute's disappearance and who, by his theft of the merchant's
card, sets up the first victim of his successor, "the man with the weed" (pp.
21–29, chap. iv). This operator in turn, after reaping his own harvest of fools,
drops a hint that prepares the same victim for the purchase of some bogus
stock in the Black Rapids Coal Company from "the man with the book" (pp.
71–73, chap. x). The book referred to—the coal company's register of stock
transfers—is spoken of as "the true book" (p. 73; cf. p. 315, chap. xliii), and
the man who carries it is described by his successor, the herb-doctor, as one
"'who, in pure goodness of heart, makes people's fortunes for them—their
everlasting fortunes, as the phrase goes—only charging his one small commission of confidence'" (p. 134, chap. xx). (There is an echo here, surely, of
Christ's "For whosoever believeth on me, he shall be saved.") The same agent
offers for sale, though somewhat more diffidently, shares in "'the New Jerusalem,'" recently founded in northern Minnesota (pp. 65–66, chap. ix). "'I
live not for myself [he assures yet another victim]; but the world will not
have confidence in me, and yet confidence in me were great gain'" (p. 97,
chap. xv). The man in gray, Calvinistically distinguished as "the righteous
man" from a passenger who is merely good (pp. 47–48, chap. vii), piously
accepts the widow's mite in behalf of his favorite charity, the Seminole
Widow and Orphan Asylum (pp. 58–59, chap. viii), no mention being made
of the fact that Indians are developed at some length later in the book
(chaps. xxv–xxviii) as a symbol of incorrigible evil. The Cosmopolitan, last
in the chain of maskers, makes his appeal chiefly, it is true, on humanitarian
grounds; but we are not allowed to forget that he is simply one in a succession of avatars of the one confidence man. There are a number of hints that
his nature is more than human, more even than Satanic. In the barber's shop,
preparing for his next to the last exploit, he takes his seat on a "throne"
which is one of three on the same dais (p. 300, chap. xlii; see also p. 307,
chap. xliii). "'*Only* a man? [he says in answer to the barber]. As if to be
but man were nothing. But don't be too sure what I am. You call me *man*,
just as the townsfolk called the angels who, in man's form, came to Lot's
house; just as the Jew rustics called the devils who, in man's form, haunted
the tombs. You can conclude nothing absolute from the human form, barber'" (pp. 299–300, chap. xlii). And when the barber (swindled despite his
skepticism and this frank warning) ruefully concludes by declaring his cus-
tomer "QUITE AN ORIGINAL," the phrase reminds us of that "mysterious imposter, . . . quite an original genius," of whom we were admonished at the
beginning to think no evil. And lest—its capitals notwithstanding—we still
miss the full significance of the barber's phrase, Melville makes it the text
of one of his elaborate "digressions" (pp. 317–19, chap. xliv), in the course
of which the word "original" is referred to its origin, with the implication
that it must be applied to nothing this side of the first cause itself: "There
would seem to be but one point in common between this sort of phenomenon
in fiction and all other sorts: it cannot be born in the author's imagination—
it being as true in literature as in zoology, that all life is from the egg." But
when all is said, the narrator remains not quite certain that he is right in
denying the Cosmopolitan the title of "original."

THE TORTOISE
IS BOTH BLACK
AND BRIGHT

Here, then, is the darker face of reality as
seen by those "nobler, sadder souls" who look behind the
world's screen of sunlight; and here, at his most inhuman, is
God as declared in the pages of His creation. It is a picture
not easily disputed. Nightmarish as it is, its truth can be supported by the disillusioned and the embittered with evidence
drawn from the daily experience of life. But the wish to estab-
lish such a case in itself argues a measure of self-delusion:
one must choose to ignore what does not fit the picture. There
are always "Two sides to a tortoise."[263] As Starbuck knowing-
ly shuts his eyes to the evidence of life's darker aspect, so
Ahab grimly turns his back on the " 'theoretic bright one.' "[264]
And truth—at least such partial truth as this—does not
invariably lead on to further truth; it may instead cut its
possessor off from the community of mankind and so shake
the certainty of all his beliefs.[265] Each step toward truth may
thus become a step away from meaning. The more determined
the seeker, the more isolated he will be; "and isolation is the
mother of illusion."[266] Being men, we need the "colored and
coloring glasses" of a man-centered outlook if the whiteness
of the absolute is not to blind us.[267] The hunger for truth is
indeed the most godlike of human desires,

but the example of many minds forever lost, like undiscoverable
Arctic explorers, amid those treacherous regions, warns us entirely
away from them; and we learn that it is not for man to follow the
trail of truth too far, since by so doing he entirely loses the directing compass of his mind; for arrived at the Pole, to whose barren-

---

[263] "The Encantadas," in *The Piazza Tales,* pp. 188–89.
[264] *Moby-Dick,* II, 190–91 (chap. xcix), 265 (cxiv), 310 (chap. cxxvii).
[265] *Pierre,* pp. 231–32 (Book IX, chap. i) ; *Moby-Dick,* II, 182 (chap. xcvi).
[266] "Rammon," in *Collected Poems,* p. 413.
[267] *Moby-Dick,* I, 244 (chap. xlii).

ness only it points, there, the needle indifferently respects all points of the horizon alike.[268]

"There is a wisdom that is woe; but there is a woe that is madness."[269] Driven to this extreme by his monomania, the Ahab who began as man's champion ends in refusing the pathetic plea of the captain of the "Rachel," banishing the weeping Pip from his presence, and shutting his heart against the memory even of his own son.[270] But not only do the natural affections atrophy and drop away from such a man: the anger called forth by his long and intense scrutiny of life's dark side begins at last to eat at his own heart. For anger must find a target somewhere.

"Would now the wind but had a body [cries Ahab]; but all the things that most exasperate and outrage mortal man, all these things are bodiless, but only bodiless as objects, not as agents. There's a most special, a most cunning, oh, a most malicious difference!"[271]

Babbalanja, " 'hunted, turns and finds no foe to fight' "; Ahab, knocked down, leaps up to find that his assailant has " 'run and hidden' "; Pierre, hurled back upon himself by the powers of earth and heaven, is stung at last into taking himself as target.[272] In a last gesture of defiance, Mortmain madly drinks of the Dead Sea's gall and lives.[273] Not all have been so fortunate. There are in this world "waters of bitterness from which one can only turn aside and be silent."[274] We may say of these men, as Sophocles said of Oedipus,

[268] *Pierre*, p. 231 (Book IX, chap. i).

[269] *Moby-Dick*, II, 182 (chap. xcvi).

[270] *Ibid.*, I, 149–50 (chap. xxvii), 229–30 (chap. xli); II, 314 (chap. cxxviii); p. 316 (chap. cxxix); pp. 329–30 (chap. cxxxii).

[271] *Ibid.*, p. 355 (chap. cxxxv).

[272] *Mardi*, II, 360 (chap. clxxxv); *Moby-Dick*, I, 210 (chap. xxxvii); *Pierre*, p. 503 (Book XXVI, chap. vi).

[273] *Clarel*, I, 315 (Part II, canto xxxiv).

[274] "Supplement" to *Battle-Pieces*, in *Poems*, p. 188.

that it was the gods who brought their bitter sufferings upon them but the hand that struck them was their own. Prometheus in them becomes his own punisher: Ahab's "intense thinking" has created in him "a vulture [that] feeds upon [his] heart forever"; and Pierre, having similarly "waked the infinite wakefulness in him[self]," can sleep only by temporarily "sheath[ing] the beak of the vulture in his hand."[275]

So, in a sense, too much knowledge may prove as dangerous as too little. Pessimist and optimist share the same error of attempting to assign to the world of experience a single and final character. As the whale upon occasion is confused by the two distinct pictures of reality shown him by his far-separated and non-fusing eyes,[276] so—to extend Melville's image —man looks out in time upon quite different prospects and mistakes each partial image for the whole. Wisdom comes, when it does, with the discovery that nature and God are too vast to be captured in any of our formulations. The Eternal Silence only *seems* to speak to us, and the world but echoes the sound of our human voices. All meaning is of man: "Nature is not so much her own . . . interpreter, as the mere supplier of that cunning alphabet, whereby selecting and combining as he pleases, each man reads his own peculiar lesson, according to his own peculiar mind and mood."[277] The breaching whale will appear to us as either Satan or an archangel, according as we are in the mood of Dante or of Isaiah.[278] It was this that Narcissus could not know: that "the ungraspable phantom of life" upon which he looked with such longing and perplexity was but his own image reflected in the fountain.[279] The Ecuadorean doubloon of the "Pequod," minted at "the middle of the world" and nailed now to the mainmast at the

275 *Moby-Dick*, I, 253 (chap. xliv) ; *Pierre*, p. 426 (Book XXII, chap. iv).

276 *Moby-Dick*, II, 61–62 (chap. lxxiv).

277 *Pierre*, p. 476 (Book XXV, chap. iv).

278 *Moby-Dick*, II, 122 (chap. lxxxvi).

279 *Ibid.*, I, 3–4 (chap. i).

ship's center, stands as an emblem of unriddled, uncommitted
nature. Its face searched for omens and auguries by Ahab,
the three mates, Queequeg, and little Pip, this " 'image of the
rounder globe, . . . like a magician's glass, to each and every
man in turn but mirrors back his own mysterious self.' "
Ahab, wilfully imposing his ego upon reality, sees and yet
does not see this truth; Queequeg notes that the coin's cryptic
characters appear also in his own tattooing but seems unable
to interpret his discovery; only mad Pip, with his thrice-re-
peated paradigm, " 'I look, you look, he looks; we look, ye
look, they look,' " seems to guess how impassable is the gulf
between the mind and its object.[280]

Yet a certain freedom comes to us with this realization.
True, " '[God] champions none. In all things, man's own
battles, man himself must fight.' "[281] "Nature is nobody's
ally; 'tis well."[282] But if the universe is not for us, neither is it
against us. And by this very fact, our state would appear to
be no worse than our fathers'. It is true that this world was
made with no thought of man's happiness. Yet there is some
comfort in knowing that "What we call Fate is even, heartless, and impartial; not a fiend to kindle bigot flames, nor a
philanthropist to espouse the cause of Greece. We may fret,
fume, and fight; but the thing called Fate everlastingly sus-
tains an armed neutrality."[283]

Queequeg, though he could not read it, wore "written out
on his body a complete theory of the heavens and earth, and
a mystical treatise on the art of attaining truth."[284] So with us.
Launched as we are upon " 'these most candid and impartial
seas,' " and foreever "sailing with sealed orders, we ourselves
are the repositories of the secret packet, whose mysterious

[280] *Ibid.*, II, 188–95 (chap. xcix).

[281] *Mardi*, II, 250 (chap. clxii).

[282] "The Stone Fleet," in *Poems*, p. 21.

[283] *White-Jacket*, p. 404 (chap. lxxv).

[284] *Moby-Dick*, II, 251 (chap. cx).

contents we long to learn. There are no mysteries out of ourselves."[285] Whatever meaning our lives are to have, we ourselves must discover and create: " 'The essence of all good
and evil is in us, not out of us. Neither poison nor honey
lodgeth in the flowers on which, side by side, bees and wasps
oft alight.' "[286] Our individual fate is not, in the end, separable
from what we are: " 'Ahab is for ever Ahab, man.' "

When all has been said, it is true that "for them who are
neither partisans, nor enthusiasts, nor theorists, nor cynics,
there are some doubts not readily to be solved. And there are
fears."[287] But there is a wisdom too—if we can attain to it—
which makes it possible to bear with both:

> Though fast youth's glorious fable flies,
> View not the world with worldling's eyes;
> Nor turn with weather of the time.
> Foreclose the coming of surprise:
> Stand where Posterity shall stand;
> Stand where the Ancients stood before,
> And dipping in lone founts thy hand,
> Drink of the never-varying lore:
> Wise once, and wise thence evermore.[288]

[285] *White-Jacket,* p. 502 ("The End").

[286] *Mardi,* II, 136 (chap. cxxxvii).

[287] "Supplement" to *Battle-Pieces,* in *Poems,* p. 186.

[288] "Lone Founts," in *Poems,* p. 267.

PART II

The Meeting

The essential self, then, as Melville conceives it, is an aboriginal and undetermined thing, owing neither its existence nor the principle of its action to the world that surrounds it. The dependence, in fact, is quite the other way about: the character which that outer world assumes when viewed as a whole is in each case largely the creation of the individual personality contemplating it. But unlike his divine model, the creator is not therefore sufficient unto himself. For if the sense of self begins in separation, it is completed in conflict. It is in the response to experience, and only in that response, that the self realizes and declares its nature.

If this is so, it will be worth our while to consider the

principal ways in which the self may attempt to deal with experience, as these are set forth in the attitudes and actions of
certain of Melville's characters. Of certain ones, let it be noted;
not all. For obviously, not every character has been conceived
with this function in mind or presented as concerned, in any
meaningful way, with the problem of moral action. The simple
doers—the Tobys and Jarls and Flasks—have no place here,
nor the innocents and the unthinking optimists—the Budds
and Delanos and Charlie Millthorpes; nor those whose nature
is already fatally fixed in evil—the Jacksons and Blands and
Claggarts. Looking instead at the behavior of those who, with
a deeper insight into the nature of reality, have in some conscious way assumed the direction of their own lives, one may
note the existence of three principal strategies.

Men may, on the one hand, enraged by what they see about
them, choose to defy the general frame of things, either in a
direct assault upon the humiliating terms of their existence or,
more often, by bearing their pain in silence while stubbornly
withholding their consent to life. They may, on the other hand,
submit, with more or less reluctance, to the resistless power of
what is, attempt to persuade themselves that all is for the best,
and in one way or another contrive to live out their lives within the limits imposed upon them. Or, finally, they may seek
to maintain, in emulation of indifferent nature herself, a state
of "armed neutrality" to life—a state involving neither immoderate hope nor despairing anger, neither submission nor
defiance.

Differing widely as individuals, the members of these three
groups may yet with some fairness be characterized in general terms. Melville's defiers are, on the whole, men of un-
usual—in some instances, of heroic—will and courage; they
err, to the extent that they may be said to err, on the side of
rashness and an immoderate anger. The submitters are notable
chiefly for a failure of will, a sort of disbelief in the worth of
their deepest self. They are a more mixed lot than the defiers:

some wholly cowardly and ignoble, some intrepid against all but the final, spiritual terrors of life; some basely self-seeking, others placing what they see as the welfare of society above their own good, prepared to sacrifice to it even the integrity of their own conscience. The members of the third group are non-submitters of a more philosophic cast than the defiers, men who press no private quarrel with the universe but who strive by a wise stoicism to maintain both their own "humanities" and their dignity as "sovereign [individuals] among the powers of heaven, hell, and earth."

It is time now to examine in some detail the actions of particular representatives of these groups. And first, of the defiers.

3. Defiance

THE WAY OF TRAGIC HEROISM

Running through all of Melville's work is the theme of banishment. Again and again in his writings we encounter the figure of the orphan, the outcast, the disinherited son. Nor, in one sense, are these figures to be regarded as exceptional. The entire race of man, if we accept the account of Scripture, lives in this world in exile and penal degradation. To think of those long centuries of human grief and to see what they have done to men is almost to credit the superstition which sees the grim "convict tortoises" of the Galapagos as men malignantly transformed and condemned to drag themselves for ages over the scorched volcanic rock in a never-to-be-satisfied quest for water.[1]

In view of his rooted belief in the inherent dignity of man and of his sense of man's present degradation at the hands of a God Who chooses to rule by force rather than by love, it is not surprising that Melville's imagination should early have seized upon and deeply considered the ancient myth of the Titans, those heroic outcasts of heaven. In taking it up, he but moved, of course, in one of the notable currents of his age. The attitude of Titanism had proved a particularly tempting one in the generations just preceding: anger at the political and intellectual repressions of the post-Revolutionary reaction had commended it to the imagination of such men as Goethe and Richter in Germany, Byron, Shelley, Blake, and Keats in England.

Broadly understood, Titanism may be defined as an attitude of uncompromising resistance to a tyrannical and resistless power. More narrowly considered, this opposition will be seen to take the form either of passive resistance or of violent counterattack. In the first instance, we have the figure of the steadfast sufferer, Prometheus chained; in the second, that of Enceladus, the furious heaven-stormer of Pierre's dream. The first is the better known. Chained to the precipice and exposed for eternity to the vulture's beak in punishment of the love which led him to steal heaven's fire as a gift for man, Prometheus scorns to buy relief at the cost of acknowledging his tormentor and surrendering his secret, the identity of Zeus' fated supplanter. Enceladus, most warlike and irreconcilable of the precipitated giants, rallies his stunned legions about him at the foot of Olympus and in hopeless fury hurls his broken body "again and yet again against the invulnerable steep."[2]

---

[1] "The Encantadas," in *The Piazza Tales*, pp. 185–86; *Clarel*, II, 170–71 (Part IV, canto iii) ; *Israel Potter*, p. 212 (chap. xxv).

[2] *Pierre*, p. 482 (Book XXV, chap. iv).

THE PROMETHEANS

Even in the narrower sense to which it is here restricted, the figure of Prometheus plays a larger symbolic role in Melville's writings than might be at first supposed. There are of course a number of explicit references to him;[3] and certain other allusions are perhaps too obvious to be missed. Few readers, for instance, will fail to recognize the godlike stance or the heroic accent of Ahab when, grasping the lightning-chains and standing "erect before the lofty tripointed trinity of flames," he utters his great prayer:

"Oh! thou clear spirit of clear fire, whom on these seas I as Persian once did worship, till in the sacramental act so burned by thee, that to this hour I bear the scar; I now know thee, thou clear spirit, and I now know thy right worship is defiance. To neither love nor reverence wilt thou be kind; and e'en for hate thou canst but kill; and all are killed. No fearless fool now fronts thee. I own thy speechless, placeless power; but to the last gasp of my earthquake life will dispute its unconditional, unintegral mastery in me. In the midst of the personified impersonal, a personality stands here. Though but a point at best; whencesoe'er I came; wheresoe'er I go; yet while I earthly live, the queenly personality lives in me, and feels her royal rights. But war is pain, and hate is woe. Come in thy lowest form of love, and I will kneel and kiss thee; but at thy highest, come as mere supernal power; and though thou launchest navies of full-freighted worlds, there's that in here that still remains indifferent. Oh, thou clear spirit, of thy fire thou madest me, and like a true child of fire, I breathe it back to thee."[4]

But titanic as he is, Ahab is yet no species to himself. He is meaningful to us for the very reason that our own offended humanity finds its voice and forgotten dignity in him. The same pride looks forth from many other faces. We see it, for instance, in Ushant, the punningly named veteran of the old

[3] *Moby-Dick*, I, 253 (chap. xliv) ; II, 237 (chap. cviii) ; *Pierre*, p. 426 (Book XXII, chap. iv).

[4] *Moby-Dick*, II, 281–82 (chap. cxix).

"Constitution" who unhesitatingly goes to the gratings and is flogged rather than comply with his captain's arbitrary command that he shave off his beard, that "token of manhood [and] . . . true badge of a warrior."[5] The Portuguese sailor, too, whom Redburn's shipmates discover dead and phosphorescently burning in the darkness of his forecastle bunk, takes on, as representative of his insulted race and class, something of titanic dimensions:

The eyes were open and fixed; the mouth was curled like a scroll, and every lean feature firm as in life; while the whole face, now wound in curls of soft blue flame, wore an aspect of grim defiance, and eternal death. Prometheus, blasted by fire on the rock.[6]

So too Hunilla, the half-breed widow marooned for three long years on the bare rock of Norfolk Isle in the Galapagos. Her signal is seen at last by a passing vessel, and the boat sent ashore for her waits while she pays a last visit to her husband's grave:

I looked into her eyes [the narrator tells us], but saw no tear. There was something which seemed strangely haughty in her air, and yet it was the air of woe. A Spanish and an Indian grief, which would not visibly lament. Pride's height in vain abased to proneness on the rack; nature's pride subduing nature's torture.

Ordered by her rescuers to leave behind her all but two of the tiny dogs who have been the only companions of her solitude, she sits silently in the boat and never looks behind her where the poor beasts run howling along the surf:

She seemed as one who, having experienced the sharpest of mortal pangs, was henceforth content to have all lesser heartstrings riven, one by one. To Hunilla, pain seemed so necessary, that pain in other beings, though by love and sympathy made her own, was unrepiningly to be borne. A heart of yearning in a frame of steel.

---

5 *White-Jacket*, pp. 459–64 (chap. lxxxvii).

6 *Redburn*, p. 317 (chap. xlviii).

A heart of earthly yearning, frozen by the frost which falleth from the sky.[7]

The figure of Prometheus seems to merge at times with that of Adam, father of our race and degraded lord of Paradise. Ahab appears both as " 'Adam, staggering beneath the piled centuries since Paradise' " and as "that captive king," mocked by "the great gods," who on his "broken throne" still "patient sits, upholding on his frozen brow the piled entablatures of ages."[8] The "invalid Titan" of *The Confidence-Man,* emerging from the wilderness with burdened step, pain-shadowed countenance, and giant form bent "like a mainmast yielding to the gale, or Adam to the thunder," seems a union of Prometheus, banished Adam, and the Wandering Jew. Boarding the "Fidèle," he is silent for a time but is stung at last by the herbdoctor's praises of his patented "Samaritan Pain Dissuader" into the scornful retort " 'You lie! Some pains cannot be eased but by producing insensibility, and cannot be cured but by producing death.' " And a moment later, he is so enraged by the lying testimonials to the nostrum that he strikes and all but fells the medicine-man divinity.[9]

Inevitably, too, the image of Prometheus must bring to mind that "second Adam" and still nobler victim of God's wrath, He

> "Whose mystic birth
> Wrecked him upon this reef of earth,
> Inclement and inhuman."[10]

Clearly we are meant to see that likeness when for the first time Ahab stands before his crew "with a crucifixion in his face; in all the nameless regal overbearing dignity of some mighty woe." His " 'soul mounts up [and] wearies with her

---

[7] "The Encantadas," in *The Piazza Tales,* pp. 233, 235.

[8] *Moby-Dick,* II, 328 (chap. cxxxii) ; I, 231 (chap. xli).

[9] *The Confidence-Man,* pp. 111–16 (chap. xvii).

[10] *Clarel,* II, 195 (Part IV, canto x).

endless hill' "; he is weighed down as by the "Iron Crown of
Lombardy"—forged, as tradition tells us, of the nails of
Christ's cross.[11]

And is the parallel really so impious? Admitted that Christ's
agony went beyond all mortal capacity to bear or even to
understand. Yet what suffering *can* be understood? And how
many times in each life is man's limit of endurance passed?
Is it not possible that our mere human desolation may in some
sense be worse than His? For

> "Through all the trials that beset,
> He leaned on an upholding arm—
> Foreknowing, too, reserves of balm.
> But how of them whose souls may claim
> Some link with Christ beyond the name,
> Which share the fate, but never share
> Aid or assurance, and nowhere
> Look for requital?"[12]

The character Bartleby may be taken as fairly representative of these. His suffering is unspectacular enough, it is true;
what could seem less titanic than the "pallidly neat, pitiably
respectable" person of the young copyist? Yet his lot is only
the more tragic by the fact that his suffering is so wholly inward, private, and incommunicable. It springs, as his easy-
going employer, the story's narrator, fails to guess, from no
"innate and incurable disorder" of the mind but from long
contemplation of a pointless existence in a meaningless universe. The other occupants of the office live out their mechanical lives completely undisturbed by the lifeless prospect about
them—the white wall of an airshaft at one window and the
black wall of a warehouse pushed up within ten feet of the
other.[13] Bartleby cannot. As Ahab saw in the white whale's
featureless brow reality's wall " 'shoved near to me,' " so

---

11 *Moby-Dick*, I, 154 (chap. xxviii) ; p. 209 (chap. xxxvii).

12 *Clarel*, II, 195 (Part IV, canto x).

13 "Bartleby," in *The Piazza Tales*, p. 21.

Bartleby in his "dead-wall reveries" vainly searches the blank for some hint of meaning. But where Ahab ends by " 'thrusting through the wall' " in an attempt to strike the mocking thing " 'behind the unreasoning mask,' " Bartleby's response is simply to withhold his consent to such a life: " 'I would prefer not to.' "[14] Having once reached this decision, he returns the same indifferent answer to both entreaty and command—to his employer, to the police, to his jailer, and finally, by his refusal to eat, to life itself. The prison has its "dead-wall" too, and Bartleby's removal to the Tombs means simply the transferral of his gaze from one wall to another. It is here in the end that the dissenter's body is found, "Strangely huddled at the base of the wall, his knees drawn up, and lying on his side, his head touching the cold stones."[15] Measured against Ahab's, his is a mild and undramatic answer, but it is defiance nonetheless. What more, in essence, did Prometheus say in refusing the demands of Zeus for his surrender than that he " 'would prefer not to' "?

The exact line between defense and offense is, in this matter as in others, not easy to define. What begins as mere passive resistance will frequently end in an active and even aggressive defiance. We have a comic instance of this progression in the actions of the householder in "The Lightning-Rod Man."[16] He begins, quietly enough, with a polite refusal of the command of "Jupiter Tonans," the lightning rod agent, that he retreat from that dangerous and wrath-tempting eminence, his hearth, which, like the huge chimney of "I and My Chimney,"[17] is the center and heart of its owner's independent existence; further threats stir him to speak meaningfully to his visitor of " 'the returning stroke . . . , when the earth, being overcharged with

---

14 *Ibid.,* p. 29. Cf. *Moby-Dick,* I, 204 (chap. xxxvi).

15 "Bartleby," in *The Piazza Tales,* p. 64.

16 "The Lightning-Rod Man," *ibid.,* pp. 171–80.

17 "I and My Chimney," in *Billy Budd and Other Prose Pieces,* pp. 276–311.

the fluid, flashes its surplus upward' "; and so the quarrel grows, to end at last with his dragging the dark lightning-king out of the door and flinging his three-tined copper scepter after him.

Ahab, in more serious vein, follows a like path from resistance to aggression. It is not, of course, in his nature to remain for long the patient sufferer, however slight the provocation. Yet we see, as late as in his prayer to the corposants,[18] that he is still ready to forget his anger and to answer love with love: the Prometheus in him has not wholly yielded to the fiercer Enceladus. But the prayer remains unanswered, and he has no choice but to return to the course of desperate opposition that ends at last in the sublime absurdity of his own death.

THE ENCELADANS

The frequency of Melville's allusions to Prometheus notwithstanding, the tragic hero as he has conceived him is more properly described as Enceladic. Not patient resistance alone, but counterattack, fierce and uncompromising, is the hallmark of his nature. In the persons of Taji, Ahab, and Pierre, Melville has given us three examples of the type. The succession is marked, as we shall see, by a growing complexity of traits and motives, but the fundamental likeness remains.

For Melville, as for others before him, the tragic hero is to be known first of all by the greatness of his gifts, by his heroic endowment of passion, energy, and will. He is man magnified. But he is also man idealized—no one-sided monster of thought or feeling but a harmonious individual whose varied gifts exist, in the beginning, in a right proportion to each other. It is not enough that he be "a man of greatly superior natural force":

---

18 *Moby-Dick*, II, 281–82 (chap. cxix).

he must be endowed with both "a globular brain and a ponderous heart."[19] He must feel life more intensely than ordinary men, but he must also look more searchingly into it.

The heroic heart makes itself evident chiefly in two ways: in a wider and quicker sympathy with the suffering of others, together with a generous readiness to relieve it, and in a seemingly limitless capacity to bear pain itself. In the grip of a deeper pain, Ahab can still weep for Pip and Pierre take thought for the wretched Delly Ulver. But it is in the hero's acceptance of his own destiny of suffering and endurance that the Promethean strain most clearly declares itself. Taji scornfully rejects the life of pleasure as a proffered alternative to his hopeless search: " 'Away! woe is its own wine. What may be mine, that will I endure, in its own essence to the quick. Let me feel the poniard if it stabs.' "[20] Ahab bears grimly up under the weight of what Starbuck recognizes as a " 'lurid woe would shrivel me up, had I it.' " Strength has its penalties:

In an instant's compass, great hearts sometimes condense to one deep pang, the sum total of those shallow pains kindly diffused through feebler men's whole lives. And so, such hearts, though summary in each one suffering; still, if the gods decree it, in their life-time aggregate a whole age of woe, wholly made up of instantaneous intensities; for even in their pointless centres, those noble natures contain the entire circumferences of inferior souls.[21]

Pierre, standing in prison amid the wreckage of his hopes, is still unbroken:

The cumbersome stone ceiling almost rested on his brow; so that the long tiers of massive cell-galleries above seemed partly piled on him. His immortal, immovable, bleached cheek was dry; but the stone cheeks of the walls were trickling.[22]

19 *Ibid.*, I, 91 (chap. xvi).

20 *Mardi*, II, 150 (chap. cxli).

21 *Moby-Dick*, I, 211 (chap. xxxviii) ; II, 339 (chap. cxxxiii).

22 *Pierre*, p. 502 (Book XXVI, chap. vi).

Seen so, he seems the image of the buried Titan, of that proud and ruined king who sits in darkness beneath the "towers of man's upper earth."[23]

The head, as has already been noted, is the active principle of man's personality. Restless and aggressive, it acknowledges for itself no destiny of suffering or forbearance. If the heart is man's Prometheus, the mind is his Enceladus. By its authority, man assumes his title to challenge all that is. Melville's tragic heroes, however else they may differ from each other, are alike in their relentless questioning of the conditions and the end of life. They will neither accept nor ignore the brute fact of evil, and in their anger they do not hesitate to drag the judge himself to the bar. Timoleon, protagonist of one of Melville's last poems, speaks for them:

> To second causes why appeal?
> Vain parleying here with fellow clods.
> To you, Arch Principals, I rear
> My quarrel, for this quarrel is with gods.[24]

They will have none of those penultimate answers urged by apologists for the Deity: they insist upon the ultimate and only meaningful answer. They would wring from God that final secret " 'that makes of [him] the everlasting mystery that he is,' " His purpose—or the frank admission that He has none—in creating an infinitude of sentient beings whose fate it is to " 'sin and suffer, but to perish.' "[25] The inescapable moral ambiguity of life is intolerable to such natures: right and wrong, they are determined, shall be as cleanly separated as in Genesis the night is from the day. They acknowledge no impediments but, like the Galapagos tortoises, drive themselves relentlessly against whatever obstacles appear in their paths—

[23] *Ibid.*, pp. 480–82 (Book XXV, chap. iv); see also *Moby-Dick*, I, 231 (chap. xli).

[24] "Timoleon," in *Poems*, p. 252.

[25] *Mardi*, II, 376 (chap. clxxxviii).

"their crowning curse . . . [this] drudging impulse to straight-
forwardness in a belittered world."[26] And they are unshaken
by failure and defeat, however final:

> "Conviction is not gone
> Though faith's gone: that which shall not be
> Still *ought* to be!"[27]

Tragedy, for the Melvillean hero, is implicit in the very
greatness of his powers. His breadth of imagination puts before him a more sweeping vision of the world's pain and injustice, and the generosity of his heart causes him to feel these
ills as his own. Mind and will, already waked to action by the
sting of his own experience, drive him on in pursuit of an
answer. But ironically, this pursuit itself leads him ever farther
away from the particular human ties and affections in whose
interest it began. Repeated disappointments and humiliations
breed a smoldering anger of a more personal sort until at last
pity gives way to a monomaniac fury which sees nothing but
the hated object. The pattern stands forth most clearly in the
career of the dedicated Indian-hater. He is one who

"in youth, or early manhood, ere the sensibilities become osseous
[suffers] some signal outrage, or, which in effect is much the same,
some of his kin have, or some friend. Now, nature all around him
by her solitudes wooing or bidding him muse upon this matter, he
accordingly does so, till the thought develops such attraction, that
much as straggling vapours troop from all sides to a storm-cloud,
so straggling thoughts of other outrages troop to the nucleus
thought, assimilate with it, and swell it. At last, taking counsel
with the elements, he comes to his resolution. An intenser Hannibal, he makes a vow, the hate of which is a vortex from whose
suction scarce the remotest chip of the guilty race may reasonably
feel secure. Next, he declares himself and settles his temporal
affairs. With the solemnity of a Spaniard turned monk, he takes
leave of his kin. . . . Last, he commits himself to the forest primeval;

---

[26] "The Encantadas," in *The Piazza Tales,* p. 191.

[27] *Clarel,* II, 285 (Part IV, canto xxx).

there, so long as life shall be his, to act upon a calm, cloistered scheme of strategical, implacable, and lonesome vengeance."[28]

We have only to read *sea* for *forest* and *Moby Dick* for *Indian* to have here a precise account of Ahab's dedication.

And we may add of either man that in the moment of that consecration his fate is already accomplished. The life which began in wholeness has fallen into a ruinous imbalance, with the mind feeding upon the heart. It could hardly have been otherwise, for men of this sort are born with a certain "half-wilful over-ruling morbidness at the bottom of [their] nature." Given the universe as it is, they have no choice but to break themselves against it. But if this compulsion is a flaw, the heroism is not something separate from it. "For all men tragically great are made so through a certain morbidness. Be sure of this, O young ambition, all mortal greatness is but disease."[29]

The first of Melville's three tragic heroes, *Mardi*'s Taji is also the least convincing. He seems at times hardly more than a preliminary sketch of the type—a sketch, too, whose outlines barely show against the bolder underpainting of a quite different figure, the hearty young whaleman whose half-finished and abandoned portrait has been left standing in the book's first sixty chapters. There is no gradual blending of the one into the other. Through all the long days in the whaleboat, the seizure of the maiden Yillah from the raft, the landing at Odo, and his elevation to demi-godhood, the narrator-hero maintains, essentially unchanged, the garrulous good humor with which he began. It is only with the mysterious disappearance of Yillah from his bower of bliss that the startling metamorphosis takes place and we suddenly face the grim and laconic Taji with whom we are henceforth to deal.

This later Taji is certainly one of the least particularized heroes in the history of fiction. The meagerness of his develop-

---

28 *The Confidence-Man*, pp. 199–200 (chap. xxvi).

29 *Moby-Dick*, I, 92 (chap. xvi)

ment, however, is less an indication of Melville's inability to create character than the consequence of experimentation with the literary device of psychological fragmentation. Taji is a shadowy character for the sufficient reason that he was never intended to be more than one-fifth of a hero, his rightful inheritance of traits having been divided at the outset of the voyage among the five companions of the search.

Melville's reason for employing this device is not hard to guess, for the added characters are clearly not required by the plot. The central action of the book's vague allegory is easily summarized: the maiden Yillah (emblematic, perhaps, of the unreflective happiness men know in their youth) is found, briefly enjoyed, inexplicably lost, and thereafter vainly sought through a kaleidoscopic succession of scenes held together only as they are representative of the variety and inconclusiveness of life. The narrative weakness of such a scheme is at once evident: there is no antagonist, no continuing conflict, no complication of plot lines, and only one possible outcome.

But Melville was far less interested in constructing a plot than in exploring "the golden Aztec glades" of his newly discovered "world of mind."[30] Such an exploration must proceed, of course, chiefly through the discussion of ideas; and since it is difficult to make more than a very few of these implicit in the action of so thin a story, the one way to give the ideas dramatic force is to assign them to a variety of characters, each representing a particular intellectual attitude or quality. Bearing in mind, too, that this is to be rather an exploration than a permanent settlement of the world of mind, what better way to mark that tentative character than to present these various spokesmen as parts of a single unrealized whole? No participant in this rambling debate, therefore, is unqualifiedly right and none is wholly wrong, though some are obviously more right than others.

The exact principle followed in the division of Taji's in-

[30] *Mardi*, II, 277 (chap. clxix).

tellectual patrimony is difficult to see. Clearly, however, Babbalanja is given the lion's share in the faculty of Reason, the
poet Yoomy is assigned Imagination, Media receives the gift
of Prudence, Mohi the historian is endowed with that lower
intellectual power which the Transcendentalists called Understanding, and Taji finally is reduced to the attribute of pure
Will. The most likely explanation is that the scheme of division
owes less to any consistent theory of the human mind than to
a wish to set up certain oppositions which might serve to en-
liven the discussion and so move the story along. Roughly
speaking, the voyagers divide into two groups, the earthbound
and the heaven-aspiring. The sensible and matter-of-fact Media
is forever pulling the reckless Babbalanja back to earth, the
inspired Yoomy scorns the dull fact-grubbing of old Mohi;
poet and philosopher display a sympathetic understanding of
each other, while king and historian unite in censuring their
excesses. Through it all the silent Taji sits by, the noncom-
mittal auditor of their debates but the one whose determination to find Yillah holds them together in the search.

It is one of the curiosities of *Mardi* that it is so little concerned with the actions and thoughts of its protagonist.
Babbalanja pours out his reflections, formed and half-formed
(even reading into the record from time to time selected
passages from his favorite authors), and both Mohi and Yoomy
speak rather more than we wish they would. But so far as the
reader can determine, Taji has no thoughts apart from the
fixed idea of Yillah's recovery. If there is an internal conflict,
it is Babbalanja's rather than Taji's: the latter is never seriously tempted from the position he takes at the time of Yillah's
disappearance.

Despite these facts, however, there is never any serious
doubt of the protagonist's identity. The thread of action upon
which all else is strung begins with Taji (the other four
voyagers having simply enlisted in his cause), is kept in sight
by Taji's repeated affirmations of purpose, and ends with his

persistence in the search beyond the point at which the others have given up. Shadow that he is, Taji is still of the same indomitable race as Ahab and Pierre. He is appalled by the hatred of the avengers whose father he slew in gaining Yillah, but he holds to his course; the arrows sent after him miss their aim—" 'But I will not mine. And whatever arrows follow, still will I hunt on.' "[31] The sensual temptress Hautia beckons him in vain:

"Sad your path, but merry Hautia's."

"Then merry may she be, whoe'er she is; and though woe be mine, I turn not from that to Hautia; nor ever will I woo her, though she woo me till I die;—though Yillah never bless my eyes."[32]

The circuit of the Mardian world once completed and no Yillah found, a humbled Babbalanja is persuaded (in Ishmael's phrase) to "lower, or at least shift, his conceit of attainable felicity" and to accept a sad tranquillity as his uttermost happiness. Media, Yoomy, and Mohi follow him in thus submitting to the necessary conditions of human life.[33]

Taji alone remains unmoved by the Serenian gospel of resignation. Babbalanja reproaches him, as in *Moby-Dick* Starbuck does Ahab, with the madness of continued search, but Taji turns from him without speaking and, "fixed as fate," embarks once more. The others—all but Babbalanja—protestingly go with him. Media, once so imperious, is forced to plead with him: " 'Taji! renounce the hunt.' " But Taji is not to be swerved from his course:

"I am the hunter, that never rests! the hunter without a home! She I seek, still flies before; and I will follow, though she lead me beyond the reef; through sunless seas; and into night and death. Her, will I seek, through all the isles and stars; and find her, whate'er betide!"[34]

[31] *Ibid.*, I, 356–58 (chap. c) ; II, 118 (chap. cxxxiv).
[32] *Ibid.*, I, 359 (chap. ci).
[33] *Ibid.*, II, 371–72 (chap. clxxxvii) ; p. 379 (chap. clxxxviii).
[34] *Ibid.*, pp. 380–82 (chap. clxxxix).

In desperation, he seeks her even in the realm of her enemy, the dark enchantress Hautia.[35] Baffled there also, and deserted at last by his companions, he seizes the helm himself and with the exultant cry " 'Now, I am my own soul's emperor; and my first act is abdication! Hail! realm of shades!' " turns the prow suicidally outward through the reef and into the unshored ocean beyond.[36]

In all this, the outline is clear enough, though the realizing touches have yet to be filled in: it is Enceladus, defiantly hurling himself against the unassailable. But when we turn to Ahab, the figure stands forth sharply and in the round. That " 'grand, ungodly, godlike man' " is of course Melville's one real triumph in the creation of character. Avoiding the schematic bareness of Taji at the one extreme and Pierre's Gothic complexities at the other, Melville has succeeded in endowing Ahab with both heroic largeness and human particularity. And yet we are told little about Ahab beyond the essentials, and even this comes to us chiefly in oblique and riddling hints.

He is a Nantucketer by birth, and originally a Quaker—now a "Quaker with a vengeance." Although led by "stillness and seclusion" to "think untraditionally and independently," he has " 'been in colleges, as well as 'mong the cannibals.' "[37] He has " 'for forty years [made] war on the horrors of the deep,' "[38] yet not always, as now, against the heavens as well. For he was, by his own testimony, long a worshipper of the good " 'till in the sacramental act' " struck down and scarred by lightning.[39] His adoration thereafter turned to anger, he becomes guilty, if we are to believe Elijah, of various wild acts of sacrilege.[40] But the hunger for vengeance has not yet wholly

---

[35] *Ibid.*, p. 384 (chap. cxc).
[36] *Ibid.*, pp. 399–400 (chap. cxcv).
[37] *Moby-Dick*, I, 91, 99 (chap. xvi).
[38] *Ibid.*, II, 328 (chap. cxxxii).
[39] *Ibid.*, p. 281 (chap. cxix).
[40] *Ibid.*, I, 116 (chap. xix).

obsessed him: at an age past fifty and after a life of isolation and conflict, he can still affirm life by taking a young wife and fathering a son.[41] It is only after this, and as a consequence of his first and nearly fatal encounter with Moby Dick, some months before Ishmael joins him, that Ahab's all-consuming anger is born.[42]

This, in sum, is all we are told of Ahab's past history, and it is not much. We know nearly as little of his physical appearance, and this comes to us in the most general terms as Ishmael watches his captain mount for the first time to the quarter-deck. The vivid impression which Ahab makes upon us is in part no doubt the work of our own imaginations, stimulated by the concreteness and the exhaustive particularity with which Melville has rendered the total shipboard scene. Ahab is real because he is an integral part of a workaday world so real that we sometimes seem to sense it kinaesthetically as we read. But more than this, Ahab lives for us through the intensity of a few great scenes (among them, "The Quarter-Deck," "The Quadrant," "The Candles," "The Symphony," and his final assault upon Moby Dick) and by the poetic force and richness of the imagery in which he is characterized. Wherever we stand in *Moby-Dick*, we are likely to be aware of his towering presence. Yet it may surprise us to note how much this is a matter simply of suggestion, how few are the times he is really there before us. Of the scenes just named (and the list would probably not vary greatly from reader to reader), all but the first come from the final quarter of the book. It is not until this point that Ahab actually moves to the front of the stage to hold it. That he dominates the earlier sections as he does is largely owing to our memory of that first volcanic display of passion on the quarter-deck when he reveals his purpose to the crew and bends their wills to his. All that needs to be done thereafter is by brief and intermittent

flashes to keep that picture vivid in our memory. Over all the
relaxed and sprawling central expanse of the book, a sense of
Ahab's intensity, his long-held-back anger, and his unguessable
reserves of will and power hangs like the shadow of an approaching typhoon.

Ahab's stature owes much, too, to the accumulated force of
image and metaphor. He is likened to a variety of natural
objects: to a mountain eagle, to "the last of the Grisly Bears
. . . in settled Missouri," to a cloud-hidden mountain peak, to
a great tree scarred by lightning, to "some lone, gigantic elm,
whose very height and strength" serve but to tempt the thunderbolt.[43] His dimensions, as he himself points out, will bear
comparison with those of nature: " 'Nor white whale, nor man,
nor fiend, can so much as graze old Ahab in his own proper
and inaccessible being. Can any lead touch yonder floor, any
mast scrape yonder roof?' "[44]

He is a king, too. In beginning the portrait of his hero,
Melville abjures the use of "all outward majestical trappings
and housings" and frankly confesses that he has here to do
not with "Emperors and Kings" but "only . . . with a poor
old whale-hunter" from Nantucket.[45] But the renunciation
serves only to mark the inward character of Ahab's kingship.
Reminders of his regality are everywhere. His name, first of
all: " 'Ahab of old, thou knowest, was a crowned king.' " And
a king, moreover, with his own aura of barbaric splendor,
rebellious idolatry, and a pride to be brought down only by
divine treachery. At his cabin table, the captain of the
"Pequod" presides like a German emperor at his coronation
banquet.[46] He walks his deck "a khan of the plank, and a king
of the sea, and a great lord of leviathans."[47] Throned on his

---

[43] *Ibid.*, II, 182 (chap. xcvi) ; I, 190 (chap. xxxiv) ; p. 155 (chap. xxviii) ;
p. 153 (chap. xxviii) ; II, 284 (chap. cxix).

[44] *Ibid.*, p. 350 (chap. cxxxiv).

[45] *Ibid.*, I, 183 (chap. xxxiii).

[46] *Ibid.*, p. 186 (chap. xxxiv).

[47] *Ibid.*, p. 160 (chap. xxx).

own "tripod of bones," he looks out like a fellow sovereign upon that " 'dark Hindoo half of nature, who of drowned bones has builded [its] separate throne somewhere in the heart of these unverdured seas.' "[48]

What Ahab sees in the white whale is not, as Starbuck mistakenly thinks, a " 'dumb brute . . . that simply smote him through blindest instinct,' " but the whole enormous power of nature "here concentrated to a point," as the whale's strength is itself all gathered into his tail.[49] But Moby Dick is more even than this to Ahab: he is a mask and expression of the Divinity—conceivably even God Himself. For who in this riddling world can tell agent from principal, or guess where the series ends? " 'There is some unsuffusing thing beyond thee, thou clear spirit [cries Ahab to the lightning], to whom all thy eternity is but time, all thy creativeness mechanical.' "[50] The whale's divinity is more than once hinted: in the ambiguity of "agent or principal" that torments Ahab, in the pronouncements of the mad prophet Gabriel, in the language with which Ishmael hails him at his first revelation, and in Ahab's farewell tribute to his stove-in vessel as " 'thou . . . only god-bullied hull.' "[51]

But whatever the meaning Ahab finally gives to him, what is certain is that he has found in Moby Dick a bodily target for the pent-up and compounded angers of a lifetime. In one form or another, that malicious and " 'inscrutable thing' " that had sought him out and maimed him was already known to him. The shock of the encounter came to him not as a sudden awakening from illusion (as their strokes to Taji and Pierre) but as the crowning indignity of a long course of outrage and humiliation suffered both in his own person and on behalf of

[48] *Ibid.*, II, 270 (chap. cxvi).

[49] *Ibid.*, I, 204 (chap. xxxvi) ; II, 119 (chap. lxxxvi).

[50] *Ibid.*, II, 282–83 (chap. cxix).

[51] *Ibid.*, I, 204 (chap. xxxvi) ; II, 43 (chap. lxxi) ; pp. 333–34 (chap. cxxxiii) ; p. 366 (chap. cxxxv).

man. What was new in his response after that encounter was not his anger, though this was greatly intensified, but the channel which that anger cut for itself during the long months of the homeward voyage when "[he] and anguish lay stretched together in one hammock" and "his torn body and gashed soul bled into one another; and so interfusing, made him mad." That which had before been bodiless had now, Ahab felt, a vulnerable body; that "intangible malignity" could now be struck:

Small reason was there to doubt, then, that ever since that almost fatal encounter, Ahab had cherished a wild vindictiveness against the whale, all the more fell for that in his frantic morbidness he at last came to identify with him, not only all his bodily woes, but all his intellectual and spiritual exasperations. The White Whale swam before him as the monomaniac incarnation of all those malicious agencies which some deep men feel eating in them, till they are left living on with half a heart and half a lung. That intangible malignity which has been from the beginning; to whose dominion even the modern Christians ascribe one-half of the worlds; which the ancient Ophites of the East reverenced in their statue devil;—Ahab did not fall down and worship it like them; but deliriously transferring its idea to the abhorred White Whale, he pitted himself, all mutilated, against it. All that most maddens and torments; all that stirs up the lees of things; all truth with malice in it; all that cracks the sinews and cakes the brain; all the subtle demonisms of life and thought; all evil, to crazy Ahab, were visibly personified, and made practically assailable in Moby Dick. He piled upon the whale's white hump the sum of all the general rage and hate felt by his whole race from Adam down; and then, as if his chest had been a mortar, he burst his hot heart's shell upon it.[52]

Ahab's tragedy lies implicit in this account of a nature which must take from the event a personal and unforgivable affront. Captain Boomer of the "Enderby" can lose an arm to the same monster, spend his convalescence drinking rum toddies with the ship's surgeon, and cheerfully call the matter

[52] *Ibid.*, I, 229–30 (chap. xli).

quits.[53] Not so Ahab. Of his first mutilation, another is born: the bone leg splinters in a Nantucket street, giving him a second and more intimate wound;[54] the gashed stump heals but leaves behind an inward sore that festers and will not close. It is this wound and not Moby Dick that is fated to destroy him. Intent upon it, he can see nothing else: mind and will crowd out heart, the single obligation of hatred increasingly takes precedence of others, and bit by bit truth is transformed into something narrower than it was.

But the change is not accomplished without a struggle. Nature has given Ahab, we recall, a "ponderous heart" as well as a "globular brain."[55] The conflict of the two—though for the most part hidden from our view—has been violent from the first. Something of this violence we have been allowed to guess from that nightmare scene in which Ahab's "eternal living principle," horrified by the flame-filled chasm opening in sleep within him, briefly escapes the tyranny of the mind and leaves the body behind to be blindly animated, as in diabolical possession, by "sheer inveteracy of will."[56]

Ahab's "monomaniac purpose" finds dramatic embodiment in the person of the strange and evil Fedallah. Not until Ahab has revealed that purpose to the crew and spiked the doubloon to the main-mast does the Parsee emerge from the darkness of the hold.[57] The watch he keeps thereafter for Moby Dick is as unintermitted as his master's. Like Ahab's purpose itself, he is never known to sleep.[58] Even at night, when the other lookouts go below, he keeps his place at the main-mast head and is thus the first to see and hail the silvery, mysteriously beckoning "spirit-spout" that leads the "Pequod" on.[59] Like

---

53 *Ibid.*, II, 196–204 (chap. c).
54 *Ibid.*, pp. 229–30 (chap. cvi).
55 *Ibid.*, I, 91 (chap. xvi).
56 *Ibid.*, pp. 252–53 (chap. xliv).
57 *Ibid.*, p. 273 (chap. xlviii).
58 *Ibid.*, II, 319–20 (chap. cxxx).
59 *Ibid.*, I, 293 (chap. li).

light, "forever . . . colorless in itself," he appears to have no proper being of his own: if he casts a shadow at all, it seems "only to blend with and lengthen Ahab's."[60] Rarely speaking in public, he and Ahab are in reality endlessly absorbed in each other. In the stillness of their night watches, they stand "far parted in the starlight" and study one another fixedly, "as if in the Parsee Ahab [sees] his forethrown shadow, in Ahab the Parsee his abandoned substance."[61] Strangely, though, the shadow seems "to have some sort of a half-hinted influence . . . [or] even authority" over the substance.[62] To the watching crew, "Ahab seemed an independent lord; the Parsee but his slave";[63] but in their secret encounters on the night deck it was different: then, "as Ahab's eyes so awed the crew's, the inscrutable Parsee's glance awed his."[64]

The opposing principle of Ahab's nature is expressed, fittingly enough, in no such single embodiment, for men are held to life not by one tie but by many. Nevertheless, Starbuck stands forth far more clearly than others as spokesman for the heart and as chief counter to Fedallah; that the two at no time confront one another merely emphasizes the inwardness of the arena in which they meet. The first mate of the "Pequod" is an admirable but a limited person, not in the end wholly adequate to the task life sets him. Brave but held from rashness by "far-off domestic memories of his young Cape Cod wife and child," spiritually perceptive but "endued with a deep natural reverence" inclining him to acceptance rather than defiance, Starbuck instinctively knows the mind to be his enemy and fears it.[65] Ahab as instinctively sees in Starbuck the one considerable human obstacle to the realization of his

60 *Ibid.*, II, 59 (chap. lxxiii).

61 *Ibid.*, p. 320 (chap. cxxx).

62 *Ibid.*, I, 291 (chap. i).

63 *Ibid.*

64 *Ibid.*, II, 319 (chap. cxxx).

65 *Ibid.*, I, 143 (chap. xxvi).

purpose, and by intellectual force rides over that opposition and "[keeping] his magnet at Starbuck's brain," long holds him in subjection.[66]

But though Ahab's end is implicit in his nature as we have seen it, his movement to the brink of catastrophe is long held back, like that of a leaf in the still reaches above a falls. During the greater part of the book, as we have noted, he is not actively present. Of the four principal parts into which the work may be divided, the first, through the sailing of the "Pequod" in chapter xxii, is devoted to Ishmael and Queequeg, with only a premonitory glance at Ahab; the second, ending with Ishmael's meditation on "The Whiteness of the Whale," presents us with the principals of the tragedy and its supporting actors but does not advance the action beyond Ahab's announcement of his purpose and his "overmanning" of Starbuck; and throughout the third and largest part of the book, chapters xliii–cv, Ahab has for tactical reasons postponed the realization of his purpose and for the time being simply waits while the ordinary business of the voyage goes forward. It is only after this, as the ship draws near those "almost final waters" of the Pacific, that he steps forward and reasserts his will.[67]

The last act of the drama is wholly Ahab's. From this point forward everything moves in a rush. In a series of swift, defiant gestures, Ahab blasphemously tempers his harpoon in human blood, exults in Fedallah's prophecies and jeers at the thought of death, smashes his "heavenly quadrant" as a sign of his abandonment of the quest for truth in favor of the pursuit of vengeance, snatches up his flaming, lightning-charged harpoon and contemptuously " 'blow[s] out the last fear,' " himself remagnetizes the compass needle the lightning

[66] *Ibid.*, pp. 204–5 (chap. xxxvi) ; p. 211 (chap. xxxviii) ; p. 266 (chap. xlvi).

[67] *Ibid.*, II, 253 (chap. cxi).

has reversed, and grimly steers on toward his enemy by level dead reckoning of log and compass.[68]

But the head is not yet undisputed master. When Starbuck finds courage on the crew's behalf to ask that the pursuit be halted while a leak in the hull is found and stopped, Ahab first threatens him, then—struck by the mate's warning of "Let Ahab beware of Ahab"—yields, and even apologizes for his harshness.[69] Even after the delirium of the harpoon's tempering, the old man can still, looking out upon a Maytime ocean's "mild blue hill-sides," feel within him stirrings of a forgotten joy and faith.[70] But the feeling is not for long: " 'Yet dost thou, darker half, rock me with a prouder, if a darker faith.' "[71] So also he is drawn to and rejects the sign of hope shown him in Queequeg's outlived coffin, calked and hung over the ship's taffrail now as a life-preserver: " 'I'll think of that. But no. So far gone am I in the dark side of earth, that its other side, the theoretic bright one, seems but uncertain twilight to me.' "[72]

The sight of poor lunatic Pip moves Ahab to stretch forth an unlooked-for, fatherly hand: " 'Here, boy; Ahab's cabin shall be Pip's home henceforth, while Ahab lives. Thou touchest my inmost centre, boy; thou art tied to me by cords woven of my heart-strings. Come, let's down.' "[73] But the head, its hated object now almost in sight, is wary of these reassertions of the heart. There is that in Pip which Ahab finds " 'too curing to my malady' "—that malady which has now become " 'my most desired health.' " When Pip interposes his childish

---

[68] *Ibid.*, p. 261 (chap. cxiii) ; pp. 271–72 (chap. cxvii) ; pp. 274–75 (chap. cxviii) ; pp. 283–84 (chap. cxix) ; pp. 297–98 (chap. cxxiv) ; pp. 299–301 (chap. cxxv).

[69] *Ibid.*, pp. 242–44 (chap. cix).

[70] *Ibid.*, p. 264 (chap. cxiv).

[71] *Ibid.*, p. 270 (chap. cxvi).

[72] *Ibid.*, p. 310 (chap. cxxvii).

[73] *Ibid.*, p. 302 (chap. cxxv).

trust and need between Ahab and his purpose, the old man is
stung to sudden anger: " 'Weep so, and I will murder thee!
have a care, for Ahab too is mad.' " So Ahab orders him below, out of his sight, with the same heartfelt if meaningless
blessing which has just accompanied his refusal of the
"Rachel's" pathetic plea for help.[74]

It is on that mild clear morning—the "symphony" of air
and sea—just preceding the sighting of Moby Dick, that the
final and decisive conflict of head and heart takes place. Everything has long pointed toward this moment. Fedallah's pledges
of victory have driven Ahab to new extremes of violence and
committed him even more firmly to his course.[75] Starbuck,
too, has drawn him more strongly since that day when he
yielded to the mate's rebuke. Preparing now to be hauled aloft
to man his own lookout for the white whale, Ahab holds in
his hand the rope on which his life is to depend, sweeps his
glance over each member of the crew, "pausing . . . long upon
Daggoo, Queequeg, Tashtego; but shunning Fedallah; and
then settling his firm relying eye upon the chief mate, [says]—
'Take the rope, sir—I give it into thy hands, Starbuck.' "[76]
And in so deciding, he has no knowledge of that night just
passed when Starbuck stood with musket leveled at his sleeping head, considered the voice of reason urging him to shoot,
and chose instead to follow the fatal counsel of his heart and
spare the old man's life.[77]

The scene on which Ahab's fate turns, or seems to turn,
opens with his leaning over the ship's side, watching his waver-
ing shadow sink and vanish in the water. It is an image of the
futility of his search itself. "But the lovely aromas in that
enchanted air . . . at last seem to dispel, for a moment, the
cankerous thing in his soul" and the old man is brought,

[74] *Ibid.*, pp. 314–16 (chap. cxxix).

[75] *Ibid.*, p. 272 (chap. cxvii) ; pp. 318–21 (chap. cxxx).

[76] *Ibid.*, p. 321 (chap. cxxx).

[77] *Ibid.*, pp. 291–93 (chap. cxxiii).

suddenly, to the verge of tears. Starbuck draws near at this moment, and Ahab reaches out to him: " 'Oh, Starbuck! it is a mild, mild wind, and a mild looking sky. On such a day—very much such a sweetness as this—I struck my first whale—a boy harpooneer of eighteen! Forty—forty—forty years ago— ago!' " And he goes on to review his life and to question at last the wisdom of the lonely and bitter path he has chosen to follow. A sense of age, of weariness, and of desolation comes over him, and in something like despair he cries:

"Close! stand close to me, Starbuck; let me look into a human eye; it is better than to gaze into sea or sky; better than to gaze upon God. By the green land; by the bright hearth-stone! this is the magic glass, man; I see my wife and child in thine eye."

Starbuck, returning his gaze, sees in his captain's eye a like vision of home and is quick to press the advantage of the moment:

"Yes, yes! no more! it is done! we head for Nantucket! Come, my Captain, study out the course, and let us away! See, see! the boy's face from the window! the boy's hand on the hill!"

But Ahab's glance was averted; like a blighted fruit tree he shook, and cast his last, cindered apple to the soil.[78]

Nothing that we could see has intervened, but suddenly all is changed. Far underground and distant, some unknown event has taken place in Ahab and the issue—perhaps never seriously in doubt—has been silently decided. The voice of the heart will not be heard again.

Ahab himself imperfectly understands the force that moves him, and would resist it if he could:

"What is it [he now asks Starbuck], what nameless, inscrutable, unearthly thing is it; what cozening, hidden lord and master, and cruel, remorseless emperor commands me; that against all natural lovings and longings, I so keep pushing, and crowding, and jamming myself on all the time; recklessly making me ready to do

[78] *Ibid.*, pp. 327–30 (chap. cxxxii).

what in my own proper, natural heart, I durst not so much as dare?"[79]

But fuller knowledge would not save him. " 'The path to my fixed purpose is laid with iron rails, whereon my soul is grooved to run.' " To change that course is not in his power— nor in that of the gods, unless they would first renounce their own purpose in making him what he is.[80] Each man plays against a packed deck. Says Stubb:

"I heard Ahab mutter, 'Here's some one thrusts these cards into these old hands of mine; swears that I must play them, and no others.' And damn me, Ahab, but thou actest right; live in the game, and die it!"[81]

But the divine joke, it now occurs to Ahab, may go farther still. If all happens of necessity, by what right do we place any one of our actions outside the fated web? Can we, in the end, call even our defiance ours? Here—his last choice made, the end nearly in sight—the old man pauses to consider this crowning irony:

"Is Ahab, Ahab? Is it I, God, or who, that lifts this arm? But if the great sun move not of himself; but is as an errand-boy in heaven; nor one single star can revolve, but by some invisible power; how then can this one small heart beat; this one small brain think thoughts; unless God does that beating, does that thinking, does that living, and not I. By heaven, man, we are turned round and round in this world, like yonder windlass, and Fate is the handspike."

To some men, such an insight might bring with it a measure of resignation; but not to Ahab. He cannot accept the annulment of individuality here implied or consent to live as agent of the same principal Who expresses Himself in the hungry rush of the albicore. There is no way for him but on. But when

---

[79] *Ibid.*, p. 330 (chap. cxxxii).

[80] *Ibid.*, I, 210 (chap. xxxvii).

[81] *Ibid.*, II, 275 (chap. cxviii).

he looks up a moment later, Starbuck is no longer beside him. He crosses the deck and once more looks down into the water. What he sees now is neither his own sinking image nor the picture of his wife and child but "two reflected, fixed eyes" staring intensely back at him. "Fedallah was motionlessly leaning over the same rail."[82]

In the mid-watch that same night Ahab scents the near presence of a sperm whale and shortly after daybreak he sights the "high sparkling hump" of Moby Dick.[83] The three-days' battle begins, and from its start, Ahab leaves Starbuck behind him and quite literally follows Fedallah—for two days the bowsman of his boat and on the fated third his guide down " 'those endless stairs' " to the sea's bottom. Once only during this time—and that after the second day's failure—does Starbuck venture to protest " 'this worse than devil's madness' " of a continued chase. But in Ahab's answer this time there is no hint that he is even touched by the plea:

"Starbuck, of late I've felt strangely moved to thee; ever since that hour we both saw—thou know'st what, in one another's eyes. But in this matter of the whale, be the front of thy face to me as the palm of this hand—a lipless, unfeatured blank. Ahab is for ever Ahab, man. This whole act's immutably decreed. 'Twas rehearsed by thee and me a billion years before this ocean rolled. Fool! I am the Fates' lieutenant; I act under orders. Look thou, underling! that thou obeyest mine.[84]

Pride, then, has made room for itself in spite of all. Much has been put in question, but the sense of self is too deep-founded to be seriously shaken. " 'Ahab is for ever Ahab, man.' " The words are both a confession and a boast. Granted that in living out " 'his own inexorable self,' " he but acts out a rehearsed part in another's play; yet that play goes forward only through his agency. He is, it now appears, no independent

---

[82] *Ibid.*, p. 330 (chap. cxxxii).

[83] *Ibid.*, pp. 332–33 (chap. cxxxiii).

[84] *Ibid.*, p. 352 (chap. cxxxiv).

power but " 'the Fates' lieutenant' " and as such condemned to " 'act under orders.' " Yet a lieutenant is still something near an equal: if he must obey orders, he also transmits and enforces them. Not quite a god, he is still something more than human. In his own person he is his subordinates' fate, and he can act with the same impersonal heartlessness as his model: " 'Ye are not other men [he tells his terrified oarsmen on the last day], but my arms and legs; and so obey me.' "[85] The head speaks here in total forgetfulness of the heart.

So isolated and so stripped of his humanities, Ahab goes to meet his death. He has watched, on earlier occasions, the stricken whale with his last strength turn to the sun, " 'how slowly, but how steadfastly, his homage-rendering and invoking brow.' " No such obeisance will be his. Poised with his last harpoon in the bow of his last broken boat, seeing in the stove and settling ship before him the mocking fulfilment of Fedallah's second pledge, Ahab knows at last the invincibility of his enemy and yet defies him:

"I turn my body from the sun. What ho, Tashtego! let me hear thy hammer [renailing the red flag of defiance to the main-truck]. Oh! ye three unsurrendered spires of mine; thou uncracked keel; and only god-bullied hull; thou firm deck, and haughty helm, and Pole-pointed prow,—death-glorious ship! must ye then perish, and without me? Am I cut off from the last fond pride of meanest ship-wrecked captains? Oh, lonely death on lonely life! Oh, now I feel my topmost greatness lies in my topmost grief. Ho, ho! from all your furthest bounds, pour ye now in, ye bold billows of my whole foregone life, and top this one piled comber of my death! Towards thee I roll, thou all-destroying but unconquering whale; to the last I grapple with thee; from hell's heart I stab at thee; for hate's sake I spit my last breath at thee. Sink all coffins and all hearses to one common pool! and since neither can be mine, let me then tow to pieces, while still chasing thee, though tied to thee, thou damned whale. *Thus*, I give up the spear!"[86]

[85] *Ibid.*, p. 361 (chap. cxxxv).

[86] *Ibid.*, p. 366 (chap. cxxxv).

The harpoon is thrown, a turn of the line catches the thrower, and Ahab disappears into the sea, tied to his enemy, cut off from his ship and all that he has loved. Oddly, though, we find in his death a sense of fulfilment, not loss. For defeat is his only who accepts defeat, and this Ahab has not done. He " 'stands forth his own inexorable self' " even in the irreversible moment of final failure. His integrity is his victory.

Pierre, the last of Melville's three tragic heroes, is both like and unlike Ahab. The points of difference, if less significant, are the more obvious. Ahab, to begin with, is an old man, Pierre a youth "just emerging from his teens"; Ahab's past history is barely suggested, while Pierre's is given in considerable, though hardly realistic, detail; Ahab's experience has made him bitter, Pierre's sheltered life has left him naïvely innocent; the older man's supreme object is knowledge of "the last things," the younger man risks all in the pursuit of unqualified virtue; tragedy comes to the first through the mind's increasing tyranny over the heart, to the second through the excesses of a generous but not yet disciplined heart. The two men are alike, on the other hand, in their capacities for intense thought and feeling, in the tensions created within them by the opposed pulls of heart and head, in their unbounded pride and defiance, and in their refusal to stop at anything less than the ultimate.

But despite these similarities, one is forced to admit that Pierre is not nearly so impressive and memorable a figure as Ahab. There are several reasons why this is so. For one thing, Ahab's greatness is in part a reflection of the strength and size of his adversary and of the immense backdrop of sea and sky against which his drama is acted out. Pierre lacks these advantages: his stage is narrow and confined, his adversary no single monster but the petty forces of worldly convention and the hidden complexities of his own nature.

Pierre suffers, too, from the continued close scrutiny to

which his thoughts and motives are subjected. Ahab is spared
this. An aura of mystery surrounds him at all times. Even when
he leaves the seclusion of his cabin, he remains shut up in a
" 'masoned, walled-town . . . exclusiveness' ";[87] spiritually, he
is as remote as the Grand Lama. We are given only the barest
essentials about him—a silhouette rather than a portrait—and
are left to fill in as we may, from hints and chance remarks, the
features left in shadow. And with less attention to detail, the
general outline looms larger. With Pierre, it is quite otherwise.
Here Melville is at pains to be explicit and analytical—at times
even condescending—and it is clear that he knows the artistic
risk he takes:

I am more frank with Pierre than the best men are with themselves.
I am all unguarded and magnanimous with Pierre; therefore you
see his weakness, and therefore only. In reserves men build imposing characters; not in revelations. He who shall be wholly honest,
though nobler than Ethan Allen; that man shall stand in danger
of the meanest mortal's scorn.[88]

In one sense, perhaps, the risk is justified. For Pierre's "topmost greatness" lies, even more clearly than Ahab's, in an
heroic defiance of the limitations of his own human nature.
But we become aware of this only upon later reflection, not in
the aesthetic moment itself. To bring a tragic hero into the
dissecting room and under the microscope adds to our knowledge, it is true, but not to the force or immediacy of the experience. What is withheld has sometimes a greater suggestive
power than what is given.

For another thing, Pierre is neither so simple nor so consistent as Ahab. The latter's character is unalterably fixed before the action begins: he is there in his entirety when he first
mounts to his quarter-deck, and all that follows thereafter is
simply an unfolding. The same cannot be said of Pierre. His
story is one of the formation, not merely the expression, of

[87] *Ibid.*, p. 328 (chap. cxxxii).

[88] *Pierre*, pp. 151–52 (Book V, chap. vii).

character, and change—even inconsistency—is of its essence. The deluded young romantic to whom we are first introduced has really very little in common with the defiant rebel of the later scenes. He is first brought forward, we discover, only as someone to be scoffed at and repudiated. Unfortunately, he is not so easily forgotten later as his author might wish, for he *is* the same person, and we cannot quite forget his original silliness even when, in the closing pages, he needs our wholly unqualified regard. And the Pierre in whose favor the first Pierre is repudiated is himself soon supplanted by another, and this one by a fourth. Clearly, Melville is working toward a quite different end from that he had achieved in *Moby-Dick:* his concern here is with the ambiguous underworld of man's moral nature. But if Pierre's complexities and contradictions are true to the facts of experience, as Melville insists they are,[89] they are nevertheless damaging to the book's singleness of effect. There are too many Pierres, and our emotional responses in the end become confused.

In its broad outline, *Pierre* is an initiation story—the account of a young man's introduction to life. As such, it belongs to a well-established tradition of nineteenth-century fiction, going back well beyond Goethe's *Wilhelm Meister*, the chief exemplar of the type. But *Pierre* departs radically from the conventions of this kind in that it is a record of the hero's growing awareness of his limitations rather than his powers, of his discovery that the world offers not so much an open field for the exercise of his talents as an insuperable barrier to their realization. Pierre's progress is indeed marked by the stripping away of illusions, but what remains in the end is not truth but only further layers of illusion.

He begins in an almost total innocence, the untouched Adam of a modern Paradise. His first unquestioning trust in life comes to an end with the revelation of impurity in the marble

[89] Ibid., p. 469 (Book XXV, chap. iii) ; see also *The Confidence-Man,* pp. 89–92 (chap. xiv).

image of his father: a cast-off illegitimate daughter makes her appearance and appeals to her brother Pierre for recognition. He reacts to this knowledge by wholly rejecting his world as a cheat and a lie and placing his faith as completely and unquestioningly in his own conscience and the dark truths thrown open to him by his sister's revelation.

What he takes to be the " 'holiest admonishings' " of his own heart now tell him that the way to acknowledge Isabel with the least pain to others is by the device of a feigned marriage. Putting aside, therefore, all selfish and prudent considerations, he abandons the girl to whom he is betrothed and commits himself to this new line of duty. Disowned by his mother, he leaves with Isabel for the city and a life of labor and poverty. But here again he finds himself betrayed, this time by the moral ambiguities of his own nature rather than his father's. Faced with the awful realization that it is in part physical passion that draws him to his sister, he feels that his unshrinking commitment to good has led only to evil and that consequently " 'the uttermost ideal of moral perfection in man is wide of the mark [of true virtue]. The demi-gods trample on trash, and Virtue and Vice are trash.' " Beyond all this, he feels, lies some unguessed higher truth which he must seek. And he thereupon dedicates himself to the writing of a book which shall show the utter worthlessness of human virtue and " 'gospelize the world anew [with] . . . deeper secrets than the Apocalypse.' "[90]

Yet he cannot reject virtue as he has the false world of his boyhood: "nothing" though it may be, he also is "a nothing" and this virtue is the law of his being.[91] Long weeks of agonizing labor at his book make it clear at last that he can neither sustain nor fully express the inhuman vision that has come to him. He knows himself now deserted by the world, by his own conscience, and by God Himself. There is no turning back, nor

[90] *Pierre*, p. 381 (Book XIX, chap. ii).

[91] *Ibid.*, p. 382 (Book XIX, chap. ii).

would he retreat if that were possible. Like Enceladus, nothing is left him but his own maimed and armless trunk, and this he hurls in a last act of desperation against the jeering world and the indifferent gods, destroying, like Ahab, both himself and those he loves.

The book is divided into three main parts in accordance with this scheme. The first part, Books I to X, is concerned with Pierre's shocked awakening to the existence of evil and his unwarranted conclusion that life's bright side is a total illusion. The second part, Books X to XX, records the fact and examines the causes, imagined and real, of his decision to commit himself wholly and irrevocably to Isabel and the dark side of life; it ends with his second great shock—the realization that evil is an inescapable part of his own nature. The third part, Books XX through XXVI, concludes the tragedy by heaping intellectual failure upon the ruins of his moral aspirations: he is denied even the last satisfaction of understanding his own fate.

On the most immediate level, Pierre's downfall results from his inability to affirm and hold steadily in view both the bright and the dark aspects of life, as these are embodied in the angelic Lucy Tartan, his betrothed, and the mysterious Isabel, his supposed half-sister. The values which attach to the two girls are complex, at times ambiguous, but the general outlines are clear. They are in almost every way opposed to each other. The blonde Lucy—her very name suggests light, as her surname Tartan hints at the unexpected complexity of light —is met at morning, and Pierre greets her with " 'I would return thy manifold good mornings, Lucy, did not that presume thou had'st lived through a night; and by Heaven, thou belong'st to the regions of an infinite day.' "[92] The dark Isabel is seen first by night, her strange letter is delivered to him in darkness, and their first appointment is, by her express com-

[92] *Ibid.*, pp. 2–3 (Book I, chaps. i–ii).

mand, at nightfall.[93] Lucy is by nature joyous and lighthearted,
Isabel mournful.[94] Lucy represents the known and familiar:
she lives in Saddle Meadows, is simple and open, and has no
secrets of any sort.[95] Isabel comes to Pierre from the sea and
from foreign parts; she would conduct him, as Yillah's ghost
does Taji, through "the great blue sluice-way into the ocean"
where all is unknown and unknowable—" 'far, far away, and
away, and away, out there where the two blues meet and are
nothing.' "[96] Lucy's values are those of the heart. Isabel,
though she herself " 'comprehend[s] nothing,' " beckons
Pierre to the world of mind, suggesting to him mysteries both
within and without.[97] Lucy, like the lowly dooryard catnip, is
an emblem of "man's earthly household peace," while Isabel
resembles the sterile immortal amaranth of the uplands, symbol of "man's ever encroaching appetite for God."[98]

On the verge of a manhood that promises a felicity as un-
flawed as his youth's, poised with his hand at the knocker of
Lucy's cottage where he has come to announce the date of their
marriage, Pierre has suddenly thrust upon him that letter of
Isabel's summoning him from "the winding tranquil vale" to
"the mountain of his Fate."[99] He has dreamed of such a sum-
mons in his boyish visions of knighthood, looking about him
"for some insulted good cause to defend" and telling himself
that " 'it must be a glorious thing to engage in a mortal quarrel on a sweet sister's behalf.' "[100] But the challenge, now that
it has actually come, is not glorious.

[93] *Ibid.*, p. 63 (Book III, chap. i) ; p. 84 (Book III, chap. iv) ; p. 89 (Book
III, chap. v).

[94] *Ibid.*, pp. 30, 32–33 (Book II, chap. ii) ; pp. 171–72 (Book VI, chap. iv).

[95] *Ibid.*, p. 54 (Book II, chap. vi).

[96] *Ibid.*, pp. 164–65 (Book VI, chap. iii) ; p. 495 (Book XXVI, chap. iii).

[97] *Ibid.*, p. 436 (Book XXIII, chap. iii) ; p. 165 (Book VI, chap. iii) ; p. 70
(Book III, chap. ii).

[98] *Ibid.*, p. 480 (Book XXV, chap. iv).

[99] *Ibid.*, p. 84 (Book III, chap. iv).

[100] *Ibid.*, pp. 16–17 (Book I, chap. iv) ; p. 7 (Book I, chap. ii).

Life has prepared him but poorly for this moment, having endowed him with everything save the knowledge of evil. He is not yet wholly himself, not yet "born from the world-husk" within which he has taken shape. His immaturity is evident in the docility with which he obeys his worldly mother, leaving to her even the determination of his own wedding date.[101] He is his mother's superior intellectually, but this power is his as yet only in potentiality. Experience has not called his critical faculty into play nor shown him the essential incompatibility of the world and the ideals he has been taught.[102] His life is that of the heart alone—all impulse, trust, and enthusiasm.

Knowing Pierre for the person he is, we might almost predict the nature of his response to Isabel's letter. The first moment of shock is followed by an impulse of disbelief: the whole thing is an " 'accursed dream, . . . a base and malicious forgery.' " But the extravagance with which he has worshiped his father's memory determines now the violence of the recoil. The very thought of his father's sin and his own bejugglement enrages him. In one instant he puts (or so he thinks) his whole past behind him and dedicates himself to truth. He has no doubt now of where he must look. Happiness having been proved false, truth must lie with sorrow: " 'Oh! falsely guided in the days of my Joy, am I now truly led in this night of my Grief?' " And having raved for a moment against Fate, he turns once again to confront this grief:

"Thou Black Knight, that with visor down, thus confrontest me, and mockest at me; lo! I strike through thy helm, and will see thy face, be it Gorgon!—Let me go, ye fond affections; all piety leave me; —I will be impious, for piety hath juggled me, and taught me to revere, where I should spurn. From all idols, I tear all veils; henceforth I will see the hidden things; and live right out in my own hidden life!"

101 *Ibid.*, pp. 19–20, 25–26 (Book I, chaps. v–vi) ; p. 78 (Book III, chap. iii).

102 *Ibid.*, pp. 288–90 (Book XIV, chap. ii).

Suddenly all doubt is gone and he is convinced—not by any external evidence but by the vehemence of his own emotions: " 'Now I feel that nothing but Truth can move me so. This letter is not a forgery. Oh! Isabel, thou art my sister; and I will love thee, and protect thee, ay, and own thee through all.' "[103]

If we see before us at this point the figure of Hamlet kneeling at the spot just occupied by his father's ghost and swearing in the cause of vengeance to erase from his memory

> all trivial fond records,
> All saws of books, all forms, all pressures past,
> That youth and observation copied there,

the likeness is not accidental. Melville has carried the parallel with Shakespeare's young hero to a point that may surprise the casual reader. Each, to begin with, has been for his world "The glass of fashion and the mould of form." Each receives a mysterious message requiring him to dedicate his life to another's quarrel. In each case, too, the message discloses impurity on the part of an honored parent—a spot of infection whose corrupting odor spreads to taint the general air and end forever "the before undistrusted moral beauty of the world."[104] The imposed task weighs heavily upon both: Hamlet's lament,

> "The time is out of joint; Oh cursed spite,
> That ever I was born to set it right!"

is later despairingly applied by Pierre to his own case.[105] Each feels an ignoble and heartless world leagued against him, and each deserts the girl he loves through a mistaken conviction that she is a part of that rejected world. With regard to action, however, the two are deliberately opposed: where Hamlet delays, Pierre applies to himself his predecessor's self-reproaches for "faltering in the fight"[106] and acts at once and disastrously.

103 *Ibid.*, pp. 90–91 (Book III, chap. vi).
104 *Ibid.*, p. 89 (Book III, chap. vi).
105 *Ibid.*, p. 235 (Book IX, chap. ii).
106 *Ibid.*, p. 237 (Book IX, chap. iv).

And finally, Melville suggests, the essence of the tragedy is in each case to be seen in the fate which presents a generous but unfinished nature with a task which it has neither the selfishness to refuse nor the strength and mature wisdom to carry out. We are to see in both " 'The flower of virtue cropped by a too rare mischance.' "[107] Of Pierre also, at the end, Fortinbras might well have said that

> he was likely, had he been put on,
> To have proved most royally.

In the hours that follow Pierre's reception of Isabel's letter, several considerations seem to him to confirm still further the truth of her story. There is the matter, first of all, of the "chair-portrait" of his father as a young man—gay, lighthearted, ambiguously smiling—a portrait whose authenticity is not to be doubted but which bears no resemblance to the official drawing-room portrait of the master of Saddle Meadows and is flatly disowned by his widow, Pierre's mother, to whom it is somehow "namelessly unpleasant and repelling."[108] Which of these two vastly different persons, Pierre had often asked himself, is really my father?[109] But when he turns now from Isabel's letter to consider again the chair-portrait and the vague legend of its origin, it seems to him that there can be only one answer. He makes no "sordid scrutiny of small pros and cons"; truth comes as sudden illumination:

In the cold courts of justice the dull head demands oaths, and holy writ proofs; but in the warm halls of the heart one single, untestified memory's spark shall suffice to enkindle such a blaze of evidence, that all the corners of conviction are as suddenly lighted up as a midnight city by a burning building, which on every side whirls its reddened brands.[110]

107 *Ibid.*, p. 191 (Book VII, chap. vi).
108 *Ibid.*, p. 99 (Book IV, chap. iii).
109 *Ibid.*, pp. 114–17 (Book IV, chap. v).
110 *Ibid.*, p. 98 (Book IV, chap. iii).

The picture and its story, he sees now, attest the truth of Isabel's letter, and that letter in turn assures him that the true image of his father is that of the strangely smiling young man of the chair-portrait.[111] Similarly, in the light thrown by the letter he can see now the falsity of his mother's world and the inhumanity of her "immense pride," so certain to obtrude itself between him and his duty; and this revelation too serves by contrast to dignify, and hence to prove right, the course to which he is called.[112] And finally, Isabel herself, when she stands before him, is her own not-to-be-doubted proof:

> Steadfastly, with his one first and last fraternal inquisition of the person of the mystic girl, Pierre now for an instant eyes her; and in that one instant sees in the imploring face ... the [subtle] expression of the portrait of his then youthful father, strangely translated, and intermarryingly blended with some before unknown, foreign feminineness. In one breath, Memory and Prophecy, and Intuition tell him—"Pierre, have no reserves; no minutest possible doubt; —this being is thy sister; thou gazest on thy father's flesh."[113]

The incomprehensibility of her story as she brokenly tells it to him serves rather to confirm than to shake his belief: the intelligible world of daylight having proved itself false, how else should truth come than clothed in an essential and unravelable mystery?[114]

The completeness of Pierre's commitment to Isabel is a measure of the violence with which he has rejected his old world. The lightning bolt of her letter has in an instant shriveled the illusions by which he has lived: "Not only [is] the long-cherished image of his father now transfigured before him from a green foliage tree into a blasted trunk," but the whole of his green world is reduced as by a forest fire to "a charred

111 *Ibid.*, pp. 118–19 (Book IV, chap. v).

112 *Ibid.*, pp. 124–27 (Book V, chap. i).

113 *Ibid.*, p. 157 (Book VI, chap. ii).

114 *Ibid.*, p. 194 (Book VII, chap. vii); pp. 198–99 (Book VII, chap. viii).

landscape within him."[115] All beauty, wealth, and delight show
now as the mere gilding on "the base rivets and the chains of
Lies," while "Ugliness and Poverty and Infamy" are revealed
as the "ministers of Truth."[116] But it is more than a negative
hatred of deceit that moves him. The appeal of his sister has
touched somehow the same chord which the Sermon on the
Mount at some time sets vibrating in "all earnest-loving
youths"—the hunger for perfection. The response of these
youths is exactly that of Pierre to Isabel:

Such emotions as that Sermon raises in the enthusiastic heart; such
emotions all youthful hearts refuse to ascribe to humanity as their
origin. This is of God! cries the heart, and in that cry ceases all
inquisition. Now, with this fresh-read Sermon in his soul, the youth
again gazes abroad upon the world. Instantly, . . . an overpowering
sense of the world's downright positive falsity comes over him; the
world seems to lie saturated and soaking with lies.

He may question the finality of this vision. He may even, on
the authority of "many good and wise people," attempt "to
refuse the evidence of his own senses" in this matter, as he once
did in the analogous case of the sun's apparent movement
around the earth; but he can be persuaded to a detached Co-
pernican belief in the world's mingled good and evil only so
long as he does not again look upon his standard of perfection.
When he does, he has no choice but to believe his senses, and
so to love good and seek to depart from evil.[117]
Of the underlying falsity of the world which Pierre rejects,
there can be little doubt: it is made painfully obvious in the
artificially heightened style in which that world is described
throughout Books I and II, in the rhapsodic optimism indi-
rectly attributed to Pierre, in the "fictitiousness" of the relations between Pierre and his mother, and in his mother's un-

115 *Ibid.*, p. 120 (Book V, chap. i).

116 *Ibid.*, p. 126 (Book V, chap. i).

117 *Ibid.*, pp. 289–90 (Book XIV, chap. ii).

christian harshness first to Delly Ulver, the fallen village girl, and then to Pierre himself.[118] But there can be little question of the mistakenness of the extreme position to which Pierre's reaction has driven him. All joy and all hope seem to him blotted out forever. Yet neither the world nor his own situation is in reality so unrelievedly dark as it appears. Disabused as he is, he is still the victim of illusion. Recent events have not so much widened his field of vision as shifted its center, and in seeing the new he has now lost sight of the old. The most evident proof of his extravagance lies before him, were he but capable of reasoning from this ground, in the simple fact of Lucy. For she is a part of that bright rejected world, yet she is not false. But Pierre cannot allow himself to think of Lucy. For the very reason that her hold upon his heart is greater than any other, she must be put aside: the world must not be permitted to use her, as with Hamlet it tried to use Ophelia, as a lure to draw him from his duty. For

> divinely dedicated as he felt himself to be; with divine commands upon him to befriend and champion Isabel, through all conceivable contingencies of Time and Chance; how could he insure himself against the insidious inroads of self-interest, and hold intact all his unselfish magnanimities, if once he should permit the distracting thought of Lucy to dispute with Isabel's the pervading possession of his soul?[119]

Truth is to be known only in its living context, not in the unnaturally isolated specimen: the sharpest outlines alter in the wider perspectives of time and experience. But Pierre, like every "young enthusiast," lacks

> that all-comprehending oneness, that calm representativeness, by which a steady philosophic mind reaches forth and draws to itself, in their collective entirety, the objects of its contemplations. . . .

[118] *Ibid.*, pp. 43–47 (Book II, chap. iv) ; pp. 17–20 (Book I, chap. v) and 246–47 (Book X, chap. i) ; pp. 140–45 (Book V, chap. iv) ; p. 258 (Book XI, chap. iii) and pp. 268–72 (Book XII, chap. ii).

[119] *Ibid.*, pp. 148–49 (Book V, chap. v).

By his eagerness, all objects are deceptively foreshortened; by his
intensity each object is viewed as detached; so that essentially and
relatively every thing is misseen by him.[120]

Half-understood hints of the twofold nature of reality have, it
is true, come to him—the thought that his father's two por-
traits may both be true if partial likenesses, the Dantean vision
of "the two mutually absorbing shapes" of man and serpent,
the momentary appearance in Lucy's eyes of "half the mourn-
fulness of Isabel's"[121]—but he is far from apprehending their
full meaning.

His pain, too, is intensified by his inexperience. His grief
seems to him final and irremediable largely because it has
come upon him so suddenly and overwhelmingly, before the
experience of lesser griefs has shown him anything of the soul's
powers of recuperation. He is capable of speaking with a mature wisdom when he begs the despairing Delly Ulver to " 'take
some little heart to thee, and bethink thee, that all thy life is
not yet lived; that Time hath surest healing in his continuous
balm. Be patient yet a little while. . . .' "[122] But he is himself
still incapable of acting upon that advice. The lesson of patience will be learned (if it is) only in depths beyond this:

It is the not impartially bestowed privilege of the more final insights, that at the same moment they reveal the depths, they do,
sometimes, also reveal—though by no means so distinctly—some
answering heights. But when only midway down the gulf, its crags
wholly conceal the upper vaults, and the wanderer thinks it all one
gulf of downward dark.[123]

Bitter as the first taste of Pierre's grief had been, it seems
to him to grow worse in the days immediately following. The
first fury gives place that same night to the "pallid compo-

120 *Ibid.*, pp. 244–45 (Book X, chap. i).

121 *Ibid.*, p. 115 (Book IV, chap. v) ; p. 119 (Book IV, chap. v) ; p. 181
(Book VII, chap. i)

122 *Ibid.*, p. 227 (Book VIII, chap. vi).

123 *Ibid.*, p. 237 (Book IX, chap. iii).

sure" of emotional exhaustion, but bit by bit the full realization of his position comes home to him: "The bitter drug is
divided into separate draughts for him: today he takes one part
of his woe; tomorrow he takes more; and so on, till the last
drop is drunk."[124] He has lost, first of all, the world-sustaining
illusion of his father's perfection.[125] Next he sees that his
mother is utterly incapable, in a moral sense, of supporting
him or even of understanding his dilemma.[126] While still reel-
ing from this blow, he is further shaken by presentiments "obscurely [involving] the everlasting peace of Lucy" and their
future happiness together;[127] he feels that he cannot, in kind-
ness, turn to her. There is one place left where he may look for
help: the church in which he has been nurtured. But when he
learns of the Reverend Mr. Falsgrave's acquiescence in the
banishment of Delly Ulver, he knows that he can hope for " 'no
earnest and world-disdaining counsel' " from that quarter. He
is left to seek that guidance " 'direct from God Himself, Who
. . . never delegates His holiest admonishings.' "[128]

But these admonishings he finds, as he considers the practical exigencies of his position, are by no means so clear as one
might expect. The outcast Isabel must be publicly acknowledged—that much is beyond question. "The deep voice of the
being of Isabel called to him from out the immense distances
of sky and air, and there seemed no veto of the earth that could
forbid her heavenly claim."[129] But how is that acknowledgment to be made? Is it really necessary that his father's repu-
tation be besmirched, that his mother's pride be humbled?
Does the one duty take precedence of all others? Pierre cannot answer. He stands confused between what seem to be the

[124] *Ibid.*, p. 146 (Book V, chap. v).

[125] *Ibid.*, pp. 89–90 (Book III, chap. vi).

[126] *Ibid.*, pp. 124–25 (Book V, chap. i).

[127] *Ibid.*, p. 147 (Book V, chap. v).

[128] *Ibid.*, p. 230 (Book VIII, chap. vii).

[129] *Ibid.*, pp. 241–42 (Book X, chap. i).

opposing voices of his conscience. All unaware that what inhibits the execution of his heavenly vow is simply the inescapable centripetal pull of his mixed nature, he is driven to fury by the thought of his own indecisiveness. Hamlet-like, he rails at himself:

"Coward and fool! Tear thyself open, and read there the confounding story of thy blind doltishness! Thy two grand resolutions—the public acknowledgement of Isabel, and the charitable withholding of her existence from thy own mother,—these are impossible adjuncts.—Likewise, thy so magnanimous purpose to screen thy father's honorable memory from reproach, and thy other intention, the open vindication of thy fraternalness to Isabel,—these also are impossible adjuncts."

It seems to him now that he is unworthy of his high calling and that no choice remains to him but to return and humble himself before the world he has scorned. Shame and frustration carry him almost to the verge of madness:

Now indeed did all the fiery floods in the *Inferno,* and all the rolling gloom in *Hamlet* suffocate him at once in flame and smoke. The cheeks of his soul collapsed in him: he dashed himself in blind fury and swift madness against the wall, and fell dabbling in the vomit of his loathed identity.[130]

From the depths of this despair, Pierre rises the next morning "stoically serene and symmetrical in soul," the warring halves of his nature seemingly reconciled. His dilemma, he now sees, has been a false one: a way exists for him to fulfil both his obligation to Isabel and his filial duty to his parents. The course he proposes involves, it is true, "a most singular act of pious imposture" but one which he thinks heaven will justify in him, "since he himself [is] to be the grand self-renouncing victim." This solution—so simple and all-resolving—is "to assume before the world, that by secret rites, Pierre Glendinning

---

[130] *Ibid.,* p. 239 (Book IX, chap. iv).

[has] already become the husband of Isabel Banford." Thus his sister will be (in some sense) acknowledged and raised to his level, his father's memory kept pure of reproach, his mother shielded from the most deadly wound to her pride, and he himself warranted in "dwelling in [Isabel's] continual company."[131]

It is not entirely hidden from Pierre that this extraordinary plan of his must necessarily bring pain upon others as well as himself. His mother, first of all, will be deeply hurt and offended by the seemingly dishonorable repudiation of his vow to Lucy. But by this very pain, she will be spared the greater anguish of knowing of her husband's dishonor. Lucy, too, must suffer in his unexplained desertion "a terrible pang . . . which in the recoil would but redouble his own." But the pain of both Lucy and his mother, as it seems to him, is not of his choosing but is simply "part of the unavoidable vast price of his enthusiastic virtue." "The loftier heroism" seems indeed to require, almost by definition, the sacrifice not of oneself only but of a loved one far dearer to one's heart.[132]

But more moves beneath the surface here than Pierre yet sees or understands. There are hints, for instance, though he himself refuses them, that fear of his mother as well as concern for her good is responsible for his decision to spare her the truth.[133] Something besides love underlies, too, his similar decision with regard to Lucy. He is well aware that the shock of his coming announcement to her would be considerably lessened were she to be told the reasons for his action. But Lucy is of all persons the one to whom he is least free to speak the truth:

If he would not reveal his father's shame to the common world, whose favorable opinion for himself, [he] now despised; how then reveal it to the woman he adored? To her, above all others, would

131 *Ibid.*, pp. 240–41 (Book X, chap. i).

132 *Ibid.*, pp. 240–49 (Book X, chaps. i–ii).

133 *Ibid.*, p. 238 (Book IX, chap. iv).

he now uncover his father's tomb, and bid her behold from what vile attaintings he himself had sprung? So Pierre turned round and tied Lucy to the same stake which must hold himself. . . .[134]

Filial piety is here not easily distinguished from the worldly pride which has so recently appalled him in his mother. The lurking element of self-love in his mother's affection for him is something Pierre now clearly sees: "She loveth me, ay;—but why? Had I been cast in a cripple's mold, how then?"[135] But it does not occur to him to wonder how he himself might have responded had his brotherly acknowledgment and aid been invoked, not by the lovely Isabel, but by some "humped, and crippled, hideous girl."[136]

It is especially here, in understanding the nature of his attraction to Isabel, that Pierre's simplistic view of reality and of his own nature misleads him. By the mere fact that events have placed her in opposition to the world by using her as an instrument to expose its lies, Isabel has become in Pierre's mind the living antithesis of all that is false—has become, in a sense, ideal truth itself. The feelings she arouses within him carry with them, in their force and novelty, their own authentication. She seems a creature less of earth than of heaven, gifted with a "marvellous power . . . over himself and his most interior thoughts and motions;—a power so hovering upon the confines of the invisible world, that it [seems] more inclined that way than this."[137] That there is something anomalous in their relation—a brother and sister wholly strange to each other—is apparent to him. He was puzzled at their first meeting by an element of unnatural restraint between them, and since then he has been uncertain of the precise nature of either her feelings or his own. But that uncertainty itself seems to him

---

[134] *Ibid.*, p. 249 (Book X, chap. ii).

[135] *Ibid.*, pp. 124–26 (Book V, chap. i).

[136] *Ibid.*, p. 151 (Book V, chap. vii).

[137] *Ibid.*, p. 212 (Book VIII, chap. iii).

evidence of the unique and holy character of the tie uniting them:

> Pierre felt that never, never would he be able to embrace Isabel with the mere brotherly embrace; while the thought of any other caress . . . was entirely vacant from his uncontaminated soul, for it had never consciously intruded there.
>
> Therefore, forever unsistered from him by the stroke of Fate, and apparently forever, and twice removed from the remotest possibility of that love which had drawn him to his Lucy; yet still the object of the ardentest and deepest emotions of his soul; therefore, to him, Isabel wholly soared out of the realms of mortalness, and for him became transfigured in the highest heaven of uncorrupted Love.[138]

But if Pierre misunderstands and overvalues his feeling for Isabel, he as seriously undervalues his love for Lucy and hers for him. Here his delusion is in a sense more wilful: only by shutting Lucy as far as possible from his consciousness has he been able to find an escape from his intolerable dilemma.

True, in his extraordinary scheme, Lucy was so intimately interwoven, that it seemed impossible for him at all to cast his future without some way having that heart's love in view. But ignorant of its quantity as yet, or fearful of ascertaining it; like an algebraist, for the real Lucy he, in his scheming thoughts, had substituted but a sign—some empty x—and in the ultimate solution of the problem, that empty x still figured; not the real Lucy.

But the heart cannot be so silenced for long. The torturing dilemma once solved, "all his resolutions clearly defined, and immovably decreed," and his future again in his own hands, Pierre's whole being relaxes from the unnatural pitch to which it has been strung. And in that unguarded moment,

> there suddenly slid into his inmost heart the living and breathing form of Lucy. His lungs collapsed; his eyeballs glared; for the sweet imagined form, so long buried alive in him, seemed now as

[138] *Ibid.*, p. 200 (Book VII, chap. viii).

gliding on him from the grave; and her light hair swept far adown her shroud.

Then, for the time, all minor things were whelmed in him; his mother, Isabel, the whole wide world; and one thing only remained to him;—this all-including query—Lucy or God?[139]

So stated, the problem can have but one solution for Pierre: once again, and this time with a more anguished sense of his loss, he renounces all hope of Lucy and keeps to his course. Swiftly, while his resolution holds, he makes known his decision, first to Lucy, then to his mother, finally to Isabel.[140] And with this announcement, Pierre has crossed his Rubicon and it is no longer in his power to turn back.

But the full meaning of his decision has not, even yet, come home to him. He is aware of the finality of that decision and in part at least of its cost, but he fails to see, rationalized as it has been into the appearance of filial piety, the human weakness which has led him to equivocate in the matter of the open acknowledgment of Isabel as his sister. Once he has made the mistake of excluding that obvious and straightforward solution, he cannot possibly go right: he must turn his back either upon "truth" or upon life. His real error, therefore, lies not in the championing of Isabel but in his choice of means. For the device of the pretended marriage not only fails, in the end, to accomplish its principal purpose—it proves as fatal to his mother as the truth could possibly have been—but it is itself in several ways productive of positive evil: it places the moral issue falsely before the world;[141] it distorts Pierre's true relationship to Isabel; it involves him, the sworn knight of truth, in a life of deception and falsity; and by cutting him off from all relationship to Lucy, it commits him as exclusively to the dark aspect of life as once he had been to the bright.

---

[139] *Ibid.*, p. 253 (Book X, chap. iii).

[140] *Ibid.*, pp. 255–58 (Book XI, chaps. ii–iii) ; pp. 266–68 (Book XII, chap. i).

[141] *Ibid.*, pp. 245–46 (Book X, chap. i).

Thrust out and disowned by his infuriated mother, Pierre prepares Isabel and their fellow outcast Delly Ulver to leave for the city in the morning, and himself removes his few personal possessions to a room in the village inn for the night. There, as he sorts his papers for the journey, his eye is caught again by the "noiseless, ever-nameless, and ambiguous, unchanging smile" of the chair-portrait of his father. Disturbing as it was before, the portrait is now, by some vague but unmistakable likeness to the living Isabel, "altogether loathsome, ineffably so, to Pierre."[142]

Why this should be is not made entirely clear. Part of it lies, we are told, in its dim intimation of "the tyranny of Time and Fate" linking the living to the dead; but a "more subtle inquisition into this deftly-winding theme" is carefully omitted.[143] What that inquiry might have disclosed has been hinted at in the scene where Pierre whispered his plan to Isabel:

The girl moved not; was done with all her tremblings; leaned closer to him, with an inexpressible strangeness of an intense love, new and inexplicable. Over the face of Pierre there shot a terrible self-revelation; he imprinted repeated burning kisses upon her; pressed hard her hand; would not let go her sweet and awful passiveness.

Then they changed; they coiled together, and entangledly stood mute.[144]

But the revelation has been but dimly understood by the innocent Pierre, and the next day he retains nothing more than a sense of "the nameless awfulness of his still imperfectly conscious, incipient, new-mingled emotion toward this mysterious being."[145]

Whatever the sources of his feeling, the fact is that Pierre, alone in the inn room, finds it unbearable "that in the smiling

---

142 *Ibid.*, pp. 273–74 (Book XII, chap. iii).
143 *Ibid.*
144 *Ibid.*, p. 268 (Book XII, chap. i).
145 *Ibid.*, p. 286 (Book XIV, chap. i).

and ambiguous portrait, her sweet mournful image should be so sinisterly becrooked, bemixed, and mutilated to him."[146] Dismembering the frame and rolling the canvas into a scroll, he places his father's portrait upon the embers of the hearth and watches it burn to nothing. Package after package of family letters and written memorials of all sorts follow the picture into the flames. It is an act of purgation and release, a total disavowal of the past:

"Thus, and thus, and thus! [he cries to his father's ghost] on thy manes I fling fresh spoils; pour out all my memory in one libation!—so, so, so—lower, lower, lower; now all is done, and all is ashes! Henceforth, cast-out Pierre hath no paternity, and no past; and since the Future is one blank to all; therefore, twice-disinherited Pierre stands untrammeledly his ever-present self!—free to do his own self-will and present fancy to whatever end!"[147]

But the past nevertheless rides with him and weighs heavily upon him when, just before dawn, he and Isabel enter the coach with Delly to begin their journey to the city. The same "stirless morning silence" of indifferent nature lies upon the woods and fields as lay there on that last untroubled morning of his life when he stood beneath Lucy's cottage window.[148] But the inner difference is immense. He has closed the door not only upon illusion but upon Lucy; and he moves now from the known to the unknown, from light to dark, from a thoughtless identity with his world to the painful isolation of self-knowledge. As the coach carries him along, he is struck suddenly with "the possibility of the mere moonshine of all his self-renouncing enthusiasm." He recalls his mother's words of banishment, Lucy's "agonizing shriek" on hearing of his marriage, and his own vaguely disquieting feeling toward Isabel. A wave of doubt sweeps over him:

[146] *Ibid.*, p. 274 (Book XII, chap. iii).
[147] *Ibid.*, p. 277 (Book XII, chap. iii).
[148] *Ibid.*, pp. 284–85 (Book XIV, chap. i) ; p. 1 (Book I, chap. i).

"Lo! I leave corpses wherever I go!" groaned Pierre to himself—
"Can then my conduct be right? Lo! by my conduct I seem threatened by the possibility of a sin anomalous and accursed, so anomalous, it may well be the one for which Scripture says, there is never
forgiveness. Corpses behind me, and the last sin before, how then
can my conduct be right?"

He becomes aware at this moment of a tattered fragment of
paper he has unconsciously picked up from the coach seat on
entering and still holds in his hand. It is Plotinus Plinlimmon's
lecture, "Chronometricals and Horologicals." Opening its
pages, he begins absently to read while the women sleep and
the coach bears all of them steadily on toward the city. It appears to be a plea for moderation and common sense in the
pursuit of virtue, and it proposes "a virtuous expediency [as]
the highest desirable or attainable earthly excellence for the
mass of men." He ends by reading and then rereading the entire pamphlet.[149]

Pierre's reaction to the work is mixed. He is deeply interested in the topic, but its central point he continues to find
puzzling. Whether this is because he may wish not to understand something that seems to expose "the intrinsic incor-
rectness and non-excellence of both the theory and the practice
of his life" or because his limited experience makes the pamphlet's principal idea incomprehensible to him, the narrator
does not attempt to settle: "It will be observed [he remarks],
that neither point of the above speculation do we, in set terms,
attribute to Pierre in connection with the rag pamphlet. Possibly both might be applicable; possibly neither."[150] A third
explanation, and one which the context would seem to support,
is that Plinlimmon's discourse may seem to Pierre, because of
its failure to recognize the fact of man's "ever-encroaching appetite for God,"[151] not to be addressed to his problem at all. "I

[149] *Ibid.*, pp. 285–88 (Book XIV, chap. i).

[150] *Ibid.*, pp. 291–92 (Book XIV, chap. ii).

[151] *Ibid.*, p. 480 (Book XXV, chap. iv).

confess [the narrator admits], that I myself can derive [from it] no conclusion which permanently satisfies those peculiar motions in my soul, to which that Lecture seems more particularly addressed. For to me it seems more the excellently illustrated restatement of a problem, than the solution of the problem itself."[152] The last page, significantly, is torn, and the whole comes to an abrupt halt on a portentous "if—."[153] But whatever the cause of his bewilderment, Pierre, after some further pondering, puts the thing aside and for the time being thinks no more about it.

A few days later, however, he has reason to remember Plinlimmon's warning. The outlook grows steadily darker for him. "The wonderful vital world-revelation so suddenly made to [him] at the Meadows" has not wholly dispelled his illusions, nor did he at the time of his great decision see all the consequences of his renunciation. In these few days he has learned still more—from the heartless refusal of his cousin and boyhood friend, Glen Stanly, to relieve or even to recognize him; from the venality and corruption of his adopted world, the city; and from a realization of his unpreparedness to earn a living for himself and his two dependents.[154]

He has brought with him a number of his youthful manuscripts, hoping, on the basis of some past success with the magazines, to sell them while undertaking a more ambitious work. But reconsidering these writings now in his twilit room in the Apostles' tower, he is so overcome with a sense of their worthlessness and falsity that he cannot bring himself even to look at them. All of them, he exclaims to Isabel, " 'like protested notes at the Banker's, . . . are jaggingly cut through and through with the protesting hammer of Truth! Oh, I am sick, sick, sick!' " Isabel's response is to draw him not toward the

---

[152] *Ibid.*, p. 293 (Book XIV, chap. ii).

[153] *Ibid.*, p. 300 (Book XIV, chap. iii).

[154] *Ibid.*, pp. 332–34 (Book XVI, chap. ii) ; pp. 334–40 (Book XVI, chap. iii) ; pp. 361–63 (Book XVIII, chap. ii).

light of a further knowledge but toward the mystery in which
she lives:

"Let the arms that never were filled but by thee, lure thee back
again, Pierre, to the peace of the twilight. . . .
She blew out the light, and made Pierre sit down by her; and
their hands were placed in each other's.
"Say, are not thy torments now gone, my brother?"
"But replaced by—by—by—Oh God, Isabel, unhand me!" cried
Pierre, starting up. "Ye heavens, that have hidden yourselves in the
black hood of night, I call to ye! If to follow Virtue to her uttermost
vista, where common souls never go; if by that I take hold on hell,
and the uttermost virtue, after all, prove but a betraying pander to
the monstrousest vice,—then close in and crush me, ye stony walls,
and into one gulf let all things tumble together!"[155]

What was only obscurely troubling to him when he first told
her of his plan of the pretended marriage has now become appallingly clear: the inward imperative on which he has acted is
at least in part mere physical passion—and passion, moreover,
for his own sister. His noblest aspirations are betrayed by the
imperfection of his own nature. Man lives in a world where,
with the best intent, it is yet impossible to do right.

Pierre's first reaction to this discovery is as immoderate as
was his earlier response to the disclosure of evil outside himself. As he then unreservedly rejected the external world, so he
now would repudiate the whole of moral reality and the bare
idea of accountability:

"Call me brother no more! [he commands Isabel] How knowest
thou I am thy brother? Did thy mother tell thee? Did my father
say so to me?—I am Pierre, and thou Isabel, wide brother and
sister in the common humanity,—no more. For the rest, let the
gods look after their own combustibles. If they have put powder-
casks in me—let them look to it! let them look to it! Ah! now I
catch glimpses, and seem to half see, somehow, that the uttermost
ideal of moral perfection in man is wide of the mark. The demi-

gods trample on trash, and Virtue and Vice are trash! Isabel, I will write such things—I will gospelize the world anew, and show them secrets deeper than the Apocalypse!—I will write it, I will write it!"

But even as he speaks, Pierre realizes the impossibility of his escaping the weight of moral responsibility. Isabel questions him:

"Thou, Pierre, speakest of Virtue and Vice; life-secluded Isabel knows neither the one nor the other, but by hearsay. What are they, in their real selves, Pierre? Tell me first what is Virtue:— begin!"
"If on that point the gods are dumb, shall a pigmy speak? Ask the air!"
"Then Virtue is nothing."
"Not that!"
"Then Vice?"
"Look: a nothing is the substance, it casts one shadow one way, and another the other way; and these two shadows cast from one nothing; these, seems to me, are Virtue and Vice."
"Then why torment thyself so, dearest Pierre?"
"It is the law."
"What?"
"That a nothing should torment a nothing; for I am a nothing. It is all a dream—we dream that we dreamed we dream."[156]

And in his realization that this is the law, the boy Pierre already sees farther than the philosopher Plinlimmon, whose doctrine of the incompatibility of human and divine virtue he has unconsciously been echoing. For it is the true irony of man's position that he can neither achieve virtue nor renounce it: as his earthly half puts perfection forever beyond his reach, so his godlike half forbids his ever being content with less. But this is a self-knowledge which brings no resignation with it but instead a deepening anger with the power that has made him as he is. He has tried once to take the kingdom of heaven by

---

156 *Ibid.*, pp. 381–82 (Book XIX, chap. ii).

storm and has been hurled back; he will try again with a different weapon—a book in which the whole truth shall at last be told.

Although the principal motif of *Pierre* so far has been the opposition of light and dark, the closely related theme of heart and head has also been prominent. The joyous and unreflective life at Saddle Meadows has been lived entirely under the dominance of the heart. It is the heart, too, that dictated Pierre's violent recoil from this world and his impulsive decision to commit himself wholly and irrevocably to Isabel and life's dark aspect. " 'The heart! the heart! 'tis God's anointed; let me pursue the heart!' " was his cry then.[157] But that pursuit has led now to the discovery that the heart is no infallible guide, and he is forced to turn elsewhere. The theme of heart and head takes on at this point an added importance which is maintained throughout the third and final part (Books XX–XXVI). Pierre's avowed object is no longer transcendent virtue (for that is now seen to be unattainable) but truth: he must understand and express the thing that has happened to him. And in realizing this purpose, he devotes himself with characteristic intensity and lack of reservation to the life of the mind. But the heart still lives and speaks within him, centripetal still pulls against centrifugal, and Pierre continues to be torn between the two halves of his nature.

The shifted emphasis in theme is announced in the opening of the third section by an account (Book XX) of Charlie Millthorpe, Pierre's boyhood friend and now the somewhat simpleminded Horatio to his Hamlet. This portrait of a shallow but warmhearted youth is obviously placed here (a good deal later than its part in the narrative might otherwise warrant) to form a contrast with the picture of Pierre, in the first few pages of Book XXI, as explorer of the world of mind. Like Pierre, Charlie has deserted the country for the city in obedience to a higher calling; like Pierre, he holds the " 'opinion [that] the

---

[157] *Ibid.*, p. 127 (Book V, chap. i).

world is all wrong,' " is on the point of " 'preaching [his] philosophy to the masses,' " and looks upon himself as " 'a Curtius [ready] to leap into the fiery gulf, and by perishing himself, save the whole empire of men.' "[158] But, unlike Pierre, Charlie is tolerated by the world, if not respected; he knows the trick of it and can survive. For "it is the glory of the bladder that nothing can sink it; [as] it is the reproach of a box of treasure, that once overboard it must down."

It is an appalling world, could he but see the whole, that Pierre encounters "on first entering into the Switzerland of his soul."[159] And it is an all but impossible task that he has set himself in "immaturely attempt[ing] a mature book"—a book, too, "to whose speedy completion two tremendous motives unitedly impelled;—the burning desire to deliver what he thought to be new, or at least miserably neglected Truth to the world; and the prospective menace of being absolutely penniless, unless by the sale of his book, he could realize money." But ignorant as yet of his unpreparedness for the task, Pierre resolutely sets forth. "All his foregone self" once again renounced, he turns from the tempest-lashed world without and devotes himself wholly to the inner world of mind. All things seem suddenly possible; he feels himself "entirely transplanted into a new and wonderful element of Beauty and Power" and does not guess that he is only resuming on another level the life of allusion he led once at Saddle Meadows.[160]

He has been at work upon his book for only a few weeks when word reaches him from the Meadows of "three most momentous events": his mother has died insane with grief, his patrimony has been inherited by Glen Stanly, and this same Glen is now the suitor of Lucy. Pierre's disregarded heart starts up once more in anguish. Guilt overwhelms him for having caused his mother's death; "an infinite quenchless rage and

---

[158] *Ibid.*, pp. 388–92 (Book XX, chap. ii).

[159] *Ibid.*, p. 396 (Book XXI, chap. i).

[160] *Ibid.*, pp. 394–95 (Book XXI, chap. i).

malice" springs up in him against the cousin who, like an imposter, has installed himself in Pierre's place and claimed his fortune and his betrothed. The doubts which came upon him as he left the Meadows return now with much greater force:

All his Faith-born, enthusiastic, high-wrought, stoic, and philosophic defenses, were now beaten down by this sudden storm of nature in his soul. For there is no faith, and no stoicism, and no philosophy, that a mortal man can possibly evoke, which will stand the final test of a real impassioned onset of Life and Passion upon him. Then all the fair philosophic or Faith-phantoms that he raised from the mist, slide away and disappear as ghosts at cock-crow. For Faith and philosophy are air, but events are brass. Amidst his gray philosophizings, Life breaks upon a man like a morning.

While this mood was on him, Pierre cursed himself for a heartless villain and an idiot fool;—heartless villain, as the murderer of his mother—idiot fool, because he had thrown away all his felicity; because he had himself, as it were, resigned his noble birthright to a cunning kinsman for a mess of pottage, which now proved all but ashes in his mouth.[161]

And as at that earlier moment of doubt, Plinlimmon's pamphlet came into his hands and seemed to mock at his presumption, so now the philosopher himself, a fellow-tenant in the Apostles' tower, appears in person to turn his look of mild indifference and scorn upon the ruin of Pierre's hopes. Imperfectly remembered, the pamphlet seems to Pierre filled with a strange and prophetic wisdom. He curses himself for having failed to understand it while there was still time, and again searches for it in vain among his belongings. Actually, as he later discovers, he is carrying it about with him in the lining of his coat. Thus "some things that men think they do not know, are . . . for all that thoroughly comprehended by them; and yet, so to speak, though contained in themselves, . . . kept a

---

[161] *Ibid.*, pp. 397–403 (Book XXI, chap. ii).

secret from themselves."[162] Whatever Pierre himself may think for the moment, he had reasons for his rash action not comprehended in Plinlimmon's utilitarian ethic.

But his present necessities of both body and soul remain and "grieve how he will, yet work he must." Pierre returns to the writing of his book and in mounting desperation drives himself on. The task grows harder rather than easier: ideas which seem utterly lucid on their first rising in the mind disclose unguessed complexities when the attempt is made to examine them more closely and to put them into words. He directs all his powers and his undivided attention to the completion of his task. No one—not even Isabel—may open the door of his study: "outer love and hate must alike be excluded" from this field.[163] He adopts a daily regimen of cold baths, sparse diet, and long hours of work, crowding his whole nature into the service of his mind. "[T]he Texas Camanche, . . . crashing like a wild deer through the green underbrush," leads a more whole and more reasonable life than Pierre, hunched over his desk.[164] It is to this that the pursuit of truth has led him. "Lo! he is fitting himself for the highest life, by thinning his blood and collapsing his heart. He is learning how to live, by rehearsing the part of death."[165]

To Pierre in this desert of intellectuality comes a letter from Lucy announcing her immediate arrival to take up a life of pure and nunlike service to him and the " 'mysterious, eversacred being' " whom he has married instead of her. She does not understand or seek to understand Pierre's reasons; she wants not the slightest return of her love. Her suffering has prepared her, she feels, to carry out " 'a celestial mission in terrestrial elements' ": she is assured as by " 'a deep, deep voice' " that Pierre is threatened by " 'some terrible jeopardy

162 *Ibid.,* pp. 404–10 (Book XXI, chap. iii).
163 *Ibid.,* p. 414 (Book XXII, chap. i).
164 *Ibid.,* p. 421 (Book XXII, chap. ii).
165 *Ibid.,* p. 425 (Book XXII, chap. iv).

. . . which [her] continual presence only can drive away.' "[166]
In keeping with her promise, she arrives at the Apostles', re-
sists the efforts of her brother Frederic and her suitor Glen
Stanly to win her back, stands firm against her mother's entreaties and abuse, and in the end accepts with perfect serenity
her mother's sentence of excommunication.[167]

In all this, the parallel with Pierre's past course is obvious.
But the difference, too, is great. Like Pierre, Lucy has made a
sacrifice of herself; but she has done so not in the cause of
some abstract and transcendent virtue but out of ordinary human love for another person. Her duty and her heart do not
lead her in opposite directions. Less intellectual than Pierre,
she is also more humble and at no time aspires beyond the
limits of her humanity. But there is nevertheless something
heroic about her—something even of a strange and unreflective wisdom. Simply by being the person she is, she exposes the
shallowness of Plinlimmon's maxims and refutes Pierre's the-
sis of the identity of virtue and vice as " 'two shadows cast
from one nothing.' "

Coming back into Pierre's life, Lucy puts visibly before him
all that was most prized and lovely in the life he has renounced.
His first reaction is one of triumph that his Lucy "should indeed, in this most tremendous of all trials, have acquitted herself with such infinite majesty"; his next feeling is one of despair at the thought of how greatly he has undervalued her and
how utterly lost to him she now is.[168] Her behavior astonishes
him. "Such wonderful strength in such wonderful sweetness"
she shows in resisting her mother that he feels, as he has at
times with Isabel, "a fascination partaking of the terrible."
The heart has its mystery and its holiness, too. Even the regal
Isabel, "as if seized by some spiritual awe, [falls] on her knees
before Lucy" in an involuntary act of homage.[169]

---

[166] *Ibid.*, pp. 429–33 (Book XXIII, chap. ii).
[167] *Ibid.*, pp. 451–58 (Book XXIV, chaps. iii–iv).
[168] *Ibid.*, pp. 433–34 (Book XXIII, chap. iii).
[169] *Ibid.*, pp. 455–56 (Book XXIV, chap. iv).

But Isabel has with difficulty been persuaded to allow Lucy to come to them at all. Her first harsh judgment of Lucy, on hearing of her plan from Pierre, seems almost an echo of Mrs. Glendinning's earlier denunciation of herself.[170] When she does yield, it is only on Pierre's representation of Lucy as his "nun-like cousin" and through fear that an outright refusal might not succeed. And even then it is her intention that Pierre shall make a choice between them—not, as Lucy intends, that both shall watch over and serve him.[171] For Isabel is determined to engross Pierre completely, though at the cost of denying him the fulfilment of his whole nature. This fierce possessiveness might have been foretold from her original unprotesting acceptance of a sacrifice "which would [it was apparent] . . . forever bar the blessed boon of marriageable love from . . . Pierre, and eternally entangle him in a fictitious alliance."[172] Fearful now of the newcomer's influence upon him, she first threatens Pierre with suicide, then maneuvers him into a display of marital affection before Lucy.[173]

And indeed, Isabel has some reason to be fearful of Lucy's influence, unconsciously exercised as it is. For "the domestic presence of Lucy [has] begun to produce a remarkable effect upon Pierre"—an effect strangely compounded of love and awe. Entirely modest as she is, she seems "nevertheless, more and more, . . . to be somehow inexplicably sliding between them, without touching them."[174] Yet for Pierre this re-awakening of the heart, like that last flowering of Ahab's "humanities," leads only to an intensification of his pain. He is, like Ahab, too " 'far gone in the dark side of earth' " ever to return to the bright. Lucy is that "insular Tahiti, full of joy

---

[170] *Ibid.*, p. 435 (Book XXIII, chap. iii) ; cf. p. 258 (Book XI, chap. iii) and pp. 270–71 (Book XII, chap. ii).

[171] *Ibid.*, pp. 436–38 (Book XXIII, chap. iii) ; cf. pp. 430, 433 (Book XXIII, chap. ii).

[172] *Ibid.*, p. 244 (Book X, chap. i).

[173] *Ibid.*, pp. 462–65 (Book XXV, chap. i).

[174] *Ibid.*, p. 470 (Book XXV, chap. iii).

and peace," which, once renounced, may never be regained. The " 'green heart-strings' " that had bound her to him are uprooted now and withered;[175] but to Isabel he is bound both by her mysterious power over him and by the compulsion of his vow. And all this while, the struggle with his book goes on, demanding the more of him as his vigor and confidence decline and his distractions mount. Neither Lucy nor Isabel can aid him here. The world at large has long since disowned him. And now as he staggers in the way, it seems to him that "the gods do likewise despise him, and own him not of their clan."[176] In this, the one labor of "his deepest, highest part, [he is] utterly without sympathy from any thing divine, human, brute, or vegetable. One in a city of hundreds of thousands . . . Pierre [is] solitary as at the Pole." Time, too, closes in on him. The need for money forces him to send the first pages prematurely to the printer and so commit what is to follow to a corresponding imperfection. The pursuit of truth is ending, as did the pursuit of virtue, in abject failure: those "deeper secrets than the Apocalypse" will not be told.

Now he began to feel that in him, the thews of a Titan were forestallingly cut by the scissors of Fate. . . . All things . . . seemed as created to mock and torment him. He seemed gifted with loftiness, merely that it might be dragged down to the mud. Still, the profound willfulness in him would not give up. Against the breaking heart, and the bursting head, . . . still he like a demi-god bore up. His soul's ship foresaw the inevitable rocks, but resolved to sail on, and make a courageous wreck.

Seeing "the everlasting elusiveness of Truth [and] the universal lurking insincerity of even the greatest and purest written thoughts," Pierre scoffs at his own book and all others. He grows cynical: "there [is] nothing he more spurn[s], than his

175 *Ibid.*, p. 443 (Book XXIII, chap. iv).
176 *Ibid.*, pp. 412–13 (Book XXII, chap. i).

own aspirations; nothing he more abhor[s] than the loftiest part of himself."[177]

In this hopeless and self-devouring mood, Pierre nevertheless writes on.

And as if all the leagued spiritual inveteracies and malices, combined with his general bodily exhaustion, were not enough, a special corporeal affliction now descended like a sky-hawk upon him. His incessant application told upon his eyes. They became so affected, that some days he wrote with the lids nearly closed, fearful of opening them wide to the light.

Still he drives himself on. "But at last he receive[s] a tremendous interior intimation, to hold off—to be still from his unnatural struggle." On a solitary walk through "the utter night-desolation" of a warehouse lane, blindness and vertigo overcome him and he falls senseless to the pavement. Recovering, he makes his way home; but disregarding the warning, he "again plie[s] heart and brain as before."

But now at last since the very blood in his body had in vain rebelled against his Titanic soul; now the only visible outward symbols of that soul—his eyes—did also turn downright traitors to him, and with more success than the rebellious blood. He had abused them so recklessly, that now they absolutely refused to look on paper. He turned them on paper, and they blinked and shut. The pupils of his eyes rolled away from him in their own orbits.

During that day he is forced to sit motionless at his desk. Relentlessly, though, the "next morning he return[s] to the charge. But again the pupils of his eyes [roll] away from him in their orbits." Once more he falls into a trance, and it is in this state that the terrifying vision of Enceladus comes to him.[178]

The setting of the dream is one familiar to Pierre from boyhood: a two-thousand-foot precipice, some few miles from

---

[177] *Ibid.*, pp. 471–72 (Book XXV, chap. iii).

[178] *Ibid.*, pp. 473–76 (Book XXV, chap. iii).

Saddle Meadows, known once by the Bunyanesque title of
"The Delectable Mountain" but later and more lastingly chris-
tened "The Mount of Titans" by some "moody, disappointed
bard." "Viewed from the [manor-house] piazza of a soft haze-
canopied summer's noon, [it] presented a long and beautiful,
but not entirely inaccessible-looking purple [front]." Somewhat more closely seen, "the precipice did not [at once] belie
its purple promise, . . . but showed the profuse aërial foliage
of a hanging forest." But as you came still nearer, "long and
frequent rents among the mass of leaves revealed horrible
glimpses of dark-dropping rocks, and mysterious mouths of
wolfish caves." All around one were enormous rocky masses,
vaguely resembling the forms of sleeping beasts.

Quitting those recumbent rocks, you still ascended toward the
hanging forest, and piercing within its lowermost fringe, . . . suddenly you stood transfixed. . . . Cunningly masked hitherto, by the
green tapestry of the interlacing leaves, a terrific towering palisade
of dark mossy massiness confronted you; and trickling with un-
evaporable moisture, distilled upon you from its beetling brow
slow thunder-showers of water-drops, chill as the last dews of death.
Now you stood and shivered in that twilight, though it were high
noon and burning August down the meads.[179]

It is the old story of illusion and reality. As in the sea, the
"most dreaded creatures glide under water, unapparent for the
most part, and treacherously hidden beneath the loveliest tints
of azure,"[180] so here

Stark desolation; ruin, remorseless and ceaseless; chills and
glooms,—all . . . lived a hidden life, curtained by that cunning
purpleness, which, from the piazza of the manor house, so beauti-
fully invested the mountain once called Delectable, but now styled
Titanic.[181]

[179] *Ibid.*, pp. 475–79 (Book XXV, chap. iv).

[180] *Moby-Dick*, I, 348 (chap. lviii).

[181] *Pierre*, p. 479 (Book XXV, chap. iv).

Falling back from these "undreamed-of glooms and steeps," one stood once more among the huge rocks scattered along the base. Before one of these

You paused; fixed by a form defiant, a form of awfulness. You saw Enceladus the Titan, the most potent of all the giants, writhing from out the imprisoning earth;—turbaned with upborne moss he writhed; still, though armless, resisting with his whole striving trunk, the Pelion and Ossa hurled back at him;—turbaned with upborne moss he writhed; still turning his unconquerable front toward that majestic mount eternally in vain assailed by him, and which, when it had stormed him off, had heaved his undoffable incubus upon him, and deridingly left him there to bay out his ineffectual howl.

All this—"the Mount of Titans, and the repulsed group of heaven-assaulters, with Enceladus in their midst shamefully recumbent at its base"—Pierre had known, if not understood, in earlier days. Now in his tormented vision, they stand before him again in more than living reality.

But no longer petrified in all their ignominious attitudes, the herded Titans now sprung to their feet; flung themselves up the slope; and anew battered at the precipice's unresounding wall. Foremost among them all, he saw a moss-turbaned, armless giant, who despairing of any other mode of wreaking his immitigable hate, turned his vast trunk into a battering-ram, and hurled his own arched-out ribs again and yet again against the invulnerable steep. "Enceladus! it is Enceladus!"—Pierre cried out in his sleep. That moment the phantom faced him; and Pierre saw Enceladus no more; but on the Titan's armless trunk, his own duplicate face and features magnifiedly gleamed upon him with prophetic discomfiture and woe. With trembling frame he started from his chair, and woke from that ideal horror to all his actual grief.[182]

Something of the meaning of that wild vision the awakened Pierre now sees, but what he sees he finds "most repulsively fateful and foreboding." That he sees no more is evidence

---

[182] *Ibid.*, pp. 480–82 (Book XXV, chap. iv).

again of his lack of "that all-comprehending oneness . . . [of the] steady philosophic mind" capable of drawing into one view the detached and distorted elements of experience.[183] It is, the narrator suggests, "because Pierre [does] not leap the final barrier of gloom; . . . [does] not willfully wrest some final comfort from the fable; [does] not flog this stubborn rock as Moses his, and force even aridity itself to quench his painful thirst,"[184] that he finds in it only additional reason for self-hatred and despair.

What a further insight might have revealed appears in the narrator's examination of the fable itself. As Enceladus was the issue of a union between Terra and "old Titan," himself the offspring of Coelus and this same Terra, his sister, so Pierre's present "reckless sky-assaulting mood" is twice tainted in its origins. From the "original organic blended heavenliness and earthliness" of Pierre's human nature was born that "mixed, uncertain, heaven-aspiring, but still not wholly earth-emancipated mood" which showed itself in his fatal attempt at "chronometrical" virtue; and of this mood, "by its terrestrial taint held down to its terrestrial mother," was born Pierre's present mood of furious determination to rise by knowledge above the illusion of good and evil. Yet—and here is the water from this rock—"the present doubly incestuous Enceladus within him . . . [is] nevertheless on one side the grandson of the sky" and shows his divine lineage in the very attempt, hopeless though it may be, "to regain his paternal birthright . . . by fierce escalade."[185]

But this possibly consoling knowledge is denied Pierre. He knows only that he is cast out by both man and God and does not suspect that this is because his nature is compounded of both. Shaken by the vision and inwardly drained by his labors, he now resolves "by an entire and violent change" of scene

---

183 *Ibid.*, pp. 244–45 (Book X, chap. i).

184 *Ibid.*, p. 483 (Book XXV, chap. v).

185 *Ibid.*, pp. 483–84 (Book XXV, chap. v).

and activity to recoup his powers for one last assault: he proposes to Isabel and Lucy a walk to the water front and a sail on the outer bay.

But there is to be no peace for Pierre. For as the three stop in at a picture gallery along the way, he and Isabel are brought to a sudden halt before a picture showing "a dark, comely, youthful man's head, portentously looking out of a dark, shaded ground, and ambiguously smiling." The catalogue identifies it only as "A stranger's head, by an unknown hand." Each is spellbound, though each for a reason unknown to the other. Isabel, seeing in it "certain shadowy traces of her own unmistakable likeness," connects it with that living being she once briefly knew as her father:

Without doubt, . . . she must have somehow vaguely fancied, that this being had always through life worn the same aspect to every body else which he had to her, for so very brief an interval of his possible existence. Solely knowing him—or dreaming of him, it may have been—under that one aspect, she could not conceive of him under any other.

But "to Pierre, this face was in part as the resurrection of the one he had burnt at the inn," yet with "an unequivocal aspect of foreignness" about it. And as the two stand wondering before it, Lucy, who had walked by it "without the least special pause," is looking up at a copy of Guido's Cenci hung directly opposite to it across the gallery: the portrait of a girl "sweetly and seraphically *blonde*, . . . [though] double-hooded, as it were, by the black crape of . . . two most horrible crimes." The bright and the dark are here fused in a single image, and the wisdom of the heart has led Lucy unerringly to it. At the dark picture on the opposing wall, meanwhile, Pierre and Isabel stare in fascination until Pierre breaks off and abruptly leads the two women from the gallery.[186]

Pierre's disquiet stays with him, even in the street. More and more, of late, Isabel's enigmatic story has seemed to him

[186] *Ibid.*, pp. 489–91 (Book XXVI, chap. i).

a mere "imaginative delirium." And now the picture of the "stranger's head" has given rise to "the most tremendous displacing and revolutionizing thoughts . . . in him"—thoughts, too, that strangely are not "wholly unwelcome to him." His whole relationship to her, and consequently the rightness of his course, is once more placed in doubt. For

setting aside all his own manifold and inter-enfolding mystic and transcendental persuasions,—originally born, as he now seemed to feel, purely of an intense and procreative enthusiasm:—an enthusiasm no longer so all-potential with him as of yore; setting all these aside, and coming to the plain, palpable facts,—how did he *know* that Isabel was his sister? Nothing that he saw in her face could he remember as having seen in his father's. The chair-portrait, *that* was the entire sum and substance of all possible . . . evidence, which peculiarly appealed to his own separate self. Yet here was another portrait of a complete stranger . . . which was just as strong an evidence as the other. Then, the original [if there was one] of this second portrait was as much the father of Isabel as the original of the chair-portrait.[187]

But he is not to be permitted even this negative certainty. For as the boat on which they have embarked upon the bay nears the outer ocean and is lifted by the swell, Isabel cries out in sudden recognition of the motion she once felt as a child when taken, as her story has it, to some faraway country. The startled Pierre sees in the incident a "striking corroboration of . . . the most surprising and improbable thing" in her whole story. But a moment later, bewildered by the "mutually neutralizing thoughts of the strange picture and the last exclamation of Isabel," he finds himself helpless either to believe or to disbelieve.[188]

His irresolution is lost in anger when, on returning home, he finds two letters waiting for him—one, from his publishers, refusing his book as " 'a swindle' " and " 'a blasphemous

---

[187] *Ibid.*, pp. 491–93 (Book XXVI, chap. ii).

[188] *Ibid.*, pp. 494–95 (Book XXVI, chap. iii).

rhapsody' "; the other, from Glen and Fred, scorning him as
" 'a villainous and perjured liar.' " Whichever way he looks
now, he is checkmated. His mother and his inheritance are
gone; Lucy, though near at hand, is forever lost to him; Isabel
he is unable either to accept or reject; both heart and head
have failed him, and his agonized attempt at truth-speaking
has ended in a botch. And now these two letters, openly snatch-
ing from him both " 'world's bread of life and world's breath
of honor,' " make clear the finality of his position.[189] Some
months before, on the verge of his great decision, Pierre had
ended his prayer to the " 'sovereign powers' " of the universe
with a prophetic threat:

"On my strong faith in ye Invisibles, I stake three whole felicities,
and three whole lives this day. If ye forsake me now,—farewell to
Faith, farewell to Truth, farewell to God; exiled for aye from God
and man, I shall declare myself an equal power with both; free to
make war on Night and Day, and all thoughts and things of mind
and matter. . . ."[190]

That moment has now come. He has nothing left to lose, no
possible way to turn.

He acts, therefore, in a burst of frantic rage and despair.
(" 'How can the prisoner reach outside except by thrusting
through the wall?' ") His own book, first of all, he nails to the
desk and spits upon. Next, pausing with outstretched arms between the opposing doors of Lucy's and Isabel's rooms, he
tells them farewell in words that are almost a curse: " 'For ye
two, my most undiluted prayer is now, that from your here
unseen and frozen chairs ye may never stir alive;—the fool of
Truth, the fool of Virtue, the fool of Fate, now quits ye forever!' "[191] Then, arming himself, he goes out in search of

189 *Ibid.*, pp. 497–98 (Book XXVI, chap. iv).
190 *Ibid.*, p. 150 (Book V, chap. vi).
191 *Ibid.*, p. 499 (Book XXVI, chap. iv).

Glen, finds him, invites his blow, and shoots him down in the open street.[192]

Standing in his prison cell that evening, Pierre contemplates his ruin. Though all is done, nothing is finished. Book and author, "mutilated stumps" both, break off abruptly, regardless of meaning—" 'Life's last chapter well stitched into the middle.' "[193] He can make little sense of what has happened to him:

"It is ambiguous still. Had I been heartless now, disowned, and spurningly portioned off the girl at Saddle Meadows, then had I been happy through a long life on earth, and perchance through a long eternity in heaven! Now, 'tis merely hell in both worlds. Well, be it hell. I will mold a trumpet of the flames, and with my breath of flame, breathe back my defiance!"[194]

He has no moment of enlightenment, no acceptance, no sense of triumph. But Plinlimmonism does not tempt him: he remains true to the law of his being.

The end comes with melodramatic swiftness. That same evening, Isabel and Lucy come to him in his cell. But he has nothing to say to them. He has declared " 'war on Night and Day,' " and has now no further need of the love or sympathy of either:

"Ye two pale ghosts [he tells them], were this the other world, ye were not welcome. Away!—Good Angel and Bad Angel both!— For Pierre is neuter now!"

Isabel's answer is at once an accusation of the world, of heaven, and of herself:

"Oh, ye stony roofs, and seven-fold stony skies!—not thou art the murderer, but thy sister hath murdered thee, my brother, oh my brother!"

---

[192] *Ibid.*, pp. 501–2 (Book XXVI, chap. v).

[193] *Ibid.*, p. 502 (Book XXVI, chap. vi) ; cf. p. 199 (Book VII, chap. viii).

[194] *Ibid.*, p. 502 (Book XXVI, chap. vi).

At these wailed words from Isabel, Lucy shrunk up like a scroll, and noiselessly fell at the feet of Pierre.

He touched her heart.—"Dead!—Girl! wife or sister, saint or fiend!"—seizing Isabel in his grasp—"in thy breast, life for infants lodgeth not, but death-milk for thee and me!—The drug!" and tearing her bosom loose, he seized the secret vial nestling there.[195]

When Fred and Millthorpe are admitted to the cell some time later, they find both Pierre and Lucy dead. And at that moment,

"All's o'er, and ye know him not!" came gasping from the wall; and from the fingers of Isabel dropped an empty vial—as if it had been a run-out sand-glass—and shivered upon the floor; and her whole form sloped sideways, and she fell upon Pierre's heart, and her long hair ran over him, and arbored him in ebon vines.[196]

He is her prisoner still—the victim of the obsessive mind, of the fascination of darkness, of the "ever-encroaching appetite for God." Had he been proof against these things, he would be safe today and happy. But he would be less noble, too, less fully human. For prudence and moderation, though virtues, are not heroic virtues; and the hero must have, above all, the courage to be foolish and to accept no measure but his own.

[195] *Ibid.*, p. 503 (Book XXVI, chap. vii).
[196] *Ibid.*, p. 505 (Book XXVI, chap. vii).

4. Submission

THE WAY OF WEAKNESS

If one considers the nature of the adversary only and not the character of the man, it is not difficult to make a case for him who chooses to submit rather than to resist. Survival itself, in such a universe as Melville has shown this to be, is no inconsiderable victory. For this is a world, clearly, that was not made with either man's comfort or his welfare in mind. What sustenance he gets, he must find for himself: the world makes no provision for him. He may protest if he wishes, but his anger will change nothing: though in desperation he should destroy himself against the wall of reality, it will not even recognize that he has existed. Who, then, will have the heart to blame him if, like the lizard or the desert rat, he adapts himself to the terrain and scales down his demands to the level of the possible? To prevail against such an enemy however briefly and by whatever strategy is an astonishing achievement. And to this extent, all of us who manage to survive—not excluding the ignorant, the foolish, the wilfully blind, the worldly compromisers, or even the outright vicious—are deserving of some credit.

But to grant this is in no sense to place the submitters and the non-submitters upon the same footing. For it is the acknowledged task of the self not merely to survive but to survive as a free, moral, and intelligent agent—to avoid annihilation, it is true, but much more, to realize something of the immense potentiality it feels within it. And that is accomplished only by bold action, by the taking of risks, by a continual affirmation of life. There is, finally, no real security in simply playing it safe. The servant in the Gospel parable who brought back his talent of silver undiminished was not, as he expected, rewarded for his prudence but condemned and thrust into the outer darkness.

THE VALOR-RUINED

The submitters, of course, are not all of one kind. There are those among them who may be thought to deserve more pity than blame. They are the ones whose yielding is a consequence not of calculated self-interest but of exhaustion or the strain of an insight disproportioned to their strength. They are the "valor-ruined," whose courage has been burned up in them by a too-sudden exposure to evil, or whose will to resist has been sapped by long and hopeless suffering.

The clearest example, perhaps, is the unfortunate whaling captain, a sort of broken Ahab, whose story Rolfe relates in *Clarel*. Proud and independent in his earlier years, this man would frequently argue metaphysics with his mate, " 'a man to creed austere resigned.' " Boldly irreligious,

> "The master ever spurned at fate,
> Calvin's or Zeno's. Always still
> Manlike he stood by man's free will
> And power to effect each thing he would,
> Did reason but pronounce it good.
> The subaltern held in humble way
> That still Heaven's overrulings sway
> Will and event."

The day comes when philosophy is put to the test: the ship strikes a hidden rock, and master and crew are forced to take to the boats. Weeks of hunger at sea drive the desperate men to cannibalism, and when another vessel at last picks up the boat, the captain is the only survivor. "Jacketed skeleton" though he is, he refuses to bow and explains his survival as a triumph of his own will. He recovers, and some months later takes out a second ship. Misfortune strikes again: in Antarctic seas, a whale staves in the side and the ship founders. Once more, after incredible hardships, he survives. But when he returns to port, he finds that no owner now will risk a ship to his command. Need reduces him at last to accept a job as night watchman on the quays. He is henceforth a humbled man,

> "not sour
> In spirit, but meek and reconciled;
> Patient he was, he none withstood;
> Oft on some secret thing would brood.
> He ate what came, though but a crust;
> In Calvin's creed he put his trust;
> Praised heaven, and said that God was good,
> And his calamity but just.
> So Sylvio Pellico from cell-door
> Forth tottering, after dungeoned years,
> Crippled and bleached, and dead his peers:
> 'Grateful, I thank the Emperor.' "[1]

[1] *Clarel*, I, 146–49 (Part I, canto xxxvii). For an account of the original of this portrait (Captain Pollard of the ill-fated "Essex") see Henry F. Pommer, "Herman Melville and the Wake of the Essex," *American Literature*, XX (November, 1948), 290–304. The Sylvio Pellico to whom the captain is here

Obscure hints connect Rolfe's whaling captain with the person of Nehemiah, the saintly old American exile and religious fanatic who serves as Clarel's first guide to the holy places of Jerusalem. Although it is evident that he has known great suffering, he too insists that God is good, keeps silent about his past, is blind to the lepers' huts around the Gate of David, omits from his recountal of the Good Samaritan's story all mention of the pitiless Levite and priest (" 'Whom God forgive, . . . / As I forget' "), devoutly awaits Christ's second coming, and in his death-dream on the Dead Sea shore sees the drowned city of Sodom rise from the waves in splendor as the heavenly Jerusalem.[2]

Something of the same reluctance to acknowledge life's darker truths is apparent in Starbuck. He is, at first thought, an odd man to discover in this company. Physically brave to the verge of audacity, he is yet not made to withstand the deeper terrors of the spirit, and his only recourse is to try to ignore them. If his subordinates, Stubb and Flask, sometimes exhibit a steadier courage, they owe this seeming superiority to their ignorance and their far more limited vision.[3] Starbuck's greater intelligence and his keener awareness of spiritual reality bring him much closer to Ahab. But he is unlike Ahab in the way he confronts that reality. There is nothing aggressive about him. His most marked characteristic is "a strong natural reverence" amounting at times almost to superstition.[4] He lives in the shadow of "the thousand-fold perils" he has encountered in the past and of the deaths of both his father and

---

compared was an Italian poet and patriot (1789–1854) imprisoned by the Austrians for political activity and released only after his health had been ruined. The figure of this "quelled enthusiast . . . / Unmanned, made meek through strenuous wrong," was of continuing interest to Melville and forms the subject of his "Pausilippo" in *Poems*, pp. 280–83.

[2] *Clarel*, I, 103 (Part I, canto xxvi) ; pp. 204–5 (Part II, canto ix) ; pp. 325–26 (Part II, canto xxxviii).

[3] *Moby-Dick*, I, 145–47 (chap. xxvii) ; II, 341 (chap. cxxxiii) ; p. 352 (chap. cxxxiv).

[4] *Ibid.*, I, 142 (chap. xxvi).

his brother at sea; he is at all times alive to "outward portents and inward presentiments."[5] Haunted by such fears, he would believe nothing but good of the world, though he knows better. On a day of quiet calm, he gazes down into the golden sea about him and murmurs: " 'Loveliness unfathomable, as ever lover saw in his young bride's eye!—Tell me not of thy teeth-tiered sharks, and thy kidnapping cannibal ways. Let faith oust fact; let fancy oust memory; I look deep down and do believe.' "[6] Ahab's " 'heaven-insulting purpose' " horrifies him by its impiety, but he cannot deny the truth of the insight forced upon him by Ahab: " 'Oh, life! 'tis in an hour like this, with soul beat down and held to knowledge,—as wild, untutored things are forced to feed—oh, life! 'tis now that I do feel the latent horror in thee!' "[7] Standing before the doubloon at the mast, he unriddles its mystic characters, but turns away in fear from what he reads there:

"A dark valley between three mighty, heaven-abiding peaks, that almost seem the Trinity, in some faint earthly symbol. So in this vale of Death, God girds us round; and over all our gloom, the sun of Righteousness still shines a beacon and a hope. If we bend down our eyes, the dark vale shows her mouldy soil; but if we lift them, the bright sun meets our glance half way, to cheer. Yet, oh, the great sun is no fixture; and if, at midnight, we would fain snatch some sweet solace from him, we gaze for him in vain! This coin speaks wisely, mildly, truly, but still sadly to me. I will quit it, lest Truth shake me falsely."[8]

Ahab, impatient with all omen-reading but his own, sees Starbuck's reverence as a kind of timorousness, as far from the point as Stubb's mechanical fearlessness: " 'Begone! Ye two are opposite poles of one thing; Starbuck is Stubb reversed, and Stubb is Starbuck; and ye two are all mankind.' "[9] But

5 *Ibid.*, pp. 142–43 (chap. xxvi).
6 *Ibid.*, II, 265 (chap. cxiv).
7 *Ibid.*, I, 212 (chap. xxxviii).
8 *Ibid.*, II, 190–91 (chap. xcix).
9 *Ibid.*, p. 341 (chap. cxxxiii).

his judgment is too harsh. If unfitted for attack, Starbuck has abundant courage to bear. When the long-dreaded moment arrives and he sees the white whale come charging down upon the ship, he stands firm and accepts the fate that comes to him in the course of duty.[10] We see in him the utmost of which "mere unaided virtue or right-mindedness"[11] is capable; that much is a great deal, but it falls short still of the true heroic.

Much farther down the scale are such unfortunates as Benito Cereno and, in one sense, the little Negro Pip. Lacking the "interior vitality" of the mate of the "Pequod," they are wholly destroyed as persons by their experience of evil. Pip's frightened glimpse into nature's inhuman void, at once the womb and grave of life, cancels all meaning for him, deprives him of reason and even of the sense of his own identity. But what is lost to him on one level is restored on another: "Man's insanity proves heaven's sense," and, like Ishmael at voyage end, Pip is reborn from the sea into a mad wisdom that places him beyond the reach of either fear or anger.[12]

Don Benito, the melancholy Spanish captain in "Benito Cereno," experiences the same shock and loss but is denied Pip's liberating insight. His revelation comes to him not in the sea but in a person. As "all evil, to crazy Ahab, [is] visibly personified . . . in Moby Dick," so for Don Benito it is gathered to a point in Babo, the leader of the rebel slaves. To look into that black face, so simple and so open to those who do not know, is for him to look over the edge of the pit. And he is transfixed by what he sees there, helpless as a bird before the snake. It is this spiritual terror, and no ordinary physical fear, that explains his helplessness in his captor's hands during the visit of the American to his ship. By a last spasmodic effort of the will as Delano's boat is leaving, he breaks the spell and throws himself overboard; he is saved and the fiendlike Babo

---

10 *Ibid.*, p. 364 (chap. cxxxv).

11 *Ibid.*, I, 230–31 (chap. xli).

12 *Ibid.*, II, 169–70 (chap. xciii).

is captured. But he has been wounded too deeply to recover: what he has seen and undergone has robbed him of the will to live. He cannot bring himself, either then or later, to look upon Babo again; the very thought of the black casts a shadow over him like death. "Twenty-nine years of age, and broken in body and mind," he does not attempt, after Babo's trial at Lima, to return to his home but retires in the company of the monk Infelez (i.e., Grief) to the monastery on nearby Mount Agonia where, some three months later, he dies.[13]

In the story of *Mardi*'s Babbalanja, we are given a much more detailed account of the steps leading to surrender. The philosopher, as we first know him, is completely self-confident. He is the skeptic, the questioner, the mocking challenger of all established opinions.[14] The historian Mohi is delighted when he can turn up an unquestioned fact, however trivial the subject. Babbalanja looks farther: " 'I am intent upon the essence of things; the mystery that lieth beyond; . . . that which is beneath the seeming; the precious pearl within the shaggy oyster. I probe the circle's center; I seek to evolve the inscrutable.' "[15] Reason is his instrument and he will not admit that any object lies beyond its reach. When Yoomy is shocked at his friend's questioning of Divine Providence, Babbalanja insists that

"[there is no] impiety in the right use of our reason, whatever the issue. Smote with superstition, shall we let it wither and die out, a dead limb to a live trunk, as the mad devotee's arm held up motionless for years? Or shall we employ it but for a paw, to help us to our bodily needs, as the brutes use their instinct? Is not reason subtle as quicksilver—live as lightning—a neighing charger to advance, but a snail to recede? Can we starve that noble instinct in us, and hope that it will survive? Better slay the body than the soul. . . . Yoomy, we are men, we are angels. And in his faculties,

13 "Benito Cereno," in *The Piazza Tales*, pp. 144, 166, 169–70.

14 *Mardi*, I, 244–46 (chap. lxix) ; pp. 275–77 (chap. lxxviii) ; p. 329 (chap. xciii) ; pp. 366–67 (chap. civ) ; II, 32 (chap. cxiii).

15 *Ibid.*, II, 36 (chap. cxiv).

[God] is but what a man would be, infinitely magnified. Let us aspire to all things. . . . What shall appall us? If eagles gaze at the sun, may not men at the gods?"

Thus encouraged, the philosopher proceeds to demonstrate, from the existence of evil, the incompatibility of God's supposed attributes of omnipresence and moral perfection, and so from the most orthodox premises arrives at the heretical conclusion that God is identical with His creation.[16]

But though he pleads with men to " 'quit this insanity' " of baseless speculation and accept a simpler faith—" 'the theology in the grass and the flower, in seed-time and harvest' "[17]— he himself will not be satisfied with a non-metaphysical religion. Such a faith is offered him in old Bardianna's formula for "A Happy Life." But though the stoic wisdom he finds in this manuscript amazes and delights him, it does not finally satisfy. Nothing can do that but the answers to the last questions, those concerning the meaning and purpose of existence. All other truths are superfluous:

"All round me, my fellow men are new-grafting their vines, and dwelling in flourishing arbors; while I am forever pruning mine, till it is become but a stump. Yet in this pruning will I persist; I will not add, I will diminish; I will train myself down to the stand- ard of what is unchangeably true. Day by day I drop off my re- dundancies; ere long I shall have stripped my ribs; when I die, they will but bury my spine. Ah! where, where, where, my lord, is the everlasting Tekana? Tell me, Mohi, where the Ephina? I may have come to the Penultimate, but where, sweet Yoomy, is the Ultimate?"[18]

One part of his mind warns him that his search is futile. He himself quotes approvingly Bardianna's dictum that " 'truth is in things, and not in words,' " and he receives without contra-

---

16 *Ibid.*, pp. 122–25 (chap. cxxxv).

17 *Ibid.*, p. 125 (chap. cxxxv).

18 *Ibid.*, pp. 78–81 (chap. cxxiv).

diction the demigod Media's reminder that " 'you mortals dwell in [this world], and it is impossible to get elsewhere.' "[19] But he nevertheless persists in his efforts to escape the gravitational pull of this earth. Just as Ahab is driven by some " 'hidden lord and master, [some] cruel, remorseless emperor' " within, so Babbalanja has his own personal devil to goad him on. This is the demon of forbidden knowledge: " 'Many things I know, not good to tell; whence they call me Azzageddi.' "[20] He is no mere playful invention of Babbalanja's, as we may at first be tempted to think. He is real, inasmuch as he represents an ungovernable inner compulsion, an enemy of the good, and the cause of much actual suffering to his host.[21] He speaks only intermittently, but he is always present, a part of his victim's very nature, to be driven out " 'only with this mortal's ghost:—together we came in, together we depart.' "[22] When he does speak ("Fugle-orum" is his countersign), it is to mock at the pretensions of earthbound man—at his science, his philosophy, and his faith in progress—or to taunt him with his dependence upon the body, his mortality, his inability to attain to meaningful Truth.[23] It is Azzageddi's mission to sting the soul into protest against the conditions of its existence; he is the sworn enemy of faith, of contentment, of earthly happiness. From his first entry upon the scene, Babbalanja's mood grows steadily darker. The gradual exhaustion of the hope of finding Yillah deepens the gloom. A sense of approaching death weighs upon all the voyagers and especially upon Babbalanja.[24] The philosopher's demon goads

---

[19] *Ibid.*, I, 329 (chap. xciii) ; II, 57, (chap. cxx).

[20] *Ibid.*, II, 114 (chap. cxxxiii) ; cf. *Moby-Dick*, II, 330 (chap. cxxxii).

[21] *Mardi*, II, 353 (chap. clxxxiv) ; pp. 369–70 (chap. clxxxviii).

[22] *Ibid.*, p. 114 (chap. cxxxiii).

[23] *Ibid.*, pp. 111–13 (chap. cxxxii) ; pp. 283–86 (chap. clxxi) ; pp. 305–7 (chap. clxxvi) ; pp. 214–16 (chap. clv) ; pp. 336–54, *passim* (chaps. clxxxi-clxxxiv) ; pp. 281–82 (chap. clxx).

[24] *Ibid.*, pp. 314–15 (chap. clxxviii) ; 355–60 (chap. clxxxv).

him almost to the verge of hysteria; he sees the end of life approaching with nothing gained, nothing understood, all his questions still unanswered.[25] Reason has promised much, but it has led only to this confusion and despair:

"No coward he, who hunted, turns and finds no foe to fight. . . . Like the stag, whose brow is beat with wings of hawks, perched in his heavenward antlers; so I, blinded, goaded, headlong, rush! this way and that; not knowing whither; one forest wide around!"[26]

The moment of surrender is now at hand.

The next morning, on a calm sea, the voyagers encounter the Serenian sage and follow him to his island, " 'the land of love.' " Landing, they hear his account of the simple and undogmatic religion of the heart which men there profess and practice. It is, in essence, a kind of Society for Ethical Culture, Christian in its origins but with all supernatural overtones carefully removed. Immortality has become a mere academic question: the Serenian faith does not require the sanctions of eternal reward or punishment:

"Brother! [the sage tells Babbalanja] were the turf our everlasting pillow, still would the Master's faith answer a blessed end;— making us more truly happy *here. That* is the first and chief result; for holy here, we must be holy elsewhere. 'Tis Mardi, to which loved Alma [i.e., Christ] gives his laws; not Paradise."

Despite this somewhat startling equation of happiness and holiness, the Serenians recognize the reality of moral evil. But far from being obsessed by it, they devote their efforts to fostering the germ of good in man's heart. It is upon the natural impulses of that heart that all is built. " 'We love [God] from an instinct in us' " and attain to righteousness by following " 'dictates, born half dormant in us, and warmed into life by Alma.' " For Alma " 'but opens unto us our own hearts. Were

25 *Ibid.*, pp. 349–51 (chap. clxxxiii) ; pp. 356–57 (chap. clxxxv).
26 *Ibid.*, p. 360 (chap. clxxxv).

his precepts strange we would recoil—not one feeling would respond; whereas, once hearkened to, our souls embrace them as with the instinctive tendrils of a vine.' " In all this, reason has its place—but " 'right-reason,' " knowing both its proper objects and its place in the whole life of man.[27]

Babbalanja finds little here that he has not already known and admired in the teachings of Bardianna, the "antique pagan." But coming to him now, in the midst of his despair, it strikes him with new force: " 'Some black cloud seems floating from me. I begin to see. I come out in the light. The sharp fang tears me less. The forked flames wane. My soul sets back like ocean streams, that sudden change their flow. Have I been sane?' " The old sage continues to speak of the joys of trust and acceptance—" 'He lays the lashings of the soul's wild aspirations after things unseen' "—and all at once the mocking philosopher is on his knees:

"Oh, Alma, Alma! prince divine! . . . in *thee*, at last, I find repose. Hope perches in my heart a dove. . . . Gone, gone! are all distracting doubts. Love and Alma now prevail. I see with other eyes:—Are these my hands? What wild, wild dreams were mine; —I have been mad. Some things there are, we must not think of. Beyond one obvious mark, all human lore is vain. . . . Reason no longer domineers; but still doth speak. All I have said ere this, that wars with Alma's precepts, I here recant. Here I kneel, and own great Oro [God] and his sovereign son."[28]

Three of his companions—Yoomy, Mohi, and Media—kneel with him; but Taji does not. Nor is he, apparently, impressed when a little later Babbalanja recounts the Dantean vision in which he has learned to put aside " 'the arrogance of knowing' " in the realization that

" 'No mind but Oro's can know all; no mind that knows not all can be content; content alone approximates to happiness. Holiness

[27] *Ibid.*, pp. 366–70 (chap. clxxxvii).

[28] *Ibid.*, pp. 369–71 (chap. clxxxvii).

comes by wisdom; and it is because great Oro is supremely wise, that He's supremely holy. But as perfect wisdom can be only Oro's; so, perfect holiness is his alone. And whoso is otherwise than perfect in his holiness, is liable to sin.' "[29]

Man's wisdom, that is to say, lies in a humble acceptance of his limits. We must put aside forever the old temptation to "be as gods, knowing good and evil." For

" 'to know all is to be all. Beatitude there is none. And the only [earthly] happiness is but exemption from great woes—no more. Great Love is sad; and heaven is Love. Sadness makes the silence throughout the realms of space; sadness is universal and eternal; but sadness is tranquillity; tranquillity the uttermost that souls may hope for.' "[30]

At sunrise the next morning on the beach the parting comes. Babbalanja does not deny that he has suffered a defeat and has settled for less than he had hoped:

"My voyage is ended. Not because what we sought is found; but that I now possess all which may be had of what I sought in Mardi. . . . Taji! for Yillah thou wilt hunt in vain; she is a phantom that but mocks thee. . . . Within our hearts is all we seek. . . . Then rove no more. Gain now, in flush of youth, that last wise thought, too often purchased by a life of woe. Be wise; be wise."[31]

The others waver, but Taji is "fixed as fate." Turning from Babbalanja without an answer, he gathers his companions about him and takes up once more the hopeless search for Yillah.[32] Suffering and despair have dictated the terms of the philosopher's surrender, and no hint of criticism is raised against him. It is not he, however, but Taji—" 'the hunter that never rests, the hunter without a home' "—who speaks the last word in the novel, and that word is defiance.

[29] *Ibid.*, p. 375 (chap. clxxxviii).
[30] *Ibid.*, p. 379 (chap. clxxxviii).
[31] *Ibid.*, p. 380 (chap. clxxxix).
[32] *Ibid.*, p. 381 (chap. clxxxix).

THE COMPROMISERS

But not all who choose the path of submission have been driven to it by weakness, suffering, or spiritual exhaustion: some men choose it out of simple cold-blooded calculation and self-interest, some others out of a larger, if still calculated, philosophy of expediency which they would justify under the name of "moral realism." We may include both, different as they are, under the one class of "the worldly compromisers." The impulses of the heart have little to do with shaping their counsels: they live by the head.

The first of these groups deserves only passing attention. The Reverend Mr. Falsgrave of Saddle Meadows provides as good an example as any. Owing the greater part of his salary to Mrs. Glendinning's generosity, this surpliced exquisite is fittingly grateful and presides with equal conscientiousness both at his benefactress' altar and at her dining table. He may feel upon occasion, as when that lady insists upon the excommunication of the erring Delly Ulver, that " 'virtue has, perhaps, an over-ardent champion in [her]' "; but he is careful not to press the case for charity beyond the limits of decorum and safety. As the allegorical brooch at his bosom suggests, he combines in admirable balance the gentleness of the dove and the wisdom of the serpent. He is no absolutist attempting " 'by one universal maxim, to embrace all moral contingencies,' " but a casuist keenly aware of the " 'millions of circumstances [that] modify all moral questions.' "[33] And he has no great difficulty in the end in disposing of the case of Delly Ulver in accordance with those circumstances most nearly affecting his own interests.[34]

The Yankee mystic of *The Confidence-Man*, having invented his own philosophy to meet his needs, is spared Falsgrave's labors of accommodation. Like Bildad, he has "long since come to the sage and sensible conclusion that a man's religion

[33] *Pierre*, pp. 135–43 (Book V, chap. iv).
[34] *Ibid.*, p. 229 (Book VIII, chap. vii).

is one thing, and this practical world quite another. This world pays dividends."[35] His kingdom, then, is frankly of this world, and success is for him the measure of value.

"Sir," said the cosmopolitan, . . . "you speak of a certain philosophy, . . . and hint of its bearing upon practical life; pray, tell me, if the study of this philosophy tends to the same formation of character with the experiences of the world?"

"It does; and that is the test of its truth; for any philosophy that, being in operation contradictory to the ways of the world, tends to produce a character at odds with it, such a philosophy must necessarily be but a cheat and a dream."[36]

And certainly Egbert, the mystic's practical disciple, is in no way unfitted by his master's teachings for success in this world. No utopian counsel of charity requires him to lessen his own fortune to help a needy friend.[37] The term "needy friend" is itself a contradiction in terms. For friends are chosen for their virtues—" 'good manners, handsome dress, and [their] parents' rank and repute of wealth.' " And obviously " 'there is something wrong about the man who wants help.' " What, after all, is failure but evidence of moral unsoundness? Hence, " 'to implore help is itself the proof of undesert of it.' " Far better, then, to treat that friend's need as a heaven-sent opportunity to better one's own fortune through a soundly secured loan at a profitable rate of interest.[38]

The same philosophy of enlightened self-interest is developed with greater explicitness and consistency in Plotinus Plinlimmon's fragmentary pamphlet, "Chronometricals and Horologicals," in *Pierre*.[39] But the satiric note is here so carefully modulated that the entire discourse has sometimes, despite Melville's repeated expressions of distaste for "the counting-room philosophy" of the Utilitarians, been taken as the au-

[35] *Moby-Dick*, II, 92–93 (chap. xvi).
[36] *The Confidence-Man*, p. 263 (chap. xxxvii).
[37] *Ibid.*, pp. 268–69 (chap. xxxix).
[38] *Ibid.*, pp. 270–74 (chap. xxxix).
[39] *Pierre*, pp. 293–300 (Book XIV, chap. iii).

thor's personal judgment upon the misguided absolutism of his hero. It is not, of course, this simple. Plinlimmon is more than a mere corrective of Pierre's enthusiasm: he stands opposed to him not merely in his "moderation" but in his total lack of feeling, of heart. The final effect of his pamphlet, as later of his character, is rather to raise than to lower Pierre in our regard. For it is difficult to imagine anything that could, by contrast, place that young man's generous extravagances in a more heroic light than this same mean-spirited counsel of imperfection.

Plinlimmon's down-to-earth gospel takes its start, oddly enough, from the insight to which Babbalanja attained only in the farthest reaches of inspired vision: that is, God's infinite superiority in wisdom and holiness to anything conceivable by man. But he pushes Babbalanja's reasoning a good step farther in concluding therefrom that the attempt to achieve perfect virtue in this world is necessarily as futile, as dangerous, and, at bottom, as impious, as the endeavor to achieve ultimate truth.

The lecture clarifies the point for us by an extended analogy: Divine wisdom and virtue are to earthly wisdom and virtue as Greenwich time is to local time. The second term in each case derives from the first but is entirely distinct from it—indeed, owes its very identity to that difference. And so long as this difference remains unchallenged, no particular difficulty will occur. But as among timepieces there are a few chronometers carrying Greenwich time into remote waters for purposes of navigation, so among men " 'there is a most rare order of human souls, which, if carried carefully in the body will almost always and everywhere give Heaven's own Truth, with some small grains of variance.' " These, and not the common horologes, are the trouble-makers:

"Now in an artificial world like ours, the soul of man is further removed from God and the Heavenly Truth, than the chronometer carried to China, is from Greenwich. And, as that chronometer, if at all accurate, will pronounce it to be 12 o'clock high-noon, when the China local watches say, perhaps, it is 12 o'clock midnight; so the chronometric soul, if in this world true to its great Greenwich in the other, will always, in its so-called intuitions of right and wrong, be contradicting the mere local standards and watch-maker's brains of this earth."[40]

But every instrument is to be judged by its usefulness to the purpose in hand and not by an absolute standard. Accordingly,

"though the chronometer carried from Greenwich to China, should truly [which is impossible] exhibit in China what the time may be in Greenwich at any moment; yet, though thereby it must necessarily contradict China time, it does by no means thence follow, that with respect to China, the China watches are at all out of the way. Precisely the reverse. For the fact of that variance is a presumption that, with respect to China, the Chinese watches must be all right; and consequently . . . the Greenwich chronometers must be wrong as to China. Besides, of what use to the Chinaman would a Greenwich chronometer, keeping Greenwich time, be? Were he thereby to regulate his daily actions, he would be guilty of all manner of absurdities:—going to bed at noon, say, when his neighbors would be sitting down to dinner. And thus, though the earthly wisdom of man be heavenly folly to God; so also, conversely, is the heavenly wisdom of God an earthly folly to man. Literally speaking, this is so. Nor does the God at the heavenly Greenwich expect common men to keep Greenwich wisdom in this remote Chinese world of ours; because such a thing were unprofitable for them here, and, indeed, a falsification of Himself, inasmuch as in that case, China time would be identical with Greenwich time, which would make Greenwich time wrong."

God, that is to say, would not be God were He not right and man wrong. And it is perhaps to remind men of this necessary opposition that God will " 'now and then send a heavenly chronometer (as a meteoric stone) into this world, uselessly as it would seem, to give the lie to all the world's time-keepers.' "[41]

[40] *Ibid.*, pp. 293–94.
[41] *Ibid.*, pp. 295–96.

The same opposition explains, too, the failure of Christ and other great religious teachers to make a lasting mark upon the human heart:

"By inference it follows, also, that he who finding in himself a chronometrical soul, seeks practically to force that heavenly time upon the earth; in such an attempt he can never succeed, with an absolute and essential success. And as for himself, if he seek to regulate his own daily conduct by it, he will but array all men's earthly time-keepers against him, and thereby work himself woe and death. Both these things are plainly evinced in the character and fate of Christ. . . . But here one thing is to be especially observed. Though Christ encountered woe in both the precept and the practice of His chronometricals, yet did He remain throughout entirely without folly or sin. Whereas, almost invariably, with inferior beings, the absolute effort to live in this world according to the strict letter of the chronometricals is, somehow, apt to involve [them] eventually in strange, *unique* follies and sins, unimagined before."[42]

But a realization of the unattainability in this world of heavenly truth and virtue ought in no sense to drive us to despair. Rather, we should, like the Calvinist non-elect, disinterestedly rejoice in the fact of God's unapproachable perfection. Nor, strictly speaking, is it true that we have no part in that glory: for as nothingness is in some sense necessary to being and evil to good, so this world is but heaven's antipodes and its " 'seeming incompatibility with God, absolutely results from its meridional correspondence with him.' "[43]

Neither does " 'this chronometrical conceit . . . involve the justification of all the acts which wicked men may perform.' " A sensible moderation ought to guard us against excesses on this side as on the other. For though to insist with the prophets that sin is death would clearly be to overstate the case, yet it is undeniably true that " 'sooner or later, in all cases, downright vice is downright woe.' "[44] But so is downright virtue:

[42] *Ibid.*, p. 296.   [43] *Ibid.*, p. 297.   [44] *Ibid.*, p. 300.

"[F]or the mass of men, the highest abstract heavenly righteousness is not only impossible, but would be entirely out of place, and positively wrong in a world like this. To turn the left cheek if the right be smitten, is chronometrical. . . . To give *all* that thou hast to the poor, this too is chronometrical. . . . Nevertheless, if a man gives with a certain self-considerate generosity to the poor; abstains from doing downright ill to any man; [and] does his convenient best in a general way to do good to his whole race,"

that man is doing all that can reasonably be expected of him.[45]

"In short, this Chronometrical and Horological conceit . . . seems to teach this: —that in things terrestrial (horological) a man must not be governed by ideas celestial (chronometrical) ; that certain minor self-renunciations in this life his own mere instinct for his own every-day general well-being will teach him to make, but he must by no means make a complete unconditional sacrifice of himself in behalf of any other being, or cause, or any conceit. . . .

"A virtuous expediency, then, seems the highest desirable or attainable earthly excellence for the mass of men, and it is the only earthly excellence that their Creator intended for them. When they go to heaven, it will be quite another thing. There, they can freely turn the left cheek, because the right cheek will never be smitten. There they can freely give all to the poor, for *there* there will be no poor to give to."[46]

But although the doctrine of worldly accommodation would thus seem to have found in Plotinus Plinlimmon its classic theoretician and apologist, we must look elsewhere if we wish to see it in action. For dwelling apart in his tower, uninvolved by any ties of affection with the human world, the "Grand Master" of the Apostles has no share in the world of passion, conflict, and action. He is not a character, strictly speaking, or even an agent, but simply an observer—"a face by itself."[47] The Yankee mystic of *The Confidence-Man,* we may recall,

45 *Ibid.*, pp. 297–98.
46 *Ibid.*, pp. 298–99.
47 *Ibid.*, pp. 404–10 (Book XXI, chap. iii).

having set forth the leading principles of his philosophy, referred further questions concerning its application to the daily
conduct of Egbert, his practical disciple.[48] In much the same
way, the student of Plinlimmonism may observe its principles
reduced to practice in the actions of the philosophic Captain
Vere of *Billy Budd*.

Such an estimate of Vere is, of course, not the most common one today. There has been for many years a tendency to
see in *Billy Budd* Melville's last "testament of acceptance," his
long-delayed recognition of necessity—almost, as it were, the
deathbed recantation of his "absolutist" errors: the author becomes his own chastened Babbalanja, kneeling on the Serenian
sands to beg forgiveness for his past impiety and madness.
(One wonders here to what extent this judgment may rest upon
a too unqualified identification of Melville with the more in-
transigent of his heroes.) In such a view, at any rate, Captain
Vere commonly assumes the stature of a tragic hero. He is
seen as a brooding and compassionate Lincoln, courageously
facing up to the hard necessities of action and responsibility,
as a sort of latter-day Abraham "resolutely offering [young
Isaac] up in obedience to the exacting behest."[49] What somehow goes unnoticed is that the action of hanging Billy is undertaken in clear opposition to Vere's own conscience and in
obedience to "the exacting behest" not of God but of social
expediency.

There are, it is true, several considerations that would seem
to invite such an interpretation: the circumstances of the
work's composition, so like those of that other supposed farewell to life, Shakespeare's *Tempest;* the quiet, unrhetorical,
and "reasonable" character of the style; the frequently equivocal nature of the narrator's comments; and, finally, one may
guess, the experience of our own generation with a like crisis

---

48 *The Confidence-Man*, pp. 262, 264 (chap. xxxvii).

49 *Billy Budd*, in *The Portable Melville*, p. 720.

he has even less confidence in the general mass: " 'With mankind' he would say 'forms, measured forms, are everything; and that is the import couched in the story of Orpheus with his lyre spell-binding the wild denizens of the wood.' And this he once applied to the disruption of forms going on across the Channel and the consequences thereof."[54] Nature has for him the connotation of disorder, and he fears it accordingly. When, anxious for an immediate conviction of Billy and alarmed by what he considers the "scruples" of his court, he reminds his officers that " 'our allegiance is [not] to Nature [but] to the King,' " he is not speaking metaphorically: the king he has in mind is George III, and he is calling upon his officers to reject the natural in favor, not of the supernatural, but of the artificial, in the form of a particular, imperfect social order. They have in fact, he reminds them, already made that choice, for

"in receiving our commissions we in the most important regards ceased to be natural free agents. When war is declared, are we the commissioned fighters previously consulted? We fight at command. If our judgments approve the war, that is but coincidence. . . . So now. For suppose condemnation to follow these present proceedings. Would it be so much we ourselves that would condemn as it would be martial law operating through us? For that law and the rigor of it, we are not responsible. Our vowed responsibility is in this: That however pitilessly that law may operate in any instance, we nevertheless adhere to it and administer it."[55]

Billy, on the other hand, has participated in no such compact, has signed away nothing. Born outside the law as a natural child, he remains "little more than a sort of upright barbarian, much . . . as Adam presumably might have been ere the urbane Serpent wriggled himself into his company." He wears, it is true, though not by choice, "the external uniform of civilization," but this is a matter of the surface only: his peculiar virtues, "pristine and unadulterate," derive "from a period

54 *Ibid.*, p. 734.

55 *Ibid.*, pp. 714–15.

prior to Cain's city and citified man."[56] Yet, he is no anarchist. His loyalty is no less true than Vere's, but it is a simpler and far less abstract thing—essentially a sort of heartfelt personal gratitude and love: " 'I have eaten the King's bread and I am true to the King.' "[57] Such a sentiment has much less to recommend it to the "thoroughly civilized" mind than has the "austere patriotism" of Claggart[58]—so serviceable to authority, so zealous for order, so irrespective of persons. And where artificial virtues are thus honored above the natural, evil is certain to prosper: "Civilization, especially if of the austerer sort, is auspicious to it. It folds itself in the mantle of respectability."[59] Each finds that it can make use of the other. A sense, upon a prior occasion, of something "superserviceable and strained" about Claggart's zeal has not led Vere to dispense with the informer's services. And in the end it is through Vere that Claggart's wish for Billy's destruction is accomplished, and by Vere's refusal to publish the truth that the lie of Claggart's fidelity and Billy's depravity gains acceptance as the authorized account.

Vere's excessive intellectuality is a second consideration aligning him with his despised but useful master-at-arms. The simple and unsophisticated Billy is an illiterate, endowed only with "that kind and degree of intelligence going along with the unconventional rectitude of a sound human creature, one to whom not yet has been proffered the questionable apple of knowledge."[60] But Claggart's "general aspect and manner" hint of an education quite above the demands of his office, and "his brow [is] of the sort phrenologically associated with more than average intellect."[61] (It is upon this forehead, "so shapely and intellectual-looking a feature in the master-at-arms," that Billy's fatal blow is later to fall.)[62] Billy's face, on the other

[56] *Ibid.*, pp. 647–49; see also p. 696.

[57] *Ibid.*, p. 709.

[58] *Ibid.*, p. 666.

[59] *Ibid.*, pp. 674–75.

[60] *Ibid.*, pp. 648–49.

[61] *Ibid.*, p. 662.

[62] *Ibid.*, p. 702.

hand, is "without the intellectual look of the pallid Claggart's, [but] none the less [is] it lit, like his, from within, though from a different source. The bonfire in his heart [makes] luminous the rose-tan in his cheek."[63]

Lacking as he is in any qualities that might be called brilliant,[64] Captain Vere is one of those who live by the head. His "philosophical austerity"[65] leaves little room for feeling. Exhibiting "a marked leaning toward everything intellectual," he reads much and thoughtfully, if within a rather narrow range, preferring those books which treat of "actual men and events" —the world as it is—to those which address the imagination.[66] These "unshared studies[,] modifying and tempering the practical training of an active career," have the effect of making him seem to certain of his fellow officers somewhat "pedantic" and remote from life—"a dry and bookish gentleman."[67] "A certain dreaminess of mood" comes over him at times which, when unavoidably broken in upon by a subordinate, may be transformed into a flash of unexpected but instantly controlled anger. Control is perhaps his most marked characteristic. Habitually grave in his bearing, he has "little appreciation of mere humor," and is by rigorous training, if not by nature, "the most undemonstrative of men."[68] His is "a mind resolute to surmount difficulties even if against primitive instincts strong as the wind and the sea."[69] The problem which Billy's impulsive act has placed before the court appears to him a practical one to be settled on purely rational grounds. Fearful of the still insufficiently "formalized humanity" of his officers, he warns them not to admit the heart to their councils:

"But the exceptional in the matter moves the hearts within you. Even so too is mine moved. But let not warm hearts betray heads that should be cool. Ashore in a criminal case will an upright

63 *Ibid.*, p. 677.
64 *Ibid.*, p. 659.
65 *Ibid.*, p. 736.
66 *Ibid.*, p. 660.

67 *Ibid.*, p. 661
68 *Ibid.*, pp. 658–59.
69 *Ibid.*, p. 713.

judge allow himself off the bench to be waylaid by some tender kinswoman of the accused seeking to touch him with her tearful plea? Well the heart, sometimes the feminine in man, here is as that piteous woman, and hard though it be, she must here be ruled out."[70]

The officers, less intellectually agile than he, seem not to notice the flaw in his analogy—at any rate do not venture to point out that what the heart asks in this case is not gratuitous mercy but ordinary justice, which is never disregardful of intent. But they remain "less convinced than agitated by the course of [his] argument."[71] When, finally, they do yield, it is not because their "scruples" have been dissipated but because they have been overawed by Vere's superior mind and crowded into action by his representations of urgency.[72] They have been given, too, their captain's personal assurance that he sympathizes with his victim as deeply as they; and in that knowledge there is perhaps some comfort for them, if no help for Billy. " 'Budd's intent or non-intent [Vere has earlier instructed them] is nothing to the purpose' "; their concern must be with his deed alone.[73] Fortunately, it is quite otherwise with the judges' act: here it is the intent and not the deed that matters. " 'I feel as you do for this unfortunate boy [Vere assures them]. But did he know our hearts, I take him to be of that generous nature that he would feel even for us on whom in this military necessity so heavy a compulsion is laid.' "[74]

The nature of that alleged compulsion deserves a more careful examination. Vere, is, to begin with, no simple impressed seaman but an officer and therefore a volunteer. He is also, as Melville is at some pains to emphasize, a mature, thoughtful, and morally sensitive man who presumably knew what he was doing when he accepted his commission and so placed himself in the service of a military code whose brutishness he abhors.[75]

[70] *Ibid.*, p. 715.

[71] *Ibid.*

[72] *Ibid.*, pp. 717–18.

[73] *Ibid.*, p. 716.

[74] *Ibid.*, p. 717.

[75] *Ibid.*, p. 716.

If, as he now intimates, his buttons and epaulets were purchased at the cost of his independence as a moral being, it must be admitted that the bargain was his own. His reason for making it seems clear enough from the evidence furnished us: he is deeply, indeed fanatically, committed to the maintenance of the established order as the sole means of preserving "the peace of the world and the true welfare of mankind."[76] And as the happiness of the human species seems to him dependent upon "lasting institutions," so these in turn rest upon the disciplined strength of the British fleet, "the right arm of a Power then all but the sole free conservative one of the Old World."[77] With so clear a view of the steps leading to "the true welfare of mankind," it is not surprising that in what seems to him a grave emergency Vere should dismiss the voice of conscience as an irrelevance,[78] relegate the whole question of moral intent to the leisured speculations of casuists and "psychologic theologians," and resign himself with an almost Plinlimmonish acquiescence to the unattainability of true justice this side of " 'the Last Assizes.' "[79]

Clearly, it is for this world that Captain Vere's most anxious cares are felt. The interests of the next world are represented locally by the chaplain, and the captain is no doubt happy to reciprocate that gentleman's religious care not to over-step the limits of his jurisdiction.[80] Like every sensible commander, he takes the navy as he finds it, accepting philosophically such established evils as impressment, spying, and flogging.[81] He conducts the business of his ship strictly according to China time; and if God chooses to send one of His Greenwich chronometers aboard, He does so at His own risk. " 'Struck dead

76 *Ibid.*, pp. 660–61, 734.

77 *Ibid.*, p. 651.

78 *Ibid.*, pp. 715–16.

79 *Ibid.*, pp. 711–12, 714, 716.

80 *Ibid.*, p. 727.

81 *Ibid.*, pp. 696–97, 666, 695, 666–67.

by an angel of God,' " Vere exclaims as he looks down at the
fallen Claggart. " 'Yet the angel must hang!' "[82] One is reminded of the answer of another practical man in an earlier
book when begged to intercede for the life of a boy condemned
to death for a cause of conscience: " 'Speak not,' said Media.
'His fate is fixed. Let [the world] stand.' "[83]

But one must be careful—as Melville himself is—not to
make a monster of Vere. He is neither a sadist nor a conscious
hypocrite. If he is cruel, if he is sometimes not wholly honest
with himself and others, these faults are rather the consequences of a principled expediency and an excessive caution.

Caution is, of course, constitutional with him. As the rule of
the heart declares itself in an impulsiveness bordering at times
on rashness, so the rule of the head is commonly evidenced by
a habit of guarded circumspection. Claggart, for instance, is
gifted with "an uncommon prudence" and brings to the ac-
complishment of his irrational aim "a cool judgment[,] sagacious and sound."[84] And Captain Vere, on his part, would
seem to be the very soul of caution. Of his personal courage, of
course, there can be no serious question: that has already
been proved in a number of naval engagements.[85] But where
the safety of his ship—and, by extension, of the fleet and civilization—seems to him concerned, he becomes suspicious and
fearful in the extreme.

The master-at-arms, it appears, knows this trait of his captain well enough and plays upon it adroitly—almost too adroitly, since he arouses his anger—when giving "evidence" against
Billy at the mainmast.[86] Vere impatiently brushes aside the
imputation of fear on his part; but the seed has been planted
with Iago-like cunning and almost immediately begins to put

[82] *Ibid.*, p. 703.

[83] *Mardi*, II, 30 (chap. cxii).

[84] *Billy Budd*, in *The Portable Melville*, pp. 680, 675.

[85] *Ibid.*, pp. 657–58.

[86] *Ibid.*, pp. 695–96.

forth shoots. Fearfulness certainly lies behind Vere's strange decision to test the informer's truthfulness by a private confrontation with the accused rather than by a formal examination of witnesses.[87] What legally admissible evidence he could hope to obtain by such a confrontation is not at all clear, but what does in point of fact happen is that he himself thereby sets up the fatal situation and invites disaster. The point was not lost upon that "self-poised character of . . . grave sense and experience," the ship's surgeon. Leaving Vere's cabin under a strict injunction of secrecy after certifying the death of the master-at-arms,

he could not help thinking how more than futile the utmost discretion sometimes proves in this human sphere, subject as it is to unforeseeable fatalities; the prudent method adopted by Captain Vere to obviate publicity and trouble having resulted in an event that necessitated the former, and, under existing circumstances in the navy, indefinitely magnified the latter.[88]

And with Claggart now dead at Billy's hand, the same spirit of fearfulness dictates the secrecy and precipitation of Vere's action in calling a drumhead court-martial: "Feeling that unless quick action were taken on it, the deed of the Foretopman, so soon as it should be known on the gun-decks, would tend to awaken any slumbering embers of the Nore [Mutiny] among the crew, a sense of the urgency of the case overruled in Captain Vere every other consideration."[89] Justice, clearly, is such a consideration. He has known from the first that " 'the angel must hang,' "[90] and in the light of this prejudgment of the case the body he convokes appears less a court of law than a convenient instrument of his will.

A not entirely disinterested prudence, the narrator hints, underlies Vere's decision to proceed against Billy by court-

[87] *Ibid.*, pp. 698–99.
[88] *Ibid.*, p. 704.
[89] *Ibid.*, p. 707.
[90] *Ibid.*, p. 703; see also p. 711.

martial rather than by the open exercise of those summary powers legally his as captain:

... though a conscientious disciplinarian he was no lover of authority for mere authority's sake. Very far was he from embracing opportunities for monopolizing to himself the perils of moral responsibility—none at least that could properly be referred to an official superior or shared with him by his official equals or even subordinates. So thinking, he was glad it would not be at variance with usage to turn the matter over to a summary court of his own officers, reserving to himself as the one on whom the ultimate accountability would rest, the right of maintaining a supervision of it, or formally or informally interposing at need.[91]

And interpose he does, repeatedly and in such a manner as to make the trial seem little more than the rehearsal of a written script. So far as actual function is concerned, the members of the court are mere bystanders: Vere is at once Billy's accuser, his jury, and his judge. The officers he has chosen, not without some misgivings of their good nature,[92] are simple, honest, and modest men, "without the faculty, [almost without] the inclination to gainsay one whom they [feel] to be an earnest man, one too not less their superior in mind than in naval rank."[93] As a result, Vere is able to manipulate them as he will, reducing the moral problem to a mere question of the mechanical infraction of a law, misrepresenting their desire for justice as overscrupulosity or baseless sentiment, confusing the issue by making the real question of the prisoner's intent seem to depend upon an understanding (by definition impossible) of "the mystery of iniquity" in Claggart, and—which proves decisive with them—impressing them with his own fears of "the practical consequences" of either an acquittal or a mitigation of the full penalty.[94] "In brief, Billy Budd was formally

91 *Ibid.*, pp. 707–8.

92 *Ibid.*, p. 708.

93 *Ibid.*, pp. 717–18.

94 *Ibid.*, pp. 711–12, 714–15, 712–14, 718, 716–17.

convicted and sentenced to be hung at the yard-arm in the early morning-watch. . . ."[95]

It is sometimes argued in Vere's defense that his fears, viewed in context and without the benefit of hindsight, are entirely reasonable and proper: he has not simply imagined either the revolutionary unrest of Europe or the recent mutinies in the British fleet. And if this is so, his defenders continue, the action he takes must be considered both wise and courageous: he has no other meaningful alternative.

Now to argue in this way is of course to beg the question of the rightness of expediency as a principle of action. The conclusion follows from the given premise only for him whose watch is set to China time. Another man, less firmly committed to the ultimate value of particular institutions, might admit Vere's estimate of the situation to be entirely correct and yet regard his choice of a course of action as unquestionably wrong.

But coming down, as White-Jacket offered to do in the manner of flogging,[96] "from the lofty mast-head of an eternal principle" to the practical level of the quarter-deck, one may note in *Billy Budd* several passages that seem plainly intended to cast doubt on the necessity for Vere's action even on grounds of expediency.

For one, Vere has not the least grain of particular evidence that disaffection actually exists aboard his ship. Claggart, for all his "ferreting genius" and his obvious wish to frighten his commander, has been able to bring forward nothing of a specific nature beyond his vague charge against Billy—which charge Vere does not believe.[97] Nor does the reader—and surely this is no oversight on Melville's part—have any evidence withheld from the captain. The general situation, it is true, is such as to justify watchfulness, but not alarm.[98] Mere possibil-

---

[95] *Ibid.*, p. 719.
[96] *White-Jacket*, p. 184 (chap. xxxvi).
[97] *Billy Budd*, in *The Portable Melville*, pp. 695–98.
[98] *Ibid.*, pp. 656–57.

ity is a long step from that near-certainty of impending revolt which moves Vere at the trial to insist upon the death penalty.[99] The *might-be*, like the *might-have-been*, "is but boggy ground to build on."[100] Vere's surmise gains little support from the behavior of the men at those three later moments when the greatest strain is placed upon their loyalties. They receive his announcement of the death sentence with the unprotesting "dumbness . . . of a seated congregation of believers in hell listening to the clergyman's announcement of his Calvinistic text."[101] At the moment of Billy's execution, they echo, like good Calvinists, "with one voice from alow and aloft," the prisoner's last cry, " 'God bless Captain Vere!' "[102] And when their shipmate's body is tipped into the sea, their mood appears less one of anger against their officers than of awe before the seeming prodigies of Billy's peaceful death and that strange "croaked requiem" of the seabirds continuing to circle "the burial-spot astern."[103] Taking all in all, it is hard to see in the captain's fears anything more than the fantasies of a mind by nature somewhat pedantically abstract[104] and by the usages of office walled off from any direct contact with the particular realities of life aboard his ship.

But were one to admit the existence of latent discontent aboard the "Indomitable," one could still question the assertion that Vere has no reasonable alternative to the course he takes. He himself, before the convoking of the court, briefly considers one such alternative: to defer "taking any action whatever respecting it, further than to keep the Foretopman a close prisoner till the ship [now on detached duty] rejoined the squadron and then submitting the matter to the judgment of his Admiral."[105] The same has already occurred, and independently, to the ship's officers and to the surgeon, the latter at least a man most guarded in the drawing of inferences.[106] But

99 *Ibid.*, p. 717.

100 *Ibid.*, p. 655.

101 *Ibid.*, p. 722.

102 *Ibid.*, p. 729.

103 *Ibid.*, p. 733.

104 *Ibid.*, p. 661.

105 *Ibid.*, p. 707.

106 *Ibid.*, p. 704–5, 730–31.

Captain Vere dismisses the thought almost as soon as it comes, "feeling that unless quick action were [to be] taken on it, the deed of the Foretopman, so soon as it should be known on the gun-decks, would tend to awaken any slumbering embers of the Nore among the crew."[107] The word *any* seems not without significance here: Vere knows of no such embers; but he is fearful, and that fear itself dictates a secrecy which forbids his seeking evidence.[108] He is in this not unlike Claggart whose covert hatred, feeding upon a suspected injury, by its very "secretiveness voluntarily cuts [itself] off from enlightenment or disillusion; and, not unreluctantly, action is taken upon surmise as upon certainty."[109]

A still stronger indication of the narrator's belief that an alternative—and a practicable alternative—exists is given us, with an elaborate apology for "divergence" from "the main road," in the implied comparison of Vere and Lord Nelson.[110] Although Vere is nowhere explicitly compared with the admiral, the qualities attributed to this " 'greatest sailor since the world began' " bring the lesser man's own qualities, by the force of contrast, unavoidably to mind.[111] When we read of Nelson's almost vainglorious splendor of appearance, we are reminded of Vere's civilian look, his "unobtrusiveness of demeanor," as of "some highly honorable discreet envoy" visiting the quarter-deck.[112] The description of Nelson as a "reckless declarer of his person in fight" reminds us that Vere is "intrepid to the verge of temerity, but never injudiciously so."[113] Nelson—for all that he is "painfully circumspect" in his

---

107 *Ibid.*, p. 707.

108 *Ibid.*, pp. 698–99, 706–7.

109 *Ibid.*, p. 680.

110 *Ibid.*, pp. 653–57.

111 The quoted phrase is twice repeated (*ibid.*, pp. 653, 655), as if for emphasis. We may note also that the guarded praise of Vere by his fellow officers (*ibid.*, p. 661) is so phrased as to invite the comparison with Lord Nelson.

112 *Ibid.*, pp. 656, 658.   113 *Ibid.*, pp. 655, 658.

preparations for battle—invites by his rashness and bravado the reproof of the "martial utilitarians" and "the Benthamites of war."[114] The lodging of such a charge against Captain Vere would strike us as preposterous; but he does not by this immunity rise in our estimation: "Personal prudence, even when dictated by quite other than selfish considerations, surely is no special virtue in a military man; while an excessive love of glory, impassioning a less burning impulse[,] the honest sense of duty, is the first."[115]

But all this is in preparation for the passage which most unmistakably points up the contrast between the two men:

Discontent foreran the Two Mutinies, and more or less it lurkingly survived them. Hence it was not unreasonable to apprehend some return of trouble sporadic or general. One instance of such apprehensions: In the same year with this story, Nelson, then Vice-Admiral Sir Horatio, being with the fleet off the Spanish coast, was directed by the Admiral in command to shift his pennant from the *Captain* to the *Theseus;* and for this reason: that the latter ship having newly arrived on the station from home where it had taken part in the Great Mutiny, danger was apprehended from the temper of the men; and it was thought that an officer like Nelson was the one, not indeed to terrorise the crew into base subjection, but to win them, by force of his mere presence and heroic personality, back to an allegiance, if not as enthusiastic as his own, yet as true. So it was that for a time on more than one quarter-deck anxiety did exist.[116]

But how different the actions to which these apprehensions led!

---

[114] *Ibid.*, pp. 654–55.   [115] *Ibid.*, p. 655.

[116] *Ibid.*, pp. 656–57. One may recall also that in an earlier book of Melville's, "the Great Sailor" is called to the stand as an expert witness against flogging, a mode of discipline to which Vere (*ibid.*, pp. 666–67) has shown himself not wholly averse: "It is well known that Lord Nelson himself, in point of policy, was averse to flogging; and that, too, when he had witnessed the mutinous effects of government abuses in the navy . . . which to the terror of all England, developed themselves at the great mutiny of the Nore: an outbreak that for several weeks jeopardized the very existence of the British navy" (*White-Jacket,* p. 186, chap. xxxvi).

To " 'respect the omens of ill' " is of course never unreasonable: " 'evil is the chronic malady of the universe; and checked in one place, breaks forth in another.' "[117] So "discontent" in some sense "lurkingly survived" its suppression at the Nore, and the possibility of its reappearance is something no responsible commander can safely ignore. This much is true. But what is perhaps " 'the grand error' " of Captain Vere, as of other doctrinaire and wholly committed men, is " 'the general supposition, that the very special Diabolus is abroad; whereas, the very special Diabolus has been abroad ever since [the world] began.' "[118] The year A.D. 1797 is not the first time the world has stood in crisis:

> "By Fate's decree
> Have not earth's vitals heaved in change
> Repeated? some wild element
> Or action been evolved? the range
> Of surface split? the deeps unpent?
> Continents in God's cauldrons cast?
> And this without effecting so
> The neutralising of the past,
> Whose rudiments persistent flow,
> From age to age transmitting, own,
> The evil with the good."[119]

And if the world has rallied from these convulsions sufficiently to continue, this is to be credited less to human foresight than to the presence, in that "persistent flow," of a " 'good which lets [the] evil last.' "[120] Since no man reads the future, "let us revere that sacred uncertainty which forever impends over men and nations."[121] The ebb and flow of good and evil is a movement to be traced not only in the general advance and retreat

[117] *Mardi*, II, 244 (chap. clxi).

[118] *Ibid.*, p. 238 (chap. clxi).

[119] *Clarel*, I, 137 (Part I, canto xxxiv).

[120] *Ibid.*, II, 240 (Part IV, canto xix).

[121] "Supplement" to *Battle-Pieces*, in *Poems*, p. 186.

of tides but in the thrust and withdrawal of each separate wave. Melville found this truth of sufficient importance to what he was saying in *Billy Budd* for him to devote his entire preface to it:

The opening proposition made by the Spirit of that Age, involved the rectification of the Old World's hereditary wrongs. In France to some extent this was bloodily effected. But what then? Straightway the Revolution itself became a wrongdoer, one more oppressive than the Kings. Under Napoleon it enthroned upstart kings, and initiated that prolonged agony of continual war whose final throe was Waterloo. During those years not the wisest could have foreseen that the outcome of all would be what to some thinkers apparently it has since turned out to be, a political advance along nearly the whole line for Europeans.

Now as elsewhere hinted, it was something caught from the Revolutionary Spirit that at Spithead emboldened the man-of-war's men to rise against real abuses, long-standing ones, and afterwards at the Nore to make inordinate and aggressive demands, successful resistance to which was confirmed only when the ringleaders were hung for an admonitory spectacle to the anchored fleet. Yet in a way analogous to the operation of the Revolution at large the Great Mutiny, though by Englishmen naturally deemed monstrous at the time, doubtless gave the first latent prompting to most important reforms in the British Navy.[122]

Could one forbid events, as the censor forbids books, the task of choosing those events would not be easy. For "in all things man sows upon the wind, which bloweth just where it listeth; for ill or good, man cannot know. Often ill comes from the good, as good from the ill."[123]

There is a sense in which *Benito Cereno* and *Billy Budd* may be said to complement each other. Each is essentially a study in blindness: as Captain Delano in the one is blind to the strength and permanence of evil, so in the other Captain Vere cannot see that good has the power to maintain itself, if never

---

[122] *Billy Budd*, in *The Portable Melville*, pp. 637–38.

[123] "The Encantadas," in *The Piazza Tales*, p. 227.

wholly to prevail, in a world where it seems always at the point
of extinction. Still less does Vere realize that it is by its own
intrinsic power that it survives and not through any devices
borrowed from its opposite. The good which in this instance
eventually comes from the evil of the young sailor's death owes
nothing at all to Vere's supposed foresight—with regard to
which that death must appear wholly futile and meaningless—
and everything to the simple fact of Billy's own goodness silently operating upon the hearts of men. It is the crowning
weakness of expediency that it so often turns out not to have
been expedient at all. Captain Vere, dying of his wound at Gi-
braltar, is perhaps fortunate in being cut off before attaining
to this humiliating knowledge and to the remorse which must
have followed it.[124] The rest of us, realizing what little control
man has over the consequences of his actions, may find in
Vere's story encouragement to risk the luxury of at least following our own conscience.

[124] *Billy Budd,* in *The Portable Melville,* p. 736.

5. *Armed Neutrality*

THE WAY OF WISDOM

The adversary against which man finds himself pitted is, it is true, finally invincible. Yet there is for Melville an immense difference of value between the submitters and the non-submitters. Greatness is not measured by success. To say this, however, is not to argue that the one worthy course of action is defiance. The heroism of that path most of us are more ready to acknowledge than to emulate. As ordinary men, we feel that we are called to a less lofty height, though perhaps a more reasonable one. The persistence of self seems to us the principal term of victory, and the hero's uncompromising anger we see as noble but leading only to self-destruction. There are some natures, we realize, so constituted that they can take no other path: they do what they must, and watching them we can only wonder and refrain from judging in a case so different from our own. But if it is not given to all of us to see and to accept our " 'topmost greatness in [our] topmost grief,' " we are not therefore driven to surrender. There remains to us a third course, nearly as difficult as the second, but more proportioned to our strength and grounded in a more balanced, if less intense, vision of reality. This is the path of acceptance, of what may be called "armed neutrality."

The attitude so named may be further described as one of resistance without defiance and acceptance without surrender, of an indifference that is not apathy and an affirmation free of all illusion. It is rooted in the single vision of dark and bright, in a firm sense of the unitary character of all experience. In a perspective so enlarged, one sees beyond the personal and the immediate into a clearer atmosphere where objects appear in their truer proportions. One sees that the world, like the ocean, "brims with natural griefs and tragedies; and into that watery immensity of terror, man's private grief is lost like a drop."[1] Melville would seem to speak from a personal experience of this sort in the quatrain "Pebbles VII," published near the end of his life:

> Healed of my hurt, I laud the inhuman Sea—
> Yea, bless the Angels Four that there convene;
> For healed I am even by their pitiless breath
> Distilled in wholesome dew named rosmarine.[2]

SPIES IN
THE WORLD'S CAMP

The state of mind of which we here speak is most explicitly set forth, if not most dramatically developed, in the brief sketch of "the easy, indifferent Haut-

---

[1] *Israel Potter*, p. 11 (chap. ii).

[2] *Poems*, p. 244.

boy," the ruined genius of Melville's story "The Fiddler." A musical prodigy who " 'in boyhood drained the whole flagon of glory,' " he is left in maturity with little money and only the lees of his fame. But neither hardship nor obscurity can dampen his genuine enjoyment of living: he is equally delighted by the freaks of a clown at the circus and the turns of an intellectual conversation with a friend. A "serene expression of leisurely, deep good sense" marks everything he says:

In most of his remarks upon a variety of topics Hautboy seemed intuitively to hit the exact line between enthusiasm and apathy. It was plain that while Hautboy saw the world pretty much as it was, yet he did not theoretically espouse its bright side nor its dark side. Rejecting all solutions, he but acknowledged facts. What was sad in the world he did not superficially gainsay; what was glad in it he did not cynically slur; and all which was to him personally enjoyable, he gratefully took to his heart. It was plain, then—so it seemed at that moment, at least—that his extraordinary cheerfulness did not arise either from deficiency of feeling or thought.[3]

Jimmy Rose is another such victor over fortune. Financially ruined, he is at first bitterly misanthropic and for some years drops out of sight; but he returns at last to live out his later years in cheerful good humor as a pensioner of his one-time equals—"peep[ing] about among the marbles and mahoganies for contumelious tea and toast where once like a very Warwick he had feasted the huzzaing world with Burgundy and venison."[4] Both he and Hautboy are men who, having died once to earthly desire, enjoy now a second life of autumnal serenity and freedom like that Lear looked for but was not to find when led off with Cordelia to prison. They, and an unknown number like them, live on as "spies in the world's camp," content to be taken by the crowd as impractical "strolling simpletons," since, being "quite done with the world, all

---

[3] "The Fiddler," in *Billy Budd and Other Prose Pieces*, p. 222–23.

[4] "Jimmy Rose," in *ibid.*, p. 267.

its mere worldly contents are become so far indifferent, that they care little of what mere worldly imprudence they may be guilty."[5]

But what is perhaps most remarkable about these men is that renunciation has not made ascetics of them. Theirs is no life of sad abnegation and denial: they relish life and affirm it as the partisans cannot. They have rediscovered, somehow, that forgotten center of stillness far within, and they take from it now a joy and a vitality which remain constant in spite of outer circumstance. Ishmael's exhortation seems realized in them:

Oh, man! admire and model thyself after the whale! Do thou, too, remain warm among ice. Do thou, too, live in this world without being of it. Be cool at the Equator; keep thy blood fluid at the Pole. Like the great dome of St. Peter's, and like the great whale, retain, O man! in all seasons a temperature of thine own.[6]

From the same secret source, clearly, springs Merrymusk's proud self-sufficiency—a spirit which finds its outward embodiment in the exultant and flamboyant crow of his "noble cock," Trumpet: "Clear, shrill, full of pluck, full of fire, full of fun, full of glee." The cock's repeated cries take their occasion from no external event: "He seemed to have nothing to do with any other concern. He replied to no other crow, but crowed solely by himself, on his own account, in solitary scorn and independence."[7] The narrator—a country gentleman weighed down by his debts, the bad weather, and a sense of universal calamity—listens to it in amazement: "Plain as cock could speak, it said: 'Let the world and all aboard of it go to pot. Do you be jolly, and never say die. What's the world compared to you? What is it anyhow but a lump of loam? Do you be jolly!' "[8] But the crow did not, for all its self-assurance,

---

[5] *Pierre*, p. 310 (Book XV, chap. i).

[6] *Moby-Dick*, II, 33 (chap. lxviii).

[7] "Cock-a-Doodle-Doo!" in *Billy Budd and Other Prose Pieces*, pp. 153–54.

[8] *Ibid.*, p. 160.

sound like the foolish, vain-glorious crow of some young sopho-
morean cock, who knew not the world, and was beginning life in
audacious gay spirits because in wretched ignorance of what might
be to come. It was the crow of a cock who crowed not without advice; the crow of a cock who knew a thing or two; the crow of a
cock who had fought the world and got the better of it, and was
now resolved to crow, though the earth should heave and the heavens should fall. It was a wise crow; an invincible crow; a philosophic crow; a crow of all crows.[9]

With this sound in his ears, the downcast narrator feels the
birth within him of a new feeling, a sort of "calm, good-natured rapture of defiance." And in much the same spirit, when
their time comes, the poor workingman Merrymusk and his invalid family die, with no trace of bitterness or regret, at the
very top of a triumphant crow.[10]

A schooled but still overflowing heart is again the secret of
one of the more interesting of the minor characters in *Clarel:*
the retired Mexican revolutionist, Don Hannibal Rohon Del
Aquaviva. Appearing in fewer than a dozen pages of the poem,
he yet serves as an effective foil to two of the principal characters, Derwent and Ungar, and so helps to define a mean between the empty optimism of the one and the unhoping bitterness of the other. That he has known suffering and loss is evident in his dangling sleeve and wooden leg, and he himself
bears eloquent witness to the extent of his disillusionment with
democracy and progress.[11] Yet "a nature bright [and] beam-
ing" as Captain Boomer's and the humorous trick of seeing
himself in perspective have preserved him from a too-exclusive
concern with either his own or the world's woes. Like his grim
Carthaginian namesake, he began by swearing upon his country's altar eternal enmity against wrong; but time has mellowed
him and he has long since forgotten his oath.

[9] *Ibid.*, pp. 152–53.

[10] *Ibid.*, pp. 170–71.

[11] *Clarel*, II, 236–38 (Part IV, canto xix).

When he first stumps onto the scene, he comes shouting a hearty echo to Ungar's overheard cry for "penalty" on sinful man; but it is not long before we realize that his is not the nature to persist in that demand. His friend Derwent offers to introduce him and begins with praise of his military exploits, but Don Hannibal cuts him short:

> "Hidalgos, I am, as ye see,
> Just a poor cripple—that is all;
> A cripple, yet contrive to hop
> Far off from Mexic liberty,
> Thank God! I lost these limbs for that;
> And would that they were mine again,
> And all were back to former state—
> I, Mexico, and poor Old Spain.
>
> .   .   .   .
>
> Oh, 'tis the sorriest thing! In me
> A *reformado* reformed ye see."

The humorless Ungar, scenting here a bitterness to match his own hatred of the leveling democracy in his America, lights up in sympathy. Derwent, more familiar with the tone, ignores the substance; he is equally certain that his friend speaks only in jest and so calls upon him to join in countering Ungar's "sore disparagement of man." But Don Hannibal turns on him:

> "You think I'll ban?
> Disparage him with all my heart!
> What villain takes the rascal's part?
> Advance the argument."[12]

Derwent is not the man to face such odds, and lightly turns aside the conversation. But Ungar will not be stopped and bursts out in a violent attack upon democracy, that "archstrumpet of an impious age." Before he is done, Don Hannibal's mood is quite altered. As Derwent later explains, " 'This man / . . . likes not grave talk, / The settled undiluted tone; /

[12] *Ibid.*, pp. 238–39 (Part IV, canto xix).

It does his humorous nature baulk.' "[13] At any rate, the Don's only comment now is a judicious remark upon the speaker's manner: " 'By Cotopaxi, a brave vent!' " he tells Ungar. And with a pinch of snuff and a murmured word of his coming dinner, he excuses himself and limps away.[14] But it is the over-earnestness that he objects to, not the facts themselves. He is ready enough to acknowledge the harsher realities, as the shocked Derwent learns a day or two later when he visits a monastery workshop and finds the old warrior comfortably ensconced in an up-ended coffin while he gossips with a friend.[15]

We may be reminded at this point of another and more important of Melville's characters, the sailor Ishmael. For to him also, no part of human experience is foreign or inadmissible:

I am tormented [he tells us] with an everlasting itch for things remote. I love to sail forbidden seas, and land on barbarous coasts. Not ignoring what is good, I am quick to perceive a horror, and could still be social with it—would they let me—since it is but well to be on friendly terms with all the inmates of the place one lodges in.[16]

But the attitude here described is not, in point of fact, a wholly accurate description of Ishmael's state of mind at the time the story begins. We must distinguish at all times between the experiencing actor and the more sophisticated narrator, between Ishmael-then and Ishmael-now. And the Ishmael to whom we are first introduced is a splenetic fellow, rather "grim about the mouth" and on far from friendly terms with even the more amiable of his fellow inmates: he can barely restrain himself from "stepping into the street and methodically knocking people's hats off." He takes to sea, it is clear, as much from a dislike of the familiar as from a love of the remote. His very

---

13 *Ibid.*, p. 242 (Part V, canto xx).

14 *Ibid.*, pp. 240–41 (Part IV, canto xix).

15 *Ibid.*, p. 258 (Part IV, canto xxv).

16 *Moby-Dick*, I, 7 (chap. i).

name, self-chosen as it clearly is, indicates the relation in which he feels himself to stand toward life and human society: he is the outcast, the wrongfully disinherited, the non-sharer in the promise. But Ishmael-now, the narrator, is a quite different person. His experiences, chief among them the witnessing of Ahab's tragedy and the loss of the "Pequod," have matured him. He no longer looms quite so large on his own horizon. Patience and good humor have taken the place of anger and rebellion. These earlier personal sorrows are neither denied nor forgotten, but he has learned to see them in a wider perspective and even with a touch of humor. Let "some old hunks of a sea-captain" order him about, if he must: his integrity as an individual is not touched. For "everybody else is one way or another served in much the same way—either in a physical or metaphysical point of view, that is; and so the universal thump is passed round, and all hands should rub each other's shoulder-blades, and be content."[17]

Something of Ishmael's movement from his first to his last state—from anger to acceptance—can be learned from a careful reading of those passages in which he is directly concerned with evaluating his own experiences. But we must not expect to uncover an exact sequence of steps composing a whole and connected action. For though Ishmael's experience does provide the frame within which the story is set, the story itself is Ahab's and not Ishmael's; and to have heightened, beyond a certain point, the coherence of the subplot would have been to draw it improperly into the foreground of the reader's attention. What Melville does instead is gradually to prepare us for the fact of Ishmael's transformation (the actual moment of which is never shown us) by the repeated statement and restatement, in so many isolated symbolic acts, of the theme of reconciliation.

The first of these acts is Ishmael's acceptance of the canni-

[17] *Ibid.,* p. 5 (chap. i).

bal Queequeg as his bedfellow and friend at Peter Coffin's inn
in New Bedford. The acquaintance, it is true, has been more
thrust upon him than sought out, but his decision to share a
blanket with this "clean, comely looking cannibal" nevertheless represents a significant step forward. Before that event,
Ishmael—friendless and almost penniless in a strange town on
"a very dark and dismal night, bitingly cold and cheerless"[18]
—feels himself already thrust forth from the congregation of
the living into that outer darkness threatened in the Gospel.
Afterward, reflecting upon the "loving and affectionate manner" in which he has been received, he is astonished at the effect upon himself: "I began to be sensible of strange feelings. I
felt a melting in me. No more my splintered heart and mad-
dened hand were turned against the wolfish world. This soothing savage had redeemed it."[19] But what is worth remembering
is that Ishmael was not wholly mistaken in his first impression
when "this head-peddling purple rascal" almost frightened him
into jumping out the window. The dried heads are real enough,
and the tomahawk peace pipe is quite as capable of splitting a
skull as of uniting two hearts. Ishmael has already in some
sense accepted the bright and dark in one.

The importance of Queequeg to the total action is not always fully realized. As Fedallah, symbol of the obsessive mind,
leads Ahab to his death, so Queequeg as the saving heart leads
Ishmael back to life and wholeness. Repeatedly, the action of
the book presents Queequeg in the role of savior—of Ishmael
from the cold at New Bedford; of the passenger swept overboard on the way to Nantucket; of the boat's crew lost at the
first lowering (among whom he sits with a lantern raised on a
waif-pole, "the sign and symbol of a man without faith, hopelessly holding up hope in the midst of despair"); of Tashtego,
drowning in the whale's head; of the ship about to be capsized

---

18 *Ibid.*, p. 9 (chap. ii).

19 *Ibid.*, p. 62 (chap. x).

by the sinking whale; and finally of Ishmael himself by suggesting the use of his outlived coffin as a life buoy.[20]

But Queequeg's pull upon Ishmael must contend with "the irresistible arm-drag" of Ahab and his crazed purpose—a pull so strong that Ishmael feels himself "a skiff in tow of a seventy-four."[21] When Ahab, in the quarter-deck scene, imposes his will upon the men, Ishmael has no wish to resist; and considering it later, he admits:

> I, Ishmael, was one of that crew; my shouts had gone up with the rest; my oath had been welded with theirs; and stronger I shouted, and more did I hammer and clinch my oath, because of the dread in my soul. A wild, mystical, sympathetical feeling was in me; Ahab's quenchless feud seemed mine.[22]

But there is a difference. Ahab hates Moby Dick out of a personal vindictiveness swollen to the conviction that in him lives incarnate the sum of all that has tormented and frustrated "the whole race from Adam down"; the white whale is for him all evil, and nothing but evil.[23] Ishmael's enmity, on the other hand, is largely the product of his fear. And what he fears most is none of "those mere obvious considerations"—the monster's reputed size, ferocity, and "intelligent malignity"—but something less tangible and almost beyond his own comprehension: "It was the whiteness of the whale that above all things appalled me." [24] Ishmael is careful, as narrator, to attribute this feeling to himself alone; there is no suggestion that the whiteness is to Ahab anything more than an identifying sign. But to Ishmael the fact that an object so terrible in itself should be dressed in the color immemorially associated with innocence,

[20] *Ibid.*, pp. 75–76 (chap. xiii); p. 284 (chap. xlviii); II, 77–79 (chap. lxxviii); pp. 98–99 (chap. lxxxi); pp. 305 (chap. cxxvi) and 368 ("Epilogue").

[21] *Ibid.*, I, 233 (chap. xli).

[22] *Ibid.*, p. 222 (chap. xli).

[23] *Ibid.*, pp. 229–30 (chap. xli).

[24] *Ibid.*, p. 234 (chap. xlii).

holiness, and divine purity is enough "to heighten [his] terror to the farthest bounds."[25] The thought awakens within him "the instinct of the knowledge of the demonism in the world."[26] And, vaguely, something even beyond this: the possibility that, "as in essence whiteness is not so much a color as the visible absence of color, and at the same time the concrete of all colors," so what awaits him here may not be simple evil (which would have, after all, its proper complement) but something more inclusive and less meaningful. There is the germ here of an insight from which Ahab's anger will forever exclude him.

Wisdom may be said to begin with the recognition of what must be. And in the daily business of whaling, Ishmael receives a practical schooling in the meaning of necessity. At first, the whole problem seems to him almost ridiculously easy. Working as Queequeg's "attendant or page" one dreamy afternoon at the task of weaving a sword-mat, he watches the rhythmic interplay of the fixed warp, his own shuttling hand placing the woof, and Queequeg's "impulsive, indifferent sword" absently packing the strands together, "slantingly, or crookedly, or strongly, or weakly, as the case may be." The whole seems to him an image of human life:

"chance, free will, and necessity—no wise incompatible—all interweavingly working together. The straight warp of necessity, not to be swerved from its ultimate course—its every alternating vibration, indeed, only tending to that; free will still free to ply her shuttle between given threads; and chance, though restrained in its play within the right lines of necessity, and sideways in its motions directed by free will, though thus prescribed to by both, chance by turns rules either, and has the last featuring blow at events."[27]

But as he weaves away and idly elaborates the terms of his analogy, the wild cry of "There she blows!" sounds from the

25 *Ibid.*, p. 236 (chap. xlii).

26 *Ibid.*, p. 243 (chap. xlii).

27 *Ibid.*, pp. 269–70 (chap. xlvii).

crosstrees above and "the ball of free will" drops from his hand. Within minutes, and without any consultation of his own wishes in the matter, he is in Starbuck's whaleboat and straining every muscle at an oar.

Ishmael's first lowering, thus abruptly announced, carries his education forward still farther. The whales taking alarm and running, the chase is drawn out until almost nightfall, when the boats manage to approach their quarry under cover of an approaching squall. At Starbuck's whispered command, his oarsmen, blindly driving themselves backforemost into "the life and death peril so close . . . ahead," pull the boat right up on the whale's back and Queequeg throws his harpoon. But squall, whale, and harpoon all strike together; the still unseen whale rolls "like an earthquake" beneath them; and the boat and its contents are scattered over the water. The boat is righted and the swimming men make their way back to it; but the storm has by now made rowing impossible, and the ship is nowhere in sight. With Queequeg holding a lighted lantern aloft on a waif-pole, they wait out the night and in the predawn mists barely escape, through Queequeg's watchfulness, being run down by the cruising "Pequod."[28]

The entire affair strikes Ishmael, as soon as he is hauled up on deck, as so preposterous that it is funny. The whole universe appears to him some "vast practical joke," though the point of it remains somewhat obscure; and worries, dangers, death itself—all seem so many "sly, good-natured hits, and jolly punches in the side bestowed by the unseen and unaccountable old joker" behind the scenes. Thinking still further on the nature of his calling, he considers how regularly he must resign his life into the hands of another, remembers that it is the prudent Starbuck and not the reckless Flask who has brought on the present disasters, and reminds himself "in what a devil's chase [he is] implicated, touching the White Whale." Everything considered, the time seems ripe for making his

[28] *Ibid.*, pp. 273–85 (chap. xlviii).

will; and summoning Queequeg as his "lawyer, executor, and legatee," he goes below to do so.

After the ceremony was concluded [he adds], I felt all the easier; a stone was rolled away from my heart. Besides, all the days I should now live would be as good as the days that Lazarus lived after his resurrection; a supplementary clean gain of so many months or weeks as the case might be. I survived myself; my death and burial were locked up in my chest. I looked around me tranquilly and contentedly, like a quiet ghost with a clean conscience sitting inside the bars of a snug family vault.[29]

Though the manner here is playful, the substance is not: it is part of the thematic pattern of death and rebirth that runs through the entire book, from Ishmael's "suicidal" putting to sea on the first page to his miraculous emergence from the "Pequod's" vortex on the last. Pip's tragic loss and paradoxical gain later repeats the theme: the old Pip, the coward who panics and leaps from boats, is disowned by the new Pip and left behind in the sea; the new Pip, carried beyond all thought of self to an indifference like his God's, thinks only of Ahab, fixes himself in his captain's chair " 'in the ship's full middle,' " and resolves to stay there, " 'though this stern strikes rocks; and they bulge through; and oysters come to join me.' "[30]

But Ishmael's education is only begun with his return from the first lowering. The lesson in the limits of free will begun with Starbuck's failure to consult him before ordering the whaleboat pulled up on the whale's back is continued for him in the episode of the monkey-rope at the cutting-in. To prepare for the stripping of the blubber, Queequeg is sent overside to work on the half-submerged and slippery surface of the dead whale; and as a means of insuring his safety, a long line is passed through his belt and attached at the other end to Ish-

---

[29] *Ibid.*, pp. 286–88 (chap. xlix).

[30] *Ibid.*, II, 169–70 (chap. xciii); p. 301 (chap. cxxv); p. 317 (chap. cxxix).

mael's belt on deck. A serious slip on Queequeg's part, then, if not checked by his anchor man, must unavoidably drag both of them down into the shark-infested water. The arrangement is at first not at all to Ishmael's taste:

So strongly and metaphysically did I conceive of my situation then, that while earnestly watching his motions, I seemed distinctly to perceive that my own individuality was now merged in a joint stock company of two; that my free will had received a mortal wound; and that another's mistake or misfortune might plunge innocent me into unmerited disaster and death. Therefore, I saw that here was a sort of interregnum in Providence; for its evenhanded equity never could have sanctioned so gross an injustice. And yet still further pondering—while I jerked him now and then from between the whale and the ship, which would threaten to jam him—still further pondering, I say, I saw that this situation of mine was the precise situation of every mortal that breathes; only, in most cases, he, one way or other, has this Siamese connection with a plurality of other mortals.[31]

So he ends in a philosophical acceptance of what cannot be avoided. Ahab, somewhat later, applying to the carpenter for a new leg, is struck by a sense of the same interdependency;[32] but for him there is humiliation and not comfort in the thought that his is "the precise situation of every mortal that breathes."

It is from a heightened awareness of this universal human bond that Ishmael takes the first impetus that begins his movement away from the dominance of Ahab's purpose. Sitting cross-legged on the deck with a circle of others one mild morning, tranquilly squeezing out the congealed lumps in a tub of sperm, Ishmael is rapt into a transport of fellowship—"a strange sort of insanity"—in which he all but loses for the time the sense of his individuality. The experience is reported with humorous overstatement, but the extravagance of the mood does not affect its basic validity nor lessen its relevance to the main theme:

[31] *Ibid.*, pp. 48–49 (chap. lxxii).
[32] *Ibid.*, pp. 239–40 (chap. cviii).

I declare to you [says the narrator], that for the time I lived as in a musky meadow; I forgot all about our horrible oath; in that inexpressible sperm, I washed my hands and heart of it; . . . while bathing in that bath, I felt divinely free from all ill-will, or petulance, or malice, of any sort whatsoever.

And his final retrospective glance at the episode makes the contrast with Ahab's monomania even clearer:

Would that I could keep squeezing that sperm for ever! For now, since by many prolonged, repeated experiences, I have perceived that in all cases man must eventually lower, or at least shift, his conceit of attainable felicity; not placing it anywhere in the intellect or the fancy; but in the wife, the heart, the bed, the table, the saddle, the fire-side, the country; now that I have perceived all this, I am ready to squeeze case eternally.[33]

But this last is a later insight, and what moves Ishmael at this moment is a transient mood. The tyranny of hatred is not so easily broken. Ishmael does, it is true, attain his freedom in the end and forgets both fear and anger to the point where one can imagine as his (as they could never possibly be Ahab's) those words which his creator, while engaged upon this book, addressed to Hawthorne: "If any of those other Powers choose to withhold certain secrets, let them; that does not impair my sovereignty in myself; that does not make me tributary."[34] But when it is that Ishmael actually makes this shift from head to heart, from resentment to acceptance, we are not told—it may be not until the last long dive of the "Pequod" has been taken. The moment is prefigured for us, however, in the account he gives us of the nearly fatal hallucination he undergoes one night as steersman.

Blubber is being boiled down in the open tryworks amidships, and as Ishmael holds the tiller and stares fixedly ahead

---

[33] *Ibid.*, p. 172 (chap. xciv).

[34] Letter to Nathaniel Hawthorne, June 1 (?), 1851, in Eleanor Melville Metcalf, *Herman Melville, Cycle and Epicycle* (Cambridge, Mass.: Harvard University Press, 1953), p. 105.

at the red flames and billowing smoke, the leaping shadows and "the Tartarean shapes of the pagan harpooners"—one of them his own friend Queequeg—stoking the fires, the hellish character of the scene is borne in upon him; all that is familiar vanishes and "the rushing *Pequod*, freighted with savages, and laden with fire, and burning a corpse, and plunging into that blackness of darkness, [seems] the material counterpart of her monomaniac commander's soul." Falling asleep so, open-eyed and on his feet, he is struck by a swing of the tiller and waked just far enough to become "horribly conscious of something fatally wrong." He tries to look, but cannot see the compass:

Nothing seemed before me but a jet gloom, now and then made ghastly by flashes of redness. Uppermost was the impression, that whatever swift, rushing thing I stood on was not so much bound to any haven ahead as rushing from all havens astern. A stark, bewildered feeling, as of death, came over me. Convulsively my hands grasped the tiller. . . .

and he wakes, "just in time to prevent the vessel from flying up into the wind, and very probably capsizing. . . ." In the hypnotic, half-waking state induced by his wild vision, he has completely lost his sense of direction and has been standing "fronting the ship's stern, with [his] back to her prow and the compass."[35]

So held by the fascination of darkness, not every sleeper, Ishmael knows, wakes in time to ward off disaster. Therefore,

Look not too long in the face of the fire, O man! Never dream with thy hand on the helm! Turn not thy back to the compass; accept the first hint of the hitching tiller; believe not the artificial fire, when its redness makes all things look ghastly. Tomorrow, in the natural sun, the skies will be bright; those who glared like devils in the forking flames, the morn will show in far other, at least gentler, relief; the glorious, golden, glad sun, the only true lamp—all others but liars!

[35] *Moby-Dick*, II, 179–81 (chap. xcvi).

But now the helm has been swung too far over in an effort to right the course, and it must go back. For darkness is no illusion:

[T]he sun hides not Virginia's Dismal Swamp, nor Rome's accursed Campagna, nor wide Sahara, nor all the millions of miles of deserts and of griefs beneath the moon. The sun hides not the ocean, which is the dark side of this earth, and which is two thirds of this earth. So, therefore, that mortal man who hath more of joy than sorrow in him, that mortal man cannot be true—not true, or undeveloped. With books the same. The truest of all men was the Man of Sorrows, and the truest of all books is Solomon's, and Ecclesiastes is the fine hammered steel of woe. "All is vanity." ALL.

And now the helm comes up again, in correction of this correction:

But even Solomon, he says, "the man that wandereth out of the way of understanding shall remain" (*i.e.* even while living) "in the congregation of the dead." Give not thyself up, then, to fire, lest it invert thee, deaden thee; as for the time it did me. There is a wisdom that is woe; but there is a woe that is madness.

But even here the wheel cannot come to rest. When the last correction seems made, we find ourselves facing still the plain fact of the heroic personality, not to be caught in any formula, not even wisdom's:

And there is a Catskill eagle in some souls that can alike dive down into the blackest gorges, and soar out of them again and become invisible in the sunny spaces. And even if he for ever flies within the gorge, that gorge is in the mountains; so that even in his lowest swoop the mountain eagle is still higher than other birds upon the plain, even though they soar.[36]

But the mountain eagles are few, and for them no man may venture to prescribe. Ishmael's counsel is rather for himself and for us, who must do what soaring we can manage above the

[36] *Ibid.*, pp. 181–82 (chap. xcvi).

plain of common life. And for us the essence of his advice is clear and simple: "Look not too long in the face of the fire, O man!—But look."

Put less cryptically, the meaning of Ishmael's experience is that life demands of us an inclusive affirmation: we must, without denying sunlight, acknowledge darkness and resolutely accept the worst. The point is borne in upon us by the book's recurrent theme of death and rebirth. We have seen it in the account of Ishmael's will-making, and may see it again in the stories of Jonah's delivery from the belly of the whale, Tashtego's from the whale's head, Pip's from his fearful and "intense concentration of self" into an indifference beyond human reason. Nowhere, though, does it speak so eloquently as in the symbol of Queequeg's coffin.

Just before the entry of the "Pequod" into the Pacific and the last act of her drama, Queequeg falls ill of a fever and lies for some days at the point of death. Thinking that his end is upon him, he asks that a coffin be made for him by the ship's carpenter. The request is granted: his measurements are taken with chalk and rule, the coffin is cut, put together, finished, and brought in for his approval. Having studied it for some time and supervised its outfitting with various funerary provisions, he asks "to be lifted into his final bed, that he [may] make trial of its comforts, if any it [has]." He lies there for a few moments with arms crossed upon his breast over his little god Yojo, and at last, seemingly satisfied, murmurs, " 'Rarmai' (it will do; it is easy)." And he asks to be taken out and put once more in his hammock. From that moment, the sick man suddenly rallies and improves, within a few days, to the point where he announces himself once again ready for action. He keeps the coffin with him, nevertheless, and spends his off-watch hours painstakingly carving into its lid those mysterious hieroglyphs in which some "departed prophet and seer of his island" once spelled out in tattoo on his body "a complete theory of the heavens and the earth, [together with] a mystical treatise on the art of attaining truth."[37]

But notwithstanding his investment of art and labor, it is Queequeg himself who suggests, after the failure of the ship's life buoy, the fitting and calking of his coffin to be hung out over the ship's taffrail against another emergency.[38] Ahab, seeing it there, reads its significance but will not acknowledge what he sees.[39] In the excitement of the three days' chase it is forgotten; but when the god-bullied "Pequod" at last goes down and drags in spinning circles after it the vanished Ahab's "lone boat, . . . and all its crew, and each floating oar, and every lance-pole . . . and smallest chip," and from the outermost rim the helplessly swimming Ishmael, it is this coffin, shot up from "the vital centre" of destruction, that offers salvation to the one survivor. "Buoyed up by that coffin," Ishmael is magically immune to the once-dreaded "demonism of this world": "I floated on a soft and dirge-like main. The unharming sharks, they glided by as if with padlocks on their mouths; the savage sea-hawks sailed with sheathed beaks. On the second day, a sail drew near, nearer, and picked me up at last."[40] Ahab and he have gone the same voyage, but where one has found death, the other has found life.

HELLENIC CHEER,
   HEBRAIC GRIEF

However important the theme of acceptance may be felt to be in *Moby-Dick*, it yet remains entirely secondary, in its imaginative impact, to the celebration of heroic defiance: the book lives in our memories, and surely this was the author's intention, as Ahab's story, not as Ishmael's.

37 *Ibid.*, pp. 247–51 (chap. cx).

38 *Ibid.*, p. 305 (chap. cxxvi).

39 *Ibid.*, p. 310 (chap. cxxvii).

40 *Ibid.*, p. 368 ("Epilogue").

But in the long poem *Clarel*, written a quarter-century later, the emphasis is different: here the search for a life-sustaining balance—a vision adequate to the needs of both heart and head—has become the central concern, and even the most eloquent of the defiers, Ungar, is so little important to the action that he is permitted to drop out almost unnoticed before the resolution is reached.[41]

The Ishmael of this work is another rootless young American with a "drizzling November in [his] soul," a voyager not of the seas, however, but of the vast deserts of nineteenth-century materialism and doubt. He is less hearty, too, more introspective, less eager for experience in and of itself. A lapsed divinity student who has come to the Holy Land in the hope of recovering his faith, he holds himself perhaps a little too conscientiously to that task. Men interest him, of course, but chiefly in their opinions and beliefs. One doubts that the laconic Queequeg would have held his attention for long.

In Jerusalem, however, Clarel meets and comes to love a young girl, Ruth, whose American father has become a convert to Judaism and brought his family here to share in the ancient promise. But raiding Arabs kill Nathan as he works at his stony acres outside the city, and his daughter is forced by the custom of her adopted people into a long period of seclusion and mourning. To fill out the interval, Clarel joins a party of pilgrims setting out on a tour of the holy places: Jericho, the Jordan, the Dead Sea, Bethlehem, Jerusalem again. The greater part of the book is an account of that tour—its sights, events, and persons, their discussions and meditations, refracted through the troubled consciousness of Clarel and focused upon the single problem of belief, of affirmation.

Of the varied group to which Clarel now joins himself, three are fellow Americans and already in some degree known to him: Nehemiah, the gentle old religious fanatic who has served as his guide about Jerusalem; Vine, a remote and richly "fu-

---

[41] *Clarel*, II, 272 (Part IV, canto xxviii).

neral man" Clarel has seen brooding among the tombs of Kedron outside the walls; and Rolfe, first met in the Garden of
Gethsemane, a genial sailor-philosopher of an independent if
still reverent turn of mind. If to these three we add two others
—Derwent, the dapper Broad Church English parson, and
Mortmain, the disillusioned European revolutionist—we have
all the principal figures of the pilgrimage but Ungar, who does
not join the party until considerably later. Each of these now
merits a somewhat closer inspection.

There is, of course, very little in Nehemiah's "poor thin
life" that can seem to Clarel at all relevant to his problem. The
good old man is a stranger both to doubt and to the realities
of his own century: he breathes the air of a vanished age and
sees about him not the lepers' huts of the present but the glory
of Solomon's Temple and King David's court,[42] not the stony
wilderness but a land flowing with milk and honey. In his dying vision, he sees Lot's city rise from its drowned foundations
and ascend in splendor as the bride of Christ.[43] When he is
gone, Clarel knows only pity.

Derwent is at first somewhat more of a puzzle to him. A
charming, lighthearted, cheerful man, he seems the very ideal
of traveling companions. Doubts trouble him, it is clear, almost as little as they do Nehemiah. But his security, one soon
sees, springs from a quite different source. He is no zealot, despite his cloth. Faith, like all things, he realizes, can be over-
done:

> "Be not extreme. Midway is best.
> Herein 'tis never as by Nile—
> From waste to garden but a stile.
> Betwixt rejection and belief,
> Shadings there are—degrees, in brief."[44]

[42] *Ibid.*, I, 103 (Part I, canto xxvi).

[43] *Ibid.*, pp. 325–26 (Part II, canto xxxviii).

[44] *Ibid.*, II, 108 (Part III, canto xxi).

He is, in opinion as in dress, the easy and cosmopolitan man of fashion:

> Imported or domestic mode,
> Thought's last adopted style he showed;
> Abreast kept with the age, the year,
> And each bright optimistic mind.[45]

Warmhearted by nature, he is still a little impatient with suffering or grief: the chirruping of birds in the English hedgerows seems to him a sufficient answer to Ungar's "jeremiad spells."[46] He looks upon Christ not as the Man of Sorrows but as " 'Pontiff of optimists supreme,' " and confesses to an aesthetic preference of the Greek cross to the more realistic Latin one.[47] Clarel's distrust of Derwent grows with his acquaintance and the two come at last to an open rupture when the student charges him with self-deceit:

> "Own, own with me, and spare to feign,
> Doubt bleeds, nor Faith is free from pain!"
> Derwent averted here his face—
> With his own heart he seemed to strive;
> Then said: "Alas, too deep you dive.
> But hear me yet for little space:
> This shaft you sink shall strike no bloom:
> The surface, ah, heaven keeps *that* green;
> Green, sunny: nature's active scene,
> For man appointed, man's true home."[48]

And looking about him at the vacant desert—"glare rived by gloom"—even Derwent feels the force of its unspoken comment and says no more. But from that hour, Clarel's uncertainty about the priest is ended.[49]

[45] *Ibid.*, I, 172 (Part II, canto i).

[46] *Ibid.*, II, 254 (Part IV, canto xxiii).

[47] *Ibid.*, p. 31 (Part III, canto yi) ; p. 91 (Part III, canto xviii).

[48] *Ibid.*, p. 109 (Part III, canto xxi).

[49] *Ibid.*, pp. 252–53 (Part IV, canto xxii).

There are three others to whom Clarel looks in hope of an answer: Vine, Rolfe, and Mortmain. Of the three, Vine seems the one of richest promise. Since their first meeting at the Herods' tomb in the Valley of Dry Bones, Vine has both attracted and baffled him. There seems something strangely contradictory about him, a "Pocahontas-wedding" of "Hellenic cheer, Hebraic grief" like that imaged in the sculptured frieze above the tomb itself:

> Palm leaves, pine-apples, grapes. These bloom,
> Involved in dearth—to puzzle us—
> As 'twere thy line, Theocritus,
> Dark Joel's text of terror threading.[50]

Closer study confirms Clarel's first impression of Vine: he is indeed a union of opposites. In him, heart and head exist in delicate balance; he is a voluptuary living under Carthusian rule:

> Under cheer
> Of opulent softness, reigned austere
> Control of self. Flesh, but scarce pride,
> Was curbed: desire was mortified;
> But less indeed by moral sway
> Than doubt if happiness through clay
> Be reachable.[51]

Generous and quick of sympathy, he is quick also to elude, and to guard his separateness. He rarely speaks, and then with few disclosures, as a nun through the convent wicket. He is sensitive to "the beauty of the world" and enjoys life as it comes, but he has no illusions; he appears

> as one
> Whose race of thought long since was run—
> For whom the spots enlarge that blot the golden sun.[52]

[50] *Ibid.*, I, 111 (Part I, canto xxviii).

[51] *Ibid.*, p. 116 (Part I, canto xxix).

[52] *Ibid.*, p. 312 (Part II, canto xxxiii).

He is committed to no theory, attempts to persuade no one. While others engage in argument, that "waste of words," he stands apart and builds "in whim of silence" a cairn of stones —"a monument to barrenness."[53] He and the laconic Arab guide ride apart from the talkative group with a common air of being "at home in dearth."

> True natives of the waste abode,
> They moved like insects of the leaf—
> Tint, tone adapted to the fief.[54]

Clarel, watching him closely day by day, feels here a kindred though higher spirit and longs for closeness and an exchange of confidence, but Vine's "ruled reserve" continues to shut him out. Finally, during a pause in a green spot along the Jordan, Clarel ventures to approach him. The older man speaks, and at some length, in light but serious comment upon the scene around them, but carefully avoids the personal. Clarel, longing as he does for brotherly nearness, is disappointed. He lets fall "some inklings" of his own perplexity and pain. Instantly Vine withdraws into shadow and is silent. The student is left to wonder at the sudden change:

> Does Vine's rebukeful dusking say—
> Why, on this vernal bank today,
> Why bring oblations of thy pain
> To one who hath his share? here fain
> Would lap him in a chance reprieve?
> Lives none can help ye; that believe.
> Art thou the first soul tried by doubt?
> Shalt prove the last? Go, live it out.
> But for thy fonder dream of love
> In man toward man—the soul's caress—
> The negatives of flesh should prove
> Analogies of non-cordialness
> In spirit.—E'en such conceits could cling

[53] *Ibid.*, II, 35 (Part III, canto vii).

[54] *Ibid.*, I, 219–20 (Part II, canto xii).

> To Clarel's dream of vain surmise
> And imputation full of sting.
> But, glancing up, unwarned he saw
> What serious softness in those eyes
> Bent on him. Shyly they withdraw.[55]

For all his air of remoteness, Vine is keenly sensitive to suffering in others: it is he, and he alone, who sees the extent of Mortmain's agony at Nehemiah's death and pities him.[56] If he is silent at such times, it is from a deep sense of the irremediability of what he sees, a knowledge, to which Clarel also comes in time, that "pain / [Is] portion inwrought with the grain" of human life.[57] His own balance is not, as the younger man assumes, something long since won and now easily maintained: there are times when, like Mortmain, he too bleeds into his armor. Clarel happens upon him alone at such a moment, still shaken by someone's allusion to the anguished face of Christ:

> Could it be Vine, and quivering so?
> 'Twas Vine. He wore that nameless look
> About the mouth—so hard to brook—
> Which in the Cenci portrait shows,
>
> . . . .
>
> A trembling over of small throes
> In weak swoll'n lips, which to restrain
> Desire is none, nor any rein.

Clarel is astonished at the intensity of feeling beneath this chastened exterior:

> Reserves laid bare? and can it be?
> The dockyard forge's silent mound,
> Played over by small nimble flame—
> Raked open, lo, the anchor's found
> In white-heat's alb.

[55] *Ibid.*, pp. 287–88 (Part II, canto xxvii).

[56] *Ibid.*, p. 328 (Part II, canto xxxix).

[57] *Ibid.*, II, 274 (Part IV, canto xxviii).

And he slips away unseen, in despair now of ever "coming at [Vine's] mystery" or knowing him other than as one knows a bird—"in shadow from the wing."[58] But he continues to observe him from a distance, and when at last Vine leaves him— in Kedron's Valley of Dry Bones, where the two first met— Clarel feels that misfortune has enabled him to take something from Vine's very silence.[59]

Less secretive than Vine but still puzzling to Clarel is Rolfe. Encountered first in the Garden of Gethsemane, he has the air of an outdoor man—a trapper, pioneer, or sailor. But he is a thinker, too:

> One read his superscription clear—
> A genial heart, a brain austere—
> And further, deemed that such a man
> Though given to study, as might seem,
> Was no scholastic partisan
> Or euphonist of Academe,
> But supplemented Plato's theme
> With daedal life in boats and tents,
> A messmate of the elements;
> And yet, more bronzed in face than mind,
> Sensitive still and frankly kind—
> Too frank, too unreserved, may be,
> And indiscreet in honesty.[60]

He is a seeker beyond the "parrot-lore" of his own day, a man of historic sense and independent mind—so independent as to seem to Clarel at times even more detached than Vine, a single seaweed adrift in the ocean.[61] This lack of commitment is central to his character: he is a critic, searching if never savage, of all fixed orthodoxies. Clarel, though he finds him "sterling" and admires his courage in facing unwelcome truths,

---

58 *Ibid.,* pp. 33–34 (Part III, canto vii).

59 *Ibid.,* p. 288 (Part IV, canto xxxii).

60 *Ibid.,* I, 121 (Part I, canto xxxi).

61 *Ibid.,* p. 122 (Part I, canto xxxi) ; p. 239 (Part II, canto xvii).

is disturbed at Rolfe's "illogical wild range / Of brain and heart's impulsive counterchange."[62] He is shocked by Rolfe's suggestion that the simple paganism of " 'that tattooed Greek / The Polynesian' " may be superior to the life of institutionalized Christianity:

> He gazed on Rolfe: Is this the man
> Whom Jordan heard in part espouse
> The appeal of that Dominican
> And Rome? and here, all sects, behold,
> All creeds involving in one fold
> Of doubt? Better a partisan!
> Earnest he seems: can union be
> 'Twixt earnestness and levity?
> Or need at last in Rolfe confess
> Thy hollow, Manysidedness![63]

But what seems in Rolfe a lack of all fixed conviction appears more clearly later as a settled opposition to all attempts to freeze experience into rigid artificial forms. Highly civilized as, in one sense, he is, his first allegiance is nevertheless to nature:

> for still the hue
> Rolfe kept of candour undefaced,
> Quoting pure nature at his need,
> As 'twere the Venerable Bede:
> An Adam in his natural ways.[64]

Man cannot hope by his "verbiage" to solve this world—"Too wild it is, too wonderful"—and how much less, therefore, that other and unseen world. The words are, in this instance, Clarel's, but the thought is acknowledged by him as Rolfe's.[65] Coming upon Derwent placidly reading his "tinted page" by

[62] *Ibid.*, p. 256 (Part II, canto xxi).
[63] *Ibid.*, II, p. 85 (Part III, canto xvi).
[64] *Ibid.*, p. 83 (Part III, canto xvi).
[65] *Ibid.*, p. 172 (Part IV, canto iii).

the Dead Sea shore, Rolfe ventures to remind him that man's basic text is that of the " 'wave and waste' " lying here about him.

> "Book-comment, though,"—
> Smiled Derwent—"were it ill to know?"
> "But how if Nature vetoes all
> Her commentators? Disenthral
> Thy heart. Look round. Are not here met
> Books and that truth no type shall set?"[66]

Rolfe is deeply suspicious of institutions. It was not Jerusalem only, he hints, but the whole city of man that wounded Christ's heart that day He

> *"Beheld*
> *The city, and wept over it:*
> Luke's words, and hard to be excelled,
> So just the brief expression there:
> Truth's rendering."[67]

Christianity has the power to move Rolfe deeply—but Christianity as he imagines it to have been in its first, best days: Christ the genial god walking abroad with peasants in a pastoral simplicity that but continued the purer elements of paganry. " 'Back rolled the world's effacing tide' " and ended that; " 'worse came—creeds, wars, stakes.' "[68] In part, that savagery now seems past: dogma has yielded for a while to opinion. But there lies in that no ground for hope that "Progress" will significantly weaken the hold of creeds and superstition upon the race. In the wake of every upheaval of the past, the priest has returned to claim his former place and

> "Hold it he shall, so long as spins
> This star of tragedies, this orb of sins."

[66] *Ibid.*, I, pp. 306–7 (Part II, canto xxxii).
[67] *Ibid.*, p. 132 (Part I, canto xxxiii).
[68] *Ibid.*, p. 254 (Part II, canto xxi).

For the power of religion, as of civilization as a whole, lies not in itself but in man's need, his helpless misery, and his inescapable ignorance of life's meaning.[69] Nature is thus the source from which even institutions draw their strength.

The total prospect, as Rolfe sees it, is far from cheerful. If nature is truer than "Civilisation['s] masque and fraud," she is yet in the end no kinder to man's hopes. And hers is a verdict, moreover, from which there is no appeal: one can only strive to accept it as that which is and which is not to be changed or understood. For a man of Rolfe's warm heart, the lesson is a hard one to master, and we find him again and again rebuking his own overearnestness and want of resignation.[70] The state to which he aspires is the indifference of nature herself, as becomes clear in the invocation he utters as the sun comes up as before over the mountains of Moab on the day of Mortmain's death:

> "Holy Morning,
> What blessed lore reservest thou,
> Withheld from man, that evermore
> Without surprise,
> But, rather, with a hurtless scorning
> In thy placid eyes,
> Thou viewest all events alike?"[71]

But wholly to learn that secret would be, perhaps, to cease to be human.

Farther, it would seem, than anyone from this desired state of indifference stands Mortmain, the "bitter Swede." He is one who, having built his whole life on a faith in man and man's perfectibility, has seen that faith betrayed and has been driven as a consequence into a mood of savage misanthropy that borders at times on insanity. What stirs his in-

---

[69] *Ibid.*, p. 126 (Part I, canto xxxi).

[70] *Ibid.*, p. 129 (Part I, canto xxxi); p. 237 (Part II, canto xvi); p. 307 (Part II, canto xxxii).

[71] *Ibid.*, II, 151–52 (Part III, canto xxxii).

terest in Christianity now, near the close of his life, is not, as
at times with Rolfe, its gospel of simple love and brotherhood
but rather its damning evidence of man's perfidy—

> " 'Twas *human,* that unanimous cry,
> 'We're fixed to hate Him—Crucify!' "—

and its insistence upon the vanity of all hope for this world:

> "The Christian plea—
> What basis has it, but that here
> Man is not happy, nor can be?
> There it confirms philosophy."[72]

Mortmain is possibly the most vividly realized figure in the
poem—a consequence, no doubt, of the fact that we know
more of his past than of any other character, Clarel included.
Like all of Melville's dark speakers, he is an Ishmael. The
illegitimate son of a Swedish noblewoman who not only disowned him but attempted, out of an unnatural hatred, to ruin
his career, Mortmain early found himself cast friendless upon
the world.

> Thus isolated, what to bind
> But the vague bond of human kind?

Coming to Paris at a time of general unrest throughout Europe (the years leading up to 1848), he became first a member
and then the leader of a revolutionary society:

> His a league
> Of frank debate and close intrigue:
> Plot, proselyte, appeal, denounce—
> Conspirator, pamphleteer, at once,
> And prophet. Wear and tear and jar
> He met with coffee and cigar:
> These kept awake the man and mood
> And dream. That uncreated Good
> He sought, whose absence is the cause

---

[72] *Ibid.,* I, 185 (Part II, canto iii).

>Of creeds and Atheists, mobs and laws.
>Precocities of heart outran
>The immaturities of brain.

But the mind in time overtook the heart and even left it behind. Experience revealing the worthlessness, blindness, and
even treachery of some of his comrades, Mortmain was driven
to re-examine his commitment and his estimate of man. Reflection upon the past confirmed his new and darker view of
the present and of the future; he renounced his apostolate to
become "oblivion's volunteer," a solitary rover of "the gray
places of the earth." It is as such that he has come now to
Palestine.[73]

But something more than a sense of personal injury and
disappointment underlies Mortmain's bitterness—

>. . . some unrenderable thing:
>'Twas not his bastardy, nor bale
>Medean in his mother pale,
>Nor thwarted aims of high design;
>But deeper—deep as nature's mine.[74]

Rolfe comes closer, perhaps, to naming it than anyone else.
The Swede, staring at the bubbles breaking in the scum along
the Dead Sea shore and brooding upon the centuries of worse
than carnal wickedness since Sodom, has been driven to curse
with Lear-like fury the very germs and moulds of life;[75] and
someone among the pilgrims has raised the question of his
sanity:

>"If mad,
>'Tis indignation at the bad,"
>Said Rolfe; "most men somehow get used
>To seeing evil, though not all
>They see; 'tis sympathetical;

[73] *Ibid.*, pp. 187–91 (Part II, canto iv).

[74] *Ibid.*, p. 191 (Part II, canto iv).

[75] *Ibid.*, pp. 320–21 (Part II, canto xxxvi).

> But never some are disabused
> Of first impressions which appal."[76]

A monomania like Ahab's grips Mortmain, drives him to take refuge from his own kind in the naked desert, leads him in thought " 'along the ocean's floor / Amid the dragon's staring crew,' " and torments him to the point where even in sleep he lies gnawing at his own hand.[77] But to turn his back, as Derwent does, upon Gethsemane would be to him a denial of truth. Suffering has given him, non-Christian that he is, a sense of Christ's pain and desolation more living than that of most believers. There are men enough, he is frank to tell Derwent,

> ". . . who with the god will sup,
> Happy to share his paschal wine.
> 'Tis well. But the ensuing cup,
> The bitter cup?"[78]

Derwent does not answer. But this cup Mortmain, at least, will have the courage not to put by; and in token of that pledge, he later kneels beside the Dead Sea, scoops the poisonous water in his palm, and drinks.[79]

The poem as a whole, of course, is concerned with Clarel's search for an acceptable philosophy and pattern of life. But it is these four characters, principally—Vine, Rolfe, Derwent, and Mortmain—who, in the interplay of their contrasting ideas and attitudes, supply the poem with most of its dramatic content and Clarel himself with a range of possible models for the conduct of his own life.[80] The total action of the poem

---

76 *Ibid.*, p. 323 (Part II, canto xxxvii).

77 *Ibid.*, p. 232 (Part II, canto xv) ; p. 321 (Part II, canto xxxvi) ; II, 74 (Part III, canto xv).

78 *Ibid.*, I, 184 (Part II, canto iii).

79 *Ibid.*, p. 315 (Part II, canto xxxiv).

80 Ungar is omitted from this number since he does not appear until Part IV of the poem, and then only as a spokesman for the same basic point of view previously represented by Mortmain.

may be said to turn upon a sequence of cantos (xxv–xxxii) at the end of Part III in which Melville, by means of a device like that of "The Doubloon" in *Moby-Dick*, leads each of these characters to declare his essential nature and so to take up a position relative to the others on a scale of value. The device is that of St. Saba's palm, symbolizing the promise of life beyond death; and the qualities by which each man is judged are the comprehensiveness of his vision of reality and the degree of his detachment from life.

The stage for this part of the action is the deep gorge of the brook Kedron where it passes the ancient monastery of Mar Saba, midway between the Dead Sea and Bethlehem. This is the same ravine, significantly, in which the pilgrimage begins and ends, Ezekiel's Valley of Dry Bones outside the walls of Jerusalem:

> . . . Kedron—word (the scholar saith)
> Importing anguish hard on death.
> And aptly may such named ravine
> Conduct unto Lot's mortal Sea
> In cleavage from Gethsemane
> Where it begins.[81]

And from the floor of this dry gorge, in its deepest and darkest part, climbs Mar Saba, its tiered levels rising one above the other up the cliffside until they lift at last into sunlight above the rim.[82] Part way up the same side of the gorge, on a small balcony cut into the wall, stands a single palm tree, miraculously green in a world of cracked and barren rock.[83] According to the legend of the monks, the palm was planted there a thousand years ago by St. Saba, the founder. The pilgrims have broken their journey by a rest of several days at the monastery, and now on their last afternoon are separately

81 *Ibid.*, p. 217 (Part II, canto xi).

82 *Ibid.*, II, 45 (Part III, canto x).

83 *Ibid.*, pp. 122–23 (Part III, canto xxv).

wandering along the paths and steps cut into the cliff across from Mar Saba; and so it is that to each of them in turn, from one vantage or another, the miraculous tree "across the interposed abyss" is suddenly revealed.

Derwent sees it first, from the very floor of Kedron to which he has descended, as Dante into Hell, in the wake of his jolly Virgil, the libertine merchant of Lesbos. The Lesbian points out the palm, far up the cliff, and adds that it was planted by the monastery's founder. Derwent is politely interested:

> "Indeed? Heaven crown him for it. Palm!
> Thou benediction in the land,
> A new millennium mayst thou stand:
> So fair, no fate would do thee harm."

But he has the tourist's wandering eye and a moment later, his attention claimed by other details of "the impressive scene," he has quite forgotten it. The two climb a little way up the opposite side and see an eagle far above let drop a black object that falls past them into the gorge. It is Mortmain's skull-cap and a moment later they see him—" 'that death's-head of all mortal men' "—seated "bareheaded brooding" on a distant crag.[84]

The two climb a little higher, casually inspect the cave of a hermit who has died insane with grief, and then turn back. To everything he sees, Derwent has the same answer, " 'Queer, 'Tis queer indeed!' " But he does not pursue the matter further, and a moment after he has arrived at the bottom again he has forgotten it all in his amusement at the "fantastic pigeon-wings" cut by his companion to illustrate " 'the step King David took' " before the Ark.[85]

Vine is next. High up the rocky wall, he halts his climb to rest, and seeing the tree across the gorge, he hails it in words of love and wonder:

[84] *Ibid.*, pp. 122–25 (Part III, canto xxv).
[85] *Ibid.*, pp. 132–34 (Part III, canto xxvii).

> "Witness to a watered land,
> Voucher of a vernal year—
> St. Saba's Palm, why there dost stand?
> Would'st thou win the desert here
> To dreams of Eden? Thy device
> Intimates a Paradise!
> Nay, thy plume would give us proof
> That thou thyself art prince thereof,
> Fair lord of that domain."

Derwent, with mechanical optimism, has forecast "a new millennium" for the tree. Vine, recalling Apollo's sacred but now vanished tree at Delos, is less hopeful:

> "Thou that pledgest heaven to me,
> Stem of beauty, shaft of light,
> Behold, thou hang'st suspended
> Over Kedron and the night!
> Shall come the fall? shall time disarm
> The grace, the glory of the Palm?"

One cannot doubt the answer. Had not this tree too its predecessors?

> "Tropic seraph! thou once gone,
> Who then shall take thy office on—
> Redeem the waste, and high appear,
> Apostle of Talassa's year
> And climes where rivers of waters run?"

But its presence here and at this moment is a fact for which one can only be grateful:

> "But braid thy tresses—yet thou'rt fair:
> Every age for itself must care:
> Braid thy green tresses; let the grim
> Awaiter find thee never dim!
> Serenely still thy glance be sent
> Plumb down from horror's battlement;
> Though the deep Fates be concerting
> A reversion, a subverting,
> Still bear thee like the Seraphim."[86]

If Vine is gladdened by the sight, it is not through any hope awakened for himself, in this world or the next. He has no thought that "horror's battlement" will melt away: whatever happens, "Kedron and the night" will, he knows, outlast life's every particular manifestation. But consciousness is a matter of intensity, not duration—of quality, not quantity; and to be wise is not merely to acknowledge darkness but to affirm, like "the brave one over there— / The Palm," the miraculous presence of life in the midst of death.

Mortmain, still seated where he was when the eagle seized his "philosopher's cap" and dropped it into the gorge, looks down and sees the small figures of Derwent and his capering friend on Kedron's floor. Comparing his own lot with that of the thoughtless dancer below, he is suddenly struck by a sense of the futility of all his thinking:

> "Wiser am I?—Curse on this store
> Of knowledge! Nay, 'twas cursed of yore.
> *Knowledge is power:* tell that to knaves;
> 'Tis knavish knowledge: the true lore
> Is impotent for earth: *'Thyself*
> *Thou canst not save: come down from cross!'*
> They cast it in His teeth. . . ."

Where turn, then? To Christ? The disproportion but recalls him to his monomania:

> "Cling to His tree, and there find hope[?]
> Me it but makes a misanthrope.
> Makes? nay, but 'twould, did not the hate
> Dissolve in pity of the fate.—
> This legend, dream, and *fact* of life!
> The drooping hands, the dancing feet
> Which in the endless series meet;
> And rumours of *No God* so rife!"[87]

[86] *Ibid.*, pp. 127–28 (Part III, canto xxvi).
[87] *Ibid.*, p. 135 (Part III, canto xxviii).

Leaving his seat, he climbs higher, stopping when the crazed monk Cyril emerges from his cave to block the way:

> "The word!"
> *"Hope,"* in derision. "Stand, delay:
> That was password for yesterday."
> *"Despair."* "Advance."
>   He, going, scanned
> The testimony of the hand
> Gnawed in the dream: "Yea, but 'tis here.
> Despair? nay, death; and what's death's cheer?
> Death means—the sea-beat gains the shore;
> He's home; his watch is called no more."

Then, turning a corner of the path:

> "But what—the Tree? O holy Palm,
> If 'tis a world where hearts wax warm
> Oftener through hate than love, and chief
> The bland thing be the adder's charm,
> And the true thing virtue's ancient grief—
> Thee yet it nourishes—even thee!
>   "Envoy, whose looks the pang assuage,
> Disclose thy heavenly embassage!
> That lily-rod which Gabriel bore
> To Mary, kneeling her before,
> Announcing a God, the mother she;
> That budded stalk from Paradise—
> Like that thou shin'st in thy device:
> And sway'st thou over here toward me—
> Toward *me* can such a symbol sway!"[88]

Astonished, he drops in the path and, still gazing upon the tree, falls into a dream of heavenly peace and certitude.

> A wind awakened him—a breath.
> He lay like light upon the heath,
> Alive though still. And all came back,
> The years outlived, with all their black;
> While bright he saw the angel-tree

[88] *Ibid.*, pp. 136–37 (Part III, canto xxviii).

> Across the gulf alluring sway:
> *Come over! be—forever be*
> *As in the trance.*

But even with the contrast thus vividly before him, he finds—surprisingly—that he cannot make the choice. His old anger is suddenly gone, and he feels within him once more something of his earlier faith in man:

> "Wilt no delay?
> Yet hear me in appeal to thee:
> When the last light shall fade from me,
> If, groping round, no hand I meet;
> Thee I'll recall—invoke thee, Palm:
> Comfort me then, thou Paraclete!
> The lull late mine beneath thy lee,
> Then, then renew, and seal the calm."

But having said this, he makes no effort to leave the spot:

> Upon the ledge of hanging stair,
> And under Vine, invisible there,
> With eyes still feeding on the Tree,
> Relapsed he lingered as in Lethe's snare.[89]

He is found there the next morning, "filmed orbs [still] fixed upon the Tree" and upon his lips—as token, it would seem, of a higher wisdom than earth's—an eagle's feather, "wafted from the skies."[90]

There remains one other of Clarel's models, and now he too appears:

> Far down see Rolfe there, hidden low
> By ledges slant. Small does he show
> (If eagles eye), small and far off. . . .

Appearing and disappearing among the rocks like a sea bird in the hollows of waves, he reaches the foot of the stone stairs and begins the ascent:

[89] *Ibid.,* pp. 137–38 (Part III, canto xxviii).
[90] *Ibid.,* p. 151 (Part III, canto xxxii).

> Up, slow
> He climbed for little space; then craved
> A respite, turned and sat; and, lo,
> The Tree in salutation waved
> Across the chasm. Remindings swell;
> Sweet troubles of emotion mount—
> Sylvan reveries. . . .

To him too the palm whispers of Paradise; but it beckons him, not forward to a life to come, but backward to an Eden already known and lost. Touched with a vague disquiet and regret, the memories of youth return. It is Typee's golden legend remembered in the desert, and implicit in it, Rolfe sees, is the tragic story of each man's inexplicable, voluntary flight from the Garden. Day by day, the story is repeated:

> "Who now adown the mountain dell
> (Till mine, by human foot untrod—
> Nor easy, like the steps to hell)
> In panic leaps the appalling crag,
> Alighting on the cloistral sod
> Where strange Hesperian orchards drag,
> Walled round by cliff and cascatelle—
> Arcades of Iris; and though lorn,
> A truant ship-boy overworn,
> Is hailed for a descended god?"

Who on that far island sees today

> "The nereids dimpling in the darkling stream?
> For whom the gambol of the tricksy dream—
> Even Puck's substantiated scene,
> Yea, much as man might hope and more than
> heaven may mean?"

Another youth now hears the plea of priest and people:

> " 'Abide, for peace is here:
> Behold, nor heat nor cold we fear,
> Nor any dearth: one happy tide—
> A dance, a garland of the year:
> Abide!' "

But though the person differs, the answer is the same. Other voices call man forth from the harmony of nature, and he must go:

> ". . . who so feels the stars annoy,
> Upbraiding him—how far astray!—
> That he abjures the simple joy,
> And hurries over the briny world away?
> "Renouncer! is it Adam's flight
> Without compulsion or the sin?
> And shall the vale avenge the slight
> By haunting thee in hours thou yet shalt win?"
> He tarried. And each swaying fan
> Sighed to his mood in threnodies of Pan.[91]

But here on this stony ledge there is no word of hope or comfort for Rolfe in what the palm whispers over Kedron.

Clarel, meanwhile, has found a way up Mar Saba's side of the gorge and has come out on the balcony of the tree itself. A monk, of serene and holy aspect, stands under it, calling the doves out of Kedron to feed from his hand. The student's first impulse is one of joy: here at last he has found peace. But the thought of Ruth returns to him, and he realizes that the life here typified gives peace only at the price of wholeness. There is still no answer capable of satisfying head and heart together.[92]

The monk is gone now. Alone, Clarel leans over the edge and sees far down and across the gulf the upturned faces of his three fellow pilgrims, each hidden from the other but all fixed, as if in worship, upon the tree above. The rock-hewn steps upon which they rest are still for a little while in sunlight and hang upon the lower darkness of the ravine like Jacob's ladder let down from heaven. Upon that ladder Vine is highest, Mortmain is under him, and Rolfe the lowest of the three. There is no sign of Derwent or his friend.[93]

[91] *Ibid.*, pp. 139–41 (Part III, canto xxix).
[92] *Ibid.*, pp. 142–45 (Part III, canto xxx).
[93] *Ibid.*, pp. 145–46 (Part III, canto xxx).

It does not, of course, occur to Clarel to look for a significance in the order of the climbers upon the stair. And were
such a thing suggested to him, he might reasonably question
the validity of an ordering that would place Rolfe—that "mind
/ Poised at self-centre and mature"—at such a distance from
Vine and at a level beneath that of the grim and monomaniac
Swede. For he knows nothing of Rolfe's inability to aspire
beyond the natural, of his failure to affirm the present or his
nostalgic preoccupation with an outgrown life which, could it
be regained, would leave him as far from wholeness as that
just proffered Clarel by the monk. Nor does the watcher know
that Mortmain, his pride of knowledge put aside, has passed,
as Rolfe has not, through the gateway of despair and come out
into a freedom where, though all is lost, nothing is regretted,
and where, having wholly given over this world, his hands are
free to reach out, at least, toward another. The placing of Vine
above the level of either of his companions, Clarel would certainly have approved; but he would perhaps have been startled
to find the ground of that pre-eminence not in the possession
of any doubt-allaying knowledge but in a renunciation greater
even than Mortmain's—a detachment not merely from the
things of this world but from any hope of consolation in the
next.

But Clarel, still hungering for certitude, cannot know this.
After all his overtures to Vine, that heart remains to him "a
fountain sealed." This is not, as he has already partly sensed,
a matter of the older man's choice: the secret behind Vine's
"gleam of oneness" is by its very nature incommunicable.
That last and most necessary wisdom—how to live—is something which no man teaches; it is to be found not in words
but in the direct and unmediated confronting of experience.
Vine can have no other message for Clarel than "Go, live it
out."

And throughout the fourth and final part of the poem, as
the cavalcade moves on from Mar Saba to Bethlehem, and

from there once again to Jerusalem, Clarel continues to swing
between the horns of his dilemma: to embrace this world or
to reject it. At times, under the influence of Rolfe's skeptic
mood, he is tempted to doubt that life has any discernible
meaning whatever.[94] But where to turn? To consume his youth
in an unending search for truth seems futile; but the alternative to this—the "common uninquiring life" of worldly rou-
tine—is not only meaningless but ignoble.[95] Cynicism offers
another path. Ungar, the New World pessimist now joining
the group, brings new and damning evidence to support
Mortmain's earlier view of man, and throws open as black a
prospect into the future as did the Old World pessimist into
the past. Clarel is again shaken:

> If man in truth be what you say [he reflects],
>
> . . . .
>
> What's left us but the senses' sway?
> Sinner, sin out life's petty lease:
> We are not worth the saving. . . .[96]

But the thought of Ruth—that "beckoning star" that seems
to hang between earth and heaven—returns to keep him from
Ungar's final bitterness. Nearly everyone he looks on seems
to Clarel more settled than he. He envies, on the one hand, the
untroubled faith and the ascetic calm of a young Tuscan monk
at the Church of the Nativity,[97] and on the other, the lighthearted and strangely innocent sensualism of a young Lyonese
met at the inn in Bethlehem.[98] In a dream, he stands between
the two—lords of luxurious Persia and of the pure but barren
sands of the desert—and cannot choose.[99] Chance knowledge
the next day reveals that the Lyonese is himself "a fugitive

[94] *Ibid.*, p. 172 (Part IV, canto iii).

[95] *Ibid.*, p. 274 (Part IV, canto xxviii).

[96] *Ibid.*, p. 253 (Part IV, canto xxii).

[97] *Ibid.*, pp. 206–7 (Part IV, canto xiii) ; p. 229 (Part IV, canto xvii).

[98] *Ibid.*, pp. 260–62 (Part IV, canto xxvi).

[99] *Ibid.*, p. 269 (Part IV, canto xxvi).

from faith" to the life of sense—a Jew by birth and a child of this same grim desert he now disowns.[100] The pulse of a new life quickens in Clarel.

The crisis comes that same night, Shrove Tuesday, as the pilgrims set out in darkness on the last stage of their journey. They ride in silence, melancholy weighing down the spirits of all but Clarel. He is caught up by a strange exuberance at the thought of Ruth waiting for him in Jerusalem. Nothing of course has been solved: there is no reason to be glad. He would be puzzled himself to explain the nature of this

> new emotion, inly held,
> That so the long contention quelled—
> Languor, and indecision, pain.
> Was it abrupt resolve? a strain
> Wiser than wisdom's self might teach?

He does not know. But whatever the source of his new decisiveness, he is at last prepared to act—to seek out Ruth and her mother and with them leave Palestine for a new beginning in some greener, happier land. The tree of knowledge is not, after all, the only tree God planted in the Garden—there is another:

> Yea, now his hand would boldly reach
> And pluck the nodding fruit to him,
> Fruit of the tree of life. If doubt
> Spin spider-like her tissue out,
> And make a snare in reason dim—
> Why hang a fly in flimsy web?[101]

A momentary doubt occurs to him: Is the heart itself to be trusted?

> May love's nice balance, finely slight,
> Take tremor from fulfilled delight?
> Can Nature such a doom dispense

[100] *Ibid.*, pp. 275–76 (Part IV, canto xxviii).

[101] *Ibid.*, p. 278 (Part IV, canto xxix).

As, after ardour's tender glow,
To make the rapture more than pall
With evil secrets in the sense[?]

But he puts the thought aside as Manichean and evil, and determines again to

Take [his] wife;
Venture, and prove the soul of life,
And let fate drive.[102]

And so resolved, he rides on through the darkness and descends once more into Kedron, "the valley of decision," where it runs beneath Jerusalem's walls. There, as they pass close to a burial party working by torchlight, Clarel's eye is caught by an embroidered scarf whose pattern he knows. Aghast, he leaps from his horse, turns back the covering from the shrouded figure on the ground, and sees Ruth's face. She and her mother, victims of grief and fever, lie there side by side.[103]

Shock and the anguished sense of loss carry him for a time almost over the edge of madness. He questions God's existence, curses the mourners and this " 'blind, blind, barren universe,' " renounces all faith as " 'perjured,' " and calls upon death to take him also. But when one of the mourners, frightened by his blasphemy, moves threateningly forward to drive him from the grave, Clarel finds his anger spent:

"Spurn—I'll endure; all spirit's fled
When one fears nothing.—Bear with me,
Yet bear!—Conviction is not gone
Though faith's gone: that which shall not be
Still *ought* to be!"[104]

And with this first small step of affirmation, he begins his slow climb up from despair.

We see Clarel at intervals only throughout the long days of

102 *Ibid.*, pp. 279–80 (Part IV, canto xxix).
103 *Ibid.*, pp. 283–84 (Part IV, canto xxx).
104 *Ibid.*, pp. 284–85 (Part IV, canto xxx).

Lent as he keeps watch alone beside the grave in Kedron. His companions—even Vine—have left him, for in this extremity no man can help another. Silent though he is, it is clear that resignation is still not his; but there is evidence that he is learning in the same school where Vine has studied before him:

> His visage calm
> Seemed not the one which late showed play
> Of passion's throe; but here divine
> No peace; ignition in the mine
> Announced is by the rush, the roar:
> These end; yet may the coal burn on—
> Still slumberous burn beneath the floor
> Of pastures where the sheep lie down.[105]

Palm Sunday's triumph goes by him unnoticed. Passion Week comes, Good Friday passes, and the morning of Easter dawns. But the sounds of the rejoicing city awaken no echo in Clarel:

> The cheer, so human, might not call
> The maiden up; *Christ is arisen:*
> But Ruth, may Ruth so burst the prison?[106]

And Easter too goes by. The brief freshet of joy dies down and once again, "sluggish, life's wonted stream flows on."

We see Clarel for the last time on the evening of Whitsuntide, a nameless member of the throng endlessly flowing in through Stephen's gate and along the crooked street called Via Crucis. Named though it is for Christ's Passion, that path was there before the city, is older even than memory, its every turn determined by

> A hint, or dictate, Nature's own,
> By man, as by the brute, obeyed.

The day Jesus toiled up it with His cross, the stones He walked on were already worn by centuries of forgotten pain. And along

---

[105] *Ibid.*, pp. 288–89 (Part IV, canto xxxii). Cf. the "dockyard forge" image by which Melville has indicated Vine's hidden intensity, *ibid.*, p. 34 (Part III, canto vii).

[106] *Ibid.*, p. 294 (Part IV, canto xxxiii).

it now, some eighteen hundred years after the Comforter's descent, there flows the same unending current of misery. Jew and Arab, merchant and slave, Turk and Christian, beggar and noble, soldier and monk, burden-carrying ass and camel,

> In varied forms of fate they wend—
> Or man or animal, 'tis one:
> Cross-bearers all, alike they tend
> And follow, slowly follow on.[107]

And Clarel, after all his questioning and all "that weary length of arguing" heard and considered, takes his place among these and is not to be distinguished from them.

But though we leave him here, his story, as the Epilogue suggests, is not yet finished. The fact of death which confronts him now with such finality has in truth been with him from the first: his journey began and ended with Kedron, the valley of the shadow of death, and each of its stages has concluded with a death touching him still more intimately—Nathan's, Nehemiah's, Mortmain's, and now Ruth's. What he has learned is what he knew before but knew less well: that death ends all. "The ancient Sphinx still keeps the porch of shade," and no man sees beyond. But if Clarel has moved, with his deeper conviction of this truth, beyond the consolation of any reasonable hope, he has put behind him also (though he does not know it) the worst extravagance of despair. Merely to persist, like Saba's green palm rising from the sterile rock, is itself a kind of affirmation. What more is faith at bottom than this same unreasoning assertion of life in the face of its opposite— the holding up, in Ishmael's image, of "an idiot candle in the heart of that almighty forlornness"?

There is of course a further reach of wisdom to which Clarel has not yet attained, and this is Vine's: the capacity for a disinterested rejoicing in the simple fact of life's brave, unavailing spectacle. But this, as we are reminded by the poem's

[107] *Ibid.*, pp. 295–96 (Part IV, canto xxxiv).

closing lines (and by their echo of Ishmael's deliverance from
the wreck of the "Pequod"), is a wisdom learned of the heart
and not the head:

> Then keep thy heart, though yet but ill-resigned—
> Clarel, thy heart, the issues there but mind;
> That like the crocus budding through the snow—
> That like a swimmer rising from the deep—
> That like a burning secret which doth go
> Even from the bosom that would hoard and keep;
> Emerge thou mayst from the last whelming sea,
> And prove that death but routs life into victory.[108]

In this, the last word of comfort that Melville can find to offer
Clarel, the latest born and most reflective of his questing heroes,
we have in all probability the best answer he was able to arrive
at for himself. It is no very positive answer, to be sure—the
prospect of pain certain, of victory a possibility at best—but
it is an honest answer and not unlike that which Ishmael found
at the end of *Moby-Dick.* Students of Melville have not given
it the attention it deserves. For it comes as the conclusion to
a complex, deeply considered, and carefully elaborated work
of art, the fruit of its author's ripest maturity, enriched by
reading and meditation, chastened by the experience of national and domestic tragedy. *Billy Budd,* however we may
choose to interpret it, is not on the same scale and does not
address itself to the same large question; it is a slighter and,
one must admit, a less perfect work. Art has no final answers,
but if it is Melville's last fully considered judgment that we
want, we must turn to *Clarel.* And quiet though it is, that
answer, in its emphasis upon endurance and affirmation, is
closer to defiance than to surrender.

[108] *Ibid.,* p. 298 (Part IV, canto xxxv).

Index